About the Author

Pete Bearder is a spoken word poet, c .... whose
work has been featured on BBC Radio 4, The World Service,
and Newsnight. He is the former National Poetry Slam Champion and has performed around the world with organisations
such as The British Council. His first collection *Numbered Boxes*
was published by Burning Eye Books in 2017, and in 2018
he was awarded The Golden Hammer Award for services to
spoken word.

www.petethetemp.co.uk

Published by Out-Spoken Press,
Future Studio,
237 Hackney Road,
London, E2 8NA

The right of Pete Bearder to be identified as the author of
this work has been asserted by them in accordance with
section 77 of the Copyright, Designs and Patents Act 1988.

A CIP record for this title is available from
the British Library.

First edition published 2019
ISBN: 978-1-9996792-5-5

Design & Art Direction
Ben Lee

Printed & Bound by:
Print Resource

Typeset in: Baskerville

Out-Spoken Press is supported using public
funding by the National Lottery through
Arts Council England.

Stage Invasion:
Poetry & the Spoken
Word Renaissance

Pete Bearder

OUT
SPOKEN
PRESS

Acknowledgements

This giant rabbit hole has come at great expense to the time I would have given to loved ones. The support and interest of friends and family has sustained this project, but above all else, I extend my heartfelt gratitude to my partner Lucy White for the faith and patience she has given me during months of working into the early morning and beyond.

The book would not have been possible without the collaboration of the eighty plus poets and poetry activists who donated poems and archival material and offered time and expertise in interviews and various correspondences.

Stage Invasion also owes much to the research of others. Lucy English of Bath Spa University mentored the project and fed back on the whole book and her guidance and expertise has been indispensable. Other researchers in this field kindly supported the project including: Tim Wells, James McKay, Russell Thompson, Sue Dymoke, Hannah Silva, Katie Ailes, Julia Novak, Patrick Turner, Jack McGowan and Corinne Fowler. Thanks also to Danny Nemu and David Lee Morgan for their feedback, as well as Mike Sanders of Manchester University and Simon Rennie of Exeter University for their historical expertise.

It has been a joy to work with Out-Spoken Press who have gone way beyond what is considered possible for a grass-roots publisher by producing a book of this nature. Special thanks to Anthony Anaxagorou (for editing and direction), Patricia Ferguson (for her diligent and informed proofreading and marketing), Yen-Yen Lu (Marketing) and Ben Lee (design and layout). Big thanks also to the many photographers who donated their work, and to Michael Partridge for his excellent cover design.

Thanks to Apples and Snakes (especially Gina Sherman and Lisa Mead) for their help in securing funding for the project. The money I received from Arts Council England has made it possible to produce this book outside of academia. Long live public funding. Long live the People's Republic of Poetry.

Contents

for Lucy

'Poetry is play at its most utopian'

—Lawrence Ferlinghetti

Introduction

I'm at Glastonbury Festival, 27 June 2014. The DJ, the violinist, the accordion player, the drummer, the brass section, the acrobats, and the fire jugglers have fallen to the floor. They appear to be dead. I walk onto the stage. Five thousand people are staring at me, confused. Moments before, they were dancing to a pyro-circus rave band called Slamboree. Who is this guy on the mic? Is he the MC? Is the show over? Nobody came here to see me, but they are just about to get me.

I launch into the opening lines of a poem. At one minute in people still seem confused, some bordering on incredulous. This has to work. The energy builds and the momentum of the piece tears through my body. I feel like something is passing into me from above. I scan the crowd, locking onto eyes. My words and hands fly outwards along with this—something—which is spilling into the crowd and flying back at me. After three minutes and fifteen seconds, the poem is over. Silence. The audience erupts in cheers. I stage-dive into their outstretched hands and the beat drops.

*

Freeze frame. How does this relatively unknown, portly, and balding poet get to stage-dive after a poem? This book is about the wave on which I, and many others, are being carried. You are this wave: a swell of poets, MCs, comics, orators, promoters, programmers, poetry activists, educators, scholars, spellcasters, healers and, perhaps most importantly, audiences. Whichever of these roles you play, you are an indispensable part of this human ecology of ritualised empathy and cultural production we call spoken word poetry.

The UK is experiencing a sea change in the way poetry is produced and consumed. As a democratic literary movement, spoken word is redefining the role of the poet in society. Poetry is happening in a proliferating diaspora of settings where this 'private art' can be found, surrounded by ordinary people—and large numbers of them—shuddering with tears, laughter, and clenched fists.

Building on the achievements of previous decades, poetry is transcending spaces like libraries, universities and bookshops to be experienced in festivals, pubs, clubs, and a widening spectrum of new media. Spoken word workshops are now even available on the NHS.[1]

Spoken word can no longer be said to be an emerging art form. For the last three years, the prestigious Ted Hughes Award has been won by poets that have grown out of slam and spoken word communities (Raymond Antrobus 2019, Jay Bernard 2018, Hollie McNish 2017). These poets follow in the footsteps of Kate Tempest who won the same award in 2013. Tempest has also been twice nominated for the Mercury Prize (an award most commonly associated with pop stars) and her work has since been featured on prime-time Friday night TV. In May 2017, Mancunian spoken word artist Tony 'Longfella' Walsh summoned tears to hundreds of thousands in a poem he performed at the Manchester bombing memorial service. The poem trended fourth in the world on Twitter.[2]

For poet Lemn Sissay, 'we are living through the most exciting time in poetry in this century and the previous century'.[3] Meanwhile, Penguin Books UK are heralding a poetic 'renaissance'.[4] These claims are not unfounded. Sales of poetry books are up by almost fifty per cent since 2014, from £8.3m in 2014 to £12.3m in 2018—a year in which two-thirds of buyers were younger than thirty-four.[5] The upsurge is being credited to poets from minority ethnic backgrounds, the world of performance and the new popularity of poetry on social media.

At some unknowable point, I estimate within the last five years, another poetic landmark was met. The viral reach of poetry on YouTube seems likely to have surpassed physical footfall to spoken word events. To date, Shane Koyczan alone has recorded almost twenty-five million views of his piece 'To This Day Project'. New technologies mean new methods of publication. As a movement that has long been extramural to the publishing industry, spoken word has been quick to exploit these new media. These experiments are not just transforming the way literature is made and accessed; they are reconfiguring the genetic code of poetry, and pioneering a new poetic interface for the human psyche.

Multi-media spoken word films are penetrating mainstream discourse. McNish's 'Embarrassed' (a poem about breastfeeding in public) reached millions of viewers online. The poem not only commented on the news but became it, triggering a string of newspaper columns and web feeds on motherhood and depictions of female nudity.[6]

Spoken word poets are everywhere. They are laureates of your cities, they are inside your schools, your radio, your TV, and Olympic opening ceremonies. Damn it, they are even selling you take-away deliveries, mortgages, and jeeps. For better, and perhaps for worse, poetry has become popular again; part of the lived conversation of British culture.

Yet, by the standards poetry criticism, viral poetry films fail as poetry. Reacting to the new cadre of poetic success stories, literary critic Rebecca Watts lashed out at the writings of Tempest and McNish as 'the open denigration of intellectual engagement and rejection of craft'. The article is threaded with sense of ownership over poetry and a perceived invasion from outsiders. Comparing their poetry to the tweets of Donald Trump, Watts condemns it as contributing to the linguistic conditions of right-wing populism.[7]

There is an urgent need to find a better language to critique spoken word. This book aims to inform this discussion from inside the movement. Founded on a recognition of spoken word poetry's achievements as a mature practice, fed by a broad range of disciplines, *Stage Invasion* dives into this literary phenomenon to explore a rich ecology of voices. It will trace spoken word's genealogy to the taproots of the oral tradition to see how it is evolving, surviving, and thriving. It will also shed light on how these rituals of verbal exchange can lead to artistic, social, and political renewal.

Some Words on Words

The fact that this operates through language deserves some attention here. Because of its centrality to human affairs, language can never be divorced from its agency in the world nor considered a mere aesthetic diversion. In the words of Martin Heidegger:

> Language is the house of Being. In its home man dwells. Those who think and those who create with words are the guardians of this home.[8]

Spoken word is not just an artistic movement, it is a generation finding a new way to metabolise the world with words. These words, says philosopher Corey Anton, are 'an extension of our nervous system', or to quote Dwight Bolinger 'the mechanism through which reality is organized'.[9]

Language is also, in essence, a tradition, or the 'collective art of expression, a summary of thousands upon thousands of individual intuitions'.[10] These are not my words, your words, or even those of Edward Sapir. Every time we speak (to steal from Mikhail Bakhtin) we 'appropriate the words of others and populate them with one's own intentions'.[11] As the octopus squirts ink when emotional, the poet casts their ink into the flow of language.

No tradition is neutral territory, and the river of language is gunboated with agendas.[12] The *who, why, where, when,* and *how* of language has always been contested. As we will see in Chapter 3, poetry has never been free of squabble. As an elevated, often very public, form of speech (with an almost religious devotion to 'the truth') it has frequently swum against the current of how we organise reality with words. Since our tribal beginnings, the poet has been simultaneously respected, feared, and derided.[13]

By extension, poetry is itself is an ideological battleground. What is poetry? Who are our great poets and who should we teach in school? These are fiercely contested issues. The poet also has a responsibility to the health of language, which everywhere is ill-used as mercenary fodder for the nefarious spell of the market, the spin doctor, the preacher, and the silver-tongued lover. We are all complicit in language, perpetrators of these sonic and pictorial nodes of energy. We all hold their potential in our hands and in our mouths.

This book will explore a new arena of linguistic innovation. It will seek to illustrate how communities are galvanising around words and how, in a myriad of small ways, this can help to reshape reality itself.

What are we Saying?

Stage Invasion will start with the story of how I fell in love with spoken word, and how I (and others) earned our credentials as 'poets' in the curious ritual of slam contests. Slam is one of the most controversial sites in UK poetry. For some it is the 'death of art'; for others it is a victory of cultural democracy. **Chapter 1: 'The Way In: Slam and the Gates of Culture'** will weigh the arguments for the *carnivalesque* in poetry. It will present slam as a rite of passage for poets and an arena of '*deliberative democracy*' for poetry more generally.

Chapter 2 will then seek to answer the biggest question in spoken word: **'What is Spoken Word?'** This chapter will navigate the dual heritages of spoken word: oral and literary, countercultural and mainstream, poetic and otherwise. What can be attributed to the 'oral tradition'? Is spoken word a style, a sensibility, or even a set of beliefs? Does it deserve its own name, or is it just poetry? In answering these questions, I will present this art form as an artistic genre in its own right, with definable features and character traits.

To complement this, **Chapter 3: 'A History of Democratic Literary Movements'** will present spoken word's canon of cultural inheritance. It will sprint through the last two hundred years of disobedient poetries: Romantics, Chartists, Modernists, the Harlem Renaissance, the Beats, Mersey poets, and the Black Arts Movement right through to the poetry of hip hop, dub, punk and alternative cabaret. These voices have played key roles in social movements that have shaped the modern world. They also demonstrate that society has rarely agreed on who poetry *belongs* to. Nor has it been able to stop people from using verse to authenticate their struggles and create their own territories of culture.

What, then, are the mechanics of this inheritance? **Chapter 4: 'The DIY Renewal of Poetry'** will ask what this field is made of, and how it succeeds in elevating voices from the bottom up. With minimal resources, spoken word is generating artistic brilliance with an informal, DIY economy that has everything to do with *people power.*

From here, **Chapter 5: 'The Journey of the Poem Through the Body'** will telescope into the neglected territory of poetry—performance. The interest here is the *body* of the performer; the organism that produces and publishes. How do physical processes inter-animate with the written word? How does spoken word speak through movement? This chapter will present spoken word as a *biodynamic* creative process, where the body is the medium for the *expression* and *transformation* of feelings.

The poem's next journey is into the crowd. At a time when poetry is saying yes to audiences, how is it adapting to live circumstance? **Chapter 6: 'The Contract of "Emotional Participation" and the Rhythms of Audience and Affect'** will attempt to answer this. Keeping the focus on physical processes, it will look at the live encounter as an intersection of coded biological and energetic transactions. Consciously and subconsciously, the performer is manipulating the nervous systems of the audience and vice versa. Through rhythms and rituals of sound, silence, eye contact, and laughter; poets and spectators are connected in a contract of 'emotional participation'. This chapter will explore 'the poem' as an energetic exchange and a process of physical attunement.

Where, then, can this participation take us? **Chapter 7: 'Reviving the Ecstatic: Live Poetry, Transcendence and Altered States of Consciousness'** has some suggestions. It will visit the curiously under-discussed connection between spoken word and *peak experience.* The terminology of trance induction is rarely used to describe spoken word. It should be. A skilled spoken word artist can enchant and spellbind an audience, conjuring states of 'collective effervescence' usually associated with the shaman, the hypnotist, or the leader of worship. This chapter will see how they do it.

Having explored the micro-dynamics of stagecraft, **Chapter 8: 'Poetry, Protest and Political Renewal'** will look at how this craft can be deployed as a force for change. Using protest as a case study, I will show how spoken word can enliven and propel social movements. Central to this is live poetry's willingness to be public and festive. Spoken word is breaking the rules, breaking the law, and even getting sentenced in court. We will see how it can occupy, hold, and transform a space with empathy, testimony, catharsis, and joy.

What follows, then, is a topography of a diverse, innovative and progressive artistic movement. This is not just a book about art, but how art can meet many of our fundamental needs. Spoken word is what I call a *remedial aesthetic:* it entertains, it heals, it connects, and it confronts. In an age of ecological and political meltdown, it may be wise to know how.

A Little Existing Literature

The study of oral cultures has a long history of neglect in academia. As a result, the discipline of performance has long been excluded from what we understand 'poetry' to be.

Until the First World War (in a society not yet distracted by radio and the moving image) performed poetry was widespread and popular, but this culture was excluded from academic consideration.[14] 'Poetry' became a strictly *textual* consideration and 'performance' was consigned to 'drama' and 'theatre' studies.[15] By the middle of the twentieth century, these trends had crystallised into the academic ideology of *New Criticism*. In advocating a 'close reading' of the text alone, New Criticism deliberately rejected any consideration of the social milieu from which it grew. The voice and biography of the author, the manner of their performance, and the context of their historical moment were judged to be inadmissible evidence.[16]

In 1960, the discussion around oral poetry changed dramatically when Milman Parry and Albert B. Lord broke the code of oral composition with *'oral-formulaic theory'*. By studying the performances of twentieth-century Slavic bards, they were able to recast our understanding of many of our most treasured 'scriptures' as belonging to an ancient *oral* discipline, with its own techniques and characteristics that were both distinct from literature and highly complex. In light of this, many now believe that 'Homer' may never have existed. Instead, 'his' entire body of work is most likely to have grown from centuries of collective oral design, transmitted through generations of bards in Ancient Greece. Oral-formulaic theory shows us how these epics (often over ten thousand lines in length) were kept alive through techniques of memorisation, and rhythmic, part-improvised retellings.[17]

Building on this work, the sixties and seventies saw a small renaissance in our understanding of oral poetry. Anthropologists coined the term 'orature' (as a counterpart to literature) to speak of the complex poetic skills of oral societies.[18] New fields such as *ethnopoetics* explored the rich verbal heritage of non-literate and indigenous societies.[19] 'Poetry' started to become de-centred from the text in a way that challenged the regime of New Criticism. Writing in 1983, linguist Paul Zumthor called out the 'specialized, ethnocentric and culturally imperialistic values' of the literary world.[20] His words point to an implicitly racist tradition within academia over what qualifies as 'poetry' and 'culture'.

The emergence of *performance studies* in the seventies further democratised our view of poetry. Performance studies developed a conception of art as a *social event*, embedded in a matrix of human interactions.[21] Central to these interactions is the human body, which became recognised as having its own things to say on matters such as gender, sex, and race.[22]

Around the same time, *socio-linguistics* was finding a science to look at 'speech communities' who lived outside the gates of 'standard' and 'official' dialects. William Labov did groundbreaking research on Afro-American verbal culture, challenging long-held assumptions of black 'verbal deprivation' and 'cultural deficit'.[23] Black American dialects, he argued, were often versatile and high-functioning verbal cultures. These cultures, like many other 'sub-cultural' speech communities, have fed into contemporary spoken word.

In spite of these reappraisals, lingering prejudices survived. David Wojahn, for example, says that performance is 'not fundamentally artistic' and condemns the 'methods of delivery and gimmickry that owe more to showbiz than to literature'.[24] This legacy of disregard has left many achievements to disappear into the fog of the canon. To this day, much academic work on poetry in performance focuses on 'the reading' or 'the recital', rather than 'the show' or 'the gig'. Among those who are writing about live poetry, there is still considerable frustration over the fixation on poetry as text. Poetry is incomplete, they argue, if 'quarantined', 'entombed' and 'petrified' in the 'verbal refrigerator' or 'prison house' of the page.[25]

Rebecca Watts's contentious 2018 attack on spoken word poets (mentioned above), shows how the legacy of New Criticism still colours how we value poetry. Watts condemns 'the "achievement" of being considered representative of a group identity that the establishment can fetishise'.[26] Her argument neglects to consider the interface between the written and spoken word, and between poetry and the conversation of society. Like appraising Bob Dylan by a transcription of his lyrics, Watts surgically removes the text from its social context.

We should perhaps not be surprised by 'the establishment's' proclivity towards established poetry. Nor should we be surprised when institutions like academia are cagey in embracing emerging art forms. What matters is that spoken word is winning its place as a subject of serious study. Anyone considering studying it can be assured that enough literature does exist. Notable examples from the UK include Trévien (2018), Novak (2011) Gräbner & Casas (eds.) (2011) and Gregory (2009). In the US these are complemented by Johnson (2017) Hoffman (2013) Somers-Willett (2009) and Bernstein (1998) to name just four. The critical discussion around spoken word is becoming more possible, with video and online recordings that capture it before it disappears into thin air. At the time of writing, the UK is experiencing a flurry of new books on this subject from Lucy English & Jack McGowan, as well as Katie Ailes, James McKay, and Hannah Silva. It is an exciting time to be working as a poet and researching spoken word.

Until now, the scene in the US has dominated the writing on spoken word both in and outside of academia. Books on 'slam' and 'spoken word' have captured the colour and vibrancy of the movement, with montages of interviews, essays, poems, and the happenings of the scene and its poets (see Glazner, 2000 and Aptowicz, 2007). The seminal work *The Spoken Word Revolution* (2003) speaks directly to poetry's lost constituency—young people.

In the UK, Munden & Wade, *Reading the Applause* (1999) and Hoyles & Hoyles, *Moving Voices: Black Performance Poetry* (2002) deserve celebration as books that have come out of the scene, though they are now around two decades old. Initiatives are now underway to chronicle the achievements and innovations of performance poetry in the UK.[27] There is also a growing DIY culture of review websites, blogs, and narrowcast interviews on podcasts and YouTube.[28] If spoken word teaches us nothing else, it is the importance of telling our own story.

Given the primacy of the spoken word to the history of poetry, as well as contemporary verse, it is astounding how little has been written about it. As we have seen, this legacy of neglect has grown out of a disembodied (bordering on necromantic) tradition of poetry criticism.

How this Book Works

In reaction to this, *Stage Invasion* will situate live poetry within the moments, places, and people that surround it. For those events where I was present, I will speak of my place in them and how the poems impacted me. This *ethnographic* method (developed by anthropology and other social sciences) recognises 'the fieldworker is never truly "invisible"' but *implicated* in what they observe.[29] As a method of research, ethnography is well suited to the *interpersonal* experience of live poetry. As any audience member knows, the 'entire person' of the observer is a 'research tool', inextricably involved in the 'empathetic participation' of the show.[30]

Stage Invasion builds on the research I did for the Writer/Teacher masters programme at Goldsmiths College, University of London. In the two and a half years I spent researching and writing the book, I have drawn on performance studies, linguistics, cultural studies, philosophy, sociology, psychotherapy, hypnotherapy, media studies, anthropology, African-American studies, and literary criticism. You do not need to have a working knowledge of any of these subjects to read this book, but you are encouraged to read the bibliography and notes. The book owes much to the research of others and, I hope, is a gateway to further study. The research also looks to newspapers, magazines, blogs, and social media posts, which can also be found in the back of the book. More broadly, *Stage Invasion* draws on fourteen years of informal research carried out as a practising spoken word artist.

This book is not a who's-who or what's-what of UK spoken word, but I have tried to incorporate as many voices as possible from the movement, mainly from English performers. These voices were harvested in interviews with fifty poets, promoters, educators, and other actors in the scene, which can be watched on dedicated YouTube and Vimeo channels.[31] Again, I encourage you to go to these videos as they explore many themes beyond the covers of this book. These interviews build on a further eighty that I recorded over four years as the UK host of the world's largest spoken word podcast, *Indiefeed Performance Poetry*, and all of this builds on hundreds of informal interviews carried out over many years: backstage, in pubs, and wandering around festivals.[32]

To gain a statistical understanding of spoken word, I recorded data from over 140 poems performed live at the Hammer & Tongue National Poetry Slam Championship. This took place over two days in January 2018 at the Royal Albert Hall in London. For each poem, I collected information on the poet, the subject matter of the piece, and the writing and performance devices used.

Summary

'*The experience of each new age requires a new confession,
and the world seems always waiting for its poet.*'
—Ralph Waldo Emerson

Art forms are ceaselessly being abandoned, reinvented, and reclaimed, but the *Spoken Word Revolution* is actually a renaissance—a re-greening made possible by deep and sprawling roots.

This book is for people who have fallen in love with spoken word but found little in libraries and bookshops that investigates poetry outside of the page or 'the recital'. It is written for those who have dedicated their lives to the art, and those who are picking up on their work. *Stage Invasion* is founded on the belief in the power of words and the social processes that assemble and share them. It is also the one thing I am qualified and obliged to give: my testimony.

Notes

1 Word/Play is a programme of performance poetry workshops for patients with mental health issues, prescribed in GP surgeries in the South West. The project is the initiative of Liv Torq and Roz Hilton, see also Chapter 8, Part 5. 'Word/Play | Take Art' https://takeart.org/word-play

2 'BBC Radio 4 - Front Row', 24 Jul. 2018, https://www.bbc.co.uk/programmes/b0bbn6vs

3 Apples and Snakes, 'Lemn Sissay', 20 Dec. 2017, (00:22:55) https://www.youtube.com/watch?v=RqgWjwLDHE0&t=1374s

4 Katie Spencer, 28 May 2017, https://news.sky.com/story/politicians-could-learn-a-lot-from-the-power-of-poetry-10895834

5 Shamaan Freeman-Powell, 28 Jan. 2019, https://www.bbc.com/news/entertainment-arts-47005108

6 Emma Cook, 13 Feb. 2016, https://www.theguardian.com/lifeandstyle/2016/feb/13/poetry-breastfeeding-and-sex

7 Watts, 'The Cult of the Noble Amateur', 2018, http://www.pnreview.co.uk/cgi-bin/scribe?item_id=1009

8 Heidegger, 'Letter on Humanism' (2000), p.83.

9 Anton, https://www.youtube.com/user/Professoranton; Bolinger, *Language, The Loaded Weapon* (2014), p.141.

10 Sapir, *Language* (1921), p.12.

11 Bakhtin, 'Discourse in the Novel' (1982), p.276.

12 Bolinger, as above.

13 See Chapter 6 of Finnegan, *Oral Poetry* (1977).

14 Harrington, *Poetry and the Public* (2002).

15 For an overview of this history see Novak, *Live Poetry* (2011), p.16–17.

16 Scholes, *The Crafty Reader* (2011).

17 Lord, *The Singer of Tales* (1960).

18 For an introduction to 'orature' see Finnegan, 'The How of Literature' (2005).

19 See Hymes, *In Vain I Tried to Tell You* (1983); Finnegan, *Oral Poetry* (1977); Tedlock, *The Spoken Word and the Work of Interpretation* (1983).

20 Zumthor, *Oral Poetry* (1990), p.16.

21 For a short overview of this history see Bauman & Briggs, 'Poetics and Performance' (1990), p.74.

22   Stiles, 'Performance' (2003).

23   Labov, 'The Logic of Nonstandard English' (1972).

24   Wojahn, '"A Kind of Vaudeville"' (1985).

25   'quarantined': Belle, 'The Poem Performed' (2003) p.14; 'entombed': Robson, *Poetry and Jazz in Concert* (1969) p.15; 'prison house': Foley, *How to Read an Oral Poem* (2002), p.26; 'verbal refrigerator': Middleton, *Distant Reading* (2005), xi.

26   Watts, 'The Cult of the Noble Amateur', 2018.

27   Online archives of UK spoken word include: 'The Apples and Snakes Story', www.spokenwordarchive.org.uk/content/new-contributions/apples-snakes-story; 'Hannah Silva | Case Studies' https://www.bl.uk/case-studies/hannah-silva# ; Tim Wells, 'Standupandspit': standupandspit.wordpress.com ; Brady, Cleary, & Willey, 'British Poetry in Performance, 1960-2008', http://projects.beyondtext.ac.uk/poetryinperformance/index.php

28   The main review site for UK performance poetry is Sabotage Reviews. YouTube channels that have come out of the spoken word scene include Muddy Feet Poetry, Process Production and Raise the Bar. Some podcasts include Lunar Poetry, The Poetry Show, Proletarian Poetry and Lies Dreaming. Other podcasts that have fallen dormant (but still have archived material) include Indiefeed Performance Poetry, Forget What you Heard (about Spoken Word), and Headstand Radio.

29   Tangherlini, '"Oral Tradition" in a Technologically Advanced World' (2003), p.137.

30   Takahashi & Olaveson cited in St John, 'Electronic Dance Music-Culture and Religion' (2006), p.15.

31   For digestible excerpts of interviews see: Stage Invasion: Poetry & the Spoken Word Renaissance Interviews - YouTube', Bearder, Peter, 2018 https://www.youtube.com/playlist?list=PLLXTjXu-0FadrRyrYerlvGpZGTMaysUW6T For full length interviews see: 'Stage Invasion: Poetry & the Spoken Word Renaissance, (Full Interviews)' on Vimeo' https://vimeo.com/album/5871870

32   Indiefeed UK podcasts have been collated on my website (though this is not the sum of UK artists featured on Indiefeed): Bearder, 'Podcasts', http://www.petethetemp.co.uk/podcasts/

Chapter 1:
The Way In: Slam and the
Gates of Culture

'Poetry is an unknown country'
—Joseph Harrington

How did I, and others like me, gain entry to the Kingdom of
Poetry and can the gates of poetic culture be renegotiated? To
begin to answer these questions, we must look at one of the most
controversial things in poetry—slam.

Slam is a live and interactive competition where poets
usually perform their own pre-written pieces to a three-minute
time limit. These performances are scored by judges who are
chosen from the audience or pre-selected as part of a panel.
The tournaments have been the target of vitriol from those
who have considered them an invasion of the world of poetry
and a cheapening of the art. Lorenzo Thomas dismisses it as
rewarding 'scatological doggerel' in events 'where drunken
audiences hoot down sensitive poems about dying grandmothers'.
Literary critic Harold Bloom has called it 'the death of art', while
novelist Martin Amis declared it poetry's 'ghoulish afterlife'.[1] Yet,
for all this talk of death, verse still lives through slam, which (like
it or not) has been part of poetry for over a third of a century.

In *Part 1: My Story—Slam as a Rite of Passage* I will tell of my
entry to spoken word through slam and look at some of the pros
and cons of using slam to baptise new poets. *Part 2: Discussing
Slam* will look at the role of slam in UK literature more generally,
and investigate its role in creating communities and spaces
for *the carnivalesque*. We will hear the arguments for and against
competitive verse and, finally, ask whether slam works as a
form of *deliberative democracy* that can bring audiences into the
conversation around poetry. *Part 3: How Big is the Slam Family?
The Tradition of Verbal Duels* will place slam in the context of oral
contests globally, and sample some of its colourful past.

Part 1: My Story—Slam as a Rite of Passage.

It's 2005 and I am descending the stairs to The Zodiac club on the Cowley Road, Oxford. Below me the slam is about to begin. The air shakes with the sinister and alluring throb of muffled hip hop. I arrive in a dark basement and am surrounded by haircuts and tattoos I wish I were cool enough to have. I feel like I have reached the beating heart of some clandestine tribe. The poetry is raw, visceral, and fiercely political. It stokes something in me, not just intellectually but emotionally and physically. There is a rowdy, heckling slam, with A.F. Harrold, Sophia Walker, and Alan Buckley taking the stage. The night is headlined by the acerbic comic barkings of the Mancunian double act Thick Richard.[2] Young, idealistic, and looking for excitement, I feel like I am in a hotbed of culture, occluded from the waters of the mainstream. Like many who discover spoken word for the first time, I am about to fall in love with it.

The slam was put on by Hammer & Tongue, an organisation founded in Oxford in 2004 off the back of a poetry benefit to raise money for the 'B52 Two' (two protesters who pleaded guilty to, and were acquitted for, sabotaging B52 bomber planes destined to commit war crimes in Iraq). In Hammer & Tongue, I found a place where art and activism cross-pollinated. Radical politics inseminated verse and vice versa. It was seeing Claire Fawcett do a poem about (and an impassioned introduction to) Climate Camp that got me into direct action politics. Spoken word enculturated me politically, and gave me a voice as an activist.

Before long I was slamming myself. In my first slam I opened with a two-minute plug for a benefit gig I was putting on. I hadn't realised that the clock had started from the moment I opened my mouth and had so many points deducted for time violation that I went into minus figures. I was told I had gained 'the lowest score ever recorded at the Oxford slam'.

I attended a series of workshops run by Hammer & Tongue's co-founder Steve Larkin who showed me that being a performance poet was something you could do with your life. I attended gigs, bought books and CDs, and travelled the country to slams and poetry gigs. I met with poets like Mark Gwynne Jones and Chloe Poems (now Gerry Potter) and quizzed them on their craft and their lives. I was inspired by the stand-up poetry of John Hegley, Elvis McGonagall and Kate Fox, enraptured by the honesty and artistry of acts like Joelle Taylor and Salena Godden, and travelled to London to see shows by people like Kat François and Zena Edwards who were among the first to be making spoken word theatre. At the Oxford slams, I saw visits from US poets like Buddy Wakefield, Taylor Mali, and Mahogany L. Browne; a new cadre of international spoken word cult celebrities.

For years I created lots of poorly written poems and called myself a 'poet' long before I was qualified to do so. I mused, memorised, and muttered to myself in train stations and bus depots and, eventually, I started winning slams. In 2009 I won the first ever Hammer & Tongue National Poetry Slam Final, a title I held for two years (they didn't have a final in 2010). Slam was my way into poetry. Raucous and accessible, it licensed the performative and entertaining side of verse.

While all this is true, poetry at slams (which are also open stages) can be of questionable quality. I know because I often won slams with well-performed but poorly-written poetry. While strongly musical, my writing was stuck in the confines of a four-four beat which came from my background as a singer-songwriter. My rhymes were predictably placed at the end of the line, and I relied heavily on (all too quickly crafted) wordplay and figurative language that was crudely thrown together. Much of the content belonged to a well-researched political tradition, but not a poetic one. In short, I hadn't done my homework. In my excitement to get on stage I was memorising poems before interrogating their every syllable.

I started to read extensively and apprenticed myself in metre, the maths of poetry, and started to see the rhythm of poetry in terms of *feet* rather than *beats*. I developed an eye for concision, precision, and the construction of metaphor. I played with forms, attended workshops, and read every textbook I could get my hands on. I read collections of poetry from cover to cover (especially poetry I didn't like) determined to loot what genius was contained in them. I realised how badly I had been writing, and how vast the discipline of verse really is.

Yet my musical training gave much to my poetry: a sense of rhythm, a phrase of breath, a physicality, and a sense of play. As Steve Larkin explained to me, performance poetry 'is halfway between speech and music'. Writing and singing lyrics gave me a working knowledge of assonance, alliteration, parallelism, and syntax. It opened my ears to the percussive qualities of language (something that beatboxing would later increase dramatically). Practically and organically, it taught me how, in Mary Oliver's words, to 'release the energy along the line' and how the right word, in the right place, can give a line its punch.[3]

Slam sharpened all of these skills to competition standard, disciplining me in the vicissitudes of audience reaction and invigorating my writing. In short, it was a rite of passage. As a young man who was driven to express my politics, it also taught me to make an art out of climbing onto raised platforms, shouting and waving my arms around. I am still trying to calm down.

Part 2: Discussing Slam

Let us take a closer look at slam in an attempt to understand why it has become such a popular and divisive force in literature. Is slam the death or the lifeblood of poetry? Are poetry and competition compatible? Where did slam come from? Why is it here and what is it doing?

Slam Credentials

The genesis of slam has been disputed in recent years. Poets like Javon Johnson point to the forgotten existence of 'poetry boxing matches' in the South Side of Chicago in the early eighties.[4] What we can be sure of is that 'slam' (and the format now associated with it) was coined and popularised by a socialist poet and construction worker called Marc Kelly Smith, who ran the first 'slam' in 1984 at Chicago's Get Me High Lounge. Smith wanted to invigorate poetry events by allowing the audience to challenge pretentiousness and complacency among the poets on stage.[5]

The slams were also conceived as democratic. Through participatory ritual, judgement is taken out of the hands of publishers and academics and put into the those of the audience.[6] Unlike the publishing industry, there were no gatekeepers to the new slam culture. By arriving in time to get their name on the list, newbies and nobodies got the chance to become slam winners.

The slam is not, however, a utopia of inclusivity. In Tim Clare's imagined debate between poets, the 'page poet' pipes up:

> If you were truly democratising poetry then
> everyone present would read and perform, listen
> to everyone else, and offer feedback. Hello?
> We already have that over here in the 'poetry
> establishment' - it's called a writing group,
> or a workshop.[7]

Smith's slams were a far cry from the workshop and the writing group. They were vaudevillian affairs where heckling was actively encouraged.[8]

Competitive elements were, however, downplayed—this was not about being a 'great poet' it was about the *game*. In levelling the playing field, Smith wanted to get new people on stage, but the aim wasn't to *certify* poets, so much as *challenge* them.[9]

It is ironic then that slam has become a major arena of what Lesley Wheeler calls 'credentialization', a way for writers and performers to have their skills validated.[10] Around the world, national and international slam can propel poets to notoriety. In the UK, the Poetry Society's annual SLAMbassadors youth slams have launched the careers of many well-known poets, including Anthony Anaxagorou, Kayo Chingonyi and Indigo Williams.

None of these poets are still slamming. Unlike countries such as Germany and the US, where it is possible to earn a living as a travelling 'slam poet', the UK slam scene is not big enough to sustain the career of a performing poet.[11] Whether for reasons of finance or because of changing tastes, most established UK poets (if they ever did slam) usually cease to do so. Slam, then, functions as an *initiation* in UK spoken word.

The 'Slam Family'

Helen Gregory argues that slam is an *art world* (a term she borrows from sociologist Howard Becker's work on *interactionism*). Slam, she argues, is the product of complex systems of human interaction which form 'local, translocal and transnational networks'. It is not just a literary *form*, but a *forum* of people (or 'for(u)m' for short).[12]

In the US, slam has created a conversation within and between cities on a landmass of over three hundred million people united by its common language. Since the mid-eighties, institutions like Poetry Slam Inc. have created an infrastructure of competitions, networks, and conventions. National and international competitions (such as National Poetry Slam or Brave New Voices) can last up to a week, and attract many thousands of participants. Young, and usually politically charged, these events are celebrated as a significant contribution to the cultural discussion.[13]

In the UK, slam is also a generative force in poetry. Since the first UK slam was started in London by Farrago Poetry in 1994, British slam has diversified into a broad pallete of formats. The annual Poets vs MCs event in Brighton pitches (you guessed it) poets against MCs.[14] Stand-Up and Slam events involve stand-up poets and stand-up comedians. Flash Slam is a forum for flash fiction, and Monologue Slam is an 'industry showcase' for actors to perform dramatic monologues.[15] These examples are not an exhaustive list.

Hammer & Tongue hold monthly slams in six cities and an annual slam at the Edinburgh Fringe.[16] These 'translocal' artistic communities serve as a touring network for established poets and upcoming slammers. Regional winners join those from other slam events at the annual UK Finals in the Royal Albert Hall, a yearly opportunity for spoken word to meet, integrate, and celebrate. What's more, the international connections

of organisations like Farrago have given slam winners the opportunity to represent themselves and their country at international
slam events.

The Place for Carnival in Poetry?

Slam is not only performed by adults at competitive events, it is
also used as an educational tool in the classroom, where poets
have discovered the slam format can enable children to find
a love of language and performance that they may not have
realised they had.

Poets like Giovanni 'Spoz' Esposito, Richard 'Dreadlock
Alien' Grant, and Joelle Taylor brought a carnival spirit into
the classroom by developing Slam Days for schools throughout
the nineties and noughties. Slam Days are rapid-fire workshops
and team exercises that propel entire year groups into bouts of
verse. Class war. Winners go on to enter inter-school slams and
win awards for themselves, their classes, and their schools. I have
seen primary-aged children turn volcanic with excitement over
slam. These lines are from Sultan (his real name), aged seven,
who performed his 'boast poem' (with every muscle in his body)
at a slam I ran in Curwen Primary School, London:

> When I go outside the police faint
> I'm so talented every singer went to jail
> When I go to Dancing the teacher lays a red carpet
> I'm so hot all the dragons retired

Slam speaks to the play, kinesis, and competitiveness of youth,
allowing poetry to be experienced as a team sport. As ritualised
drama, it embraces elements of poetry that the teaching of
English has neglected: cheering, booing, and the stamping of feet.

Slam scholar Tyler Hoffman argues that these rituals belong
to the ancient human aesthetic of *the carnivalesque* (a literary mode
that was coined by Russian literary critic Mikhail Bakhtin).[17]
Slam inverts official culture and ways of speaking to indulge
in laughter and the profane. For a moment, the world is turned
upside down. To 'take the holy art of poetry and thrust it in

the spotlight of gladiatorial combat' (to quote Bob Holman) is to allow a playful irreverence that is at right angles to what we often associate with 'poetry' and 'literature'.[18] Through slam, the Spoken Word Renaissance reintroduces poetry to the *festive* and the *revelrous*.

Such cultural practices were suppressed in Northern European culture when the modern world was stirring in the sixteenth to eighteenth centuries. During this time, carnivals and other popular celebrations were wiped from the streets by religious and political elites.[19] Popular oral culture (like that of street corner ballad singers) was often clamped down on as vulgar and licentious. Historian L.I. Davies argues that the 'learned' and rational values of the 'Enlightenment' were also infused with a fear of 'the mob'.[20] By this analysis, slam can be seen to counteract what David Fleming calls the 'play deprivation' of Western culture (more on this in later chapters).[21]

In her poem, 'Crowd Pleaser', Brenda Read-Brown defends her craft from the objection that poetry should be temperate or 'right on':

> I'm not here to rant and rage,
> or whinge about my woes and worries -
> I earn my place on the stage
> with jokes and feel-good stories.
> Crowd-pleaser, I hear them sneer.
> She's a crowd-pleaser; nothing more.
> And the lords of poetry slam the door.
> Well, let's face it, a poet pleasing a crowd?
> The thought turns your stomach;
> it shouldn't be allowed. [22]

Read-Brown's sarcasm at stomach-churning pleasure came from being publicly attacked as 'a crowd pleaser' when she became poet laureate of Gloucestershire in 2012. The poem goes on to tell of the elderly and terminally ill patients she has worked with, their lack of self-pity and their wicked sense of humour. At the end of the poem, one of them asks her to '*write a poem to make my mourners laugh.*' In this surprisingly poignant poem, the ludic and the carnivalesque become not just entertainment, but therapy for the remote and atomised in her community. 'Crowd Pleaser' shows that the carnivalesque meets a need in young and old alike.

The Controversy of Competition

The competitive element of slam has made it the target of scorn, and not just from within the 'literary establishment'. Amiri Baraka, one of the principal poets of the Black Arts Movement (see Chapter 3) dismissed slam because:

> ...they make poetry a carnival, the equivalent of a strong man act. They will do to the poetry movement what they did to rap, give it a quick shot in the butt and elevate it to commercial showiness, emphasising the most backward elements.[23]

For Lemn Sissay, one of the UK's most famous poet-performers, 'the judging of a poem out of ten reduces what it is to be a poet'. Sissay even accuses it of preventing the growth of 'an entire generation of poets'.[24] Even youth slam pioneer Joelle Taylor believes that slam has drifted from the ethos she sought to cultivate in the early noughties. Too many poets are 'competing to be the best in the room' instead of getting up to 'own their own voices'.[25] Taylor's criticism should be considered in the context of youth slams that do, by design, minimise competition to encourage new voices. Yet there is a tension between slam's competition and that core value of spoken word—community. Slam is a transgression from the radical roots of performance poetry, says Cornelia Gräbner. Its 'basic element' (competition) is 'counterproductive' to social movements 'because it supplants the politically much more effective practice of solidarity'.[26]

There is certainly currency in these objections. In the nineties and noughties (when US slam became commercially lucrative), North American slam celebrity Taylor Mali became infamous for his calculated approach to winning. Mali even published a tongue-in-cheek pamphlet on team-slam strategy which included tips like 'Don't Lead with your Lesbian'.[27] As we will explore in Chapter 2, the slam format can lead to the following of 'winning formulas' that many believe have infected spoken word with a particular style of 'slammy'.

Like all competitive formats, slam holds potential for sweaty egos and hyper-masculine peacocking. I once saw a slam contestant in the Netherlands light a joint on stage and launch into a five-minute polemic about drug laws. After being told to put it out, he continued his rant until a thickening cringe induced half of the audience to leave. The organisers eventually muted his mic and made a repossession of the stage and the 'poet' left in a huff. In the ensuing interval, everyone was fuming.

Yet these exceptions prove the rule. Anyone who has attended a poetry slam will be familiar with the strong sense of mutual respect and community that they cultivate. For one expert in the oral tradition, James Foley, slam rules are 'channels for some very focused social dynamics'. Slams are, he argues, highly ritualised processes, every aspect of which is 'an appeal to tradition'.[28] The 'MC spiel' of the host introduces rules and expectations to the participants (everyone in the room). They also convey the ethos of the slam ideal, discrediting the competitive elements with stock reminders: 'the point is not the points, the point is the poetry'. Before the competition commences, the 'Sacrificial Poet' (an experienced performer who performs but does not compete) is used to calibrate the judges to ensure fair and consistent scoring. Any scores below a 5 out of 10 are usually formally discouraged.

It should also be pointed out that poetic competition is not exclusive to slam. North American slammer and academic Jeffrey McDaniel compares slams to manuscript competitions (that often charge hefty entrance fees) as well as competitions for arts funding, which are decided by panels of experts who score applicants with points.[29] Former Hammer & Tongue National Champion Theresa Lola compares her win to other poetry competitions she has entered:

> That was the most intense experience I ever
> had, but I love it because it made me respect the
> craft more. It made me a better performer... For
> a poetry prize, for example, you hand in one
> poem. But with slam, you perform a new poem
> every round. The audience are *right there* as the
> decision is being made. With a poetry prize, you
> just receive an email.[30]

Whether it is formalised or not, this contest is present in poetry anyway, says McDaniel. Slam recognises and makes light of implied hierarchies which can be seen in the placement of names on publicity material, or the 'running order' of acts where the 'biggest names' feature last and longest.[31] Not only that, but slam temporarily flattens and even overturns hierarchies. This could explain why established poets don't slam.

In summary, there are legitimate objections to slams from within the spoken word community that deserve to be engaged with. Perhaps the best way slam can do this is to contain the competition in an envelope of lightheartedness which explicitly names the slam for what it is—a gimmick to get poets on stage and (playfully) challenge them. In recognition of this, critics of slam should discriminate between slams that succeed in this and those that don't. Poetry, after all, is a territory with many border crossings.

Slam as 'Deliberative Democracy'

I have often found criticism to dissipate in the polite applause of performance, but slam ignites an argument. Did the winner deserve to win? What type of poet, or poem, always wins these things? Who else should have won and why? The disagreements that happen at the bar or on the journey home are part of what slam is.

This discussion is a type of deliberative democracy, a debate that counteracts power monopolies of experts and representatives. To quote David Lee Morgan, 'it's a difference of opinion that makes an education'. By pitching poetic against poetic, and technique against technique, slam lets the audience participate in the validation of art. The result is a 'fluid' space of competing aesthetics, none of which ever wins outright, argues Joseph Harrington. Putting poetry into a constant state of *contest* and *re-becoming* leads him to suggest that poetry is 'not the prize but the contest itself'.[32]

Hammer & Tongue, as a matter of principle, makes judges out of randomly selected audience members who are not given any criteria for judging. The only qualification for being picked is that they are 'not sleeping with, or have formerly slept with the poet'. The model is founded on a democratic principle which, for Harrington, 'makes the public judge, makes judgement public and publicizes the diversity of judgement within a public'.[33] It is also an appeal to intuition that resists a rational assessment of poetry and the loaded assessments of cultural insiders.

The competition, however, and the method by which it is judged, is premised on a (self-consciously) absurd idea. Good art is a subjective preference, and the decisions of the five judges (chosen randomly) can never truly represent an audience. As the slam saying goes 'the best poet always loses'. In recognition of this, spectators are ritually encouraged to jeer and cheer their opinions at judges. In extreme cases, judges in the US have been known to resign their roles due to audience pressure though I have never known of British audiences taking slam so seriously.[34]

The litany of meta-slam parody events in the UK suggests a recognition of slam's futility in certifying 'winning' poetry. At The Anti Slam, the worst poetry wins, in a comic, cringe-worthy celebration of shabbiness. The event also serves as a live satire on performance poetry (see Chapter 2, Part 2.4). In 2017, Raise the Bar ran a slam at the Edinburgh Fringe called Verses, a two-headed contest of poets presenting improvised poems on subjects pulled from a hat. Points were ultimately determined with mini-games (related to the poem's content) between each round. If the theme of the poems was 'recreation', contestants would have to throw a dart at each other. If the theme was 'growing up', they might have to make something out of play-dough.

Yet perhaps the most ingenious inversion of the slam competition is that of the Dice Slam. A series of these were run by Midlands-based poet Bohdan Piasecki, who borrowed the idea from the Dutch poet Bernhard Christiansen. Here scores are given by the rolling of dice. A panel of judges then tries to justify the dice's score and show why it is the best possible numerical assessment of the work. The winner emerges at the end of the night when the audience votes for their favourite judge.

Even if we could invent a system of judging that fairly and accurately reflects the will of the audience, is this even desirable? Jesse Donaldson criticises the reduction of poetry's worth to scorecards because 'you don't get any specific or useful criticism from those numbers'.[35] However, Donaldson doesn't offer any alternative performance formats that *do* present critical feedback. Indeed, it is hard to see how an open mic or a reading might offer a performer more 'specific or useful criticism' than they would find at a slam.

Some slams use panels of judges composed of established poets applying judging criteria, such as *quality of writing*, *quality of performing*, and *strength of audience response*. One slam in Israel would ask slammers to give two performances of the same poem (with a panel discussion in between to debate the piece).[36] In the same spirit, the Word N Sound slam, in Johannesburg, gives performers feedback (delivered live on stage) from the host Thabiso 'Afurakan' Mohare. Chris Redmond remembers the night from his tour of South Africa:

> He'd be giving *crits!*...: 'Man, y'know, I love this,
> and I love this, but you could tighten that up, and
> that was far too long, and have you tried this?' ...
> And it came from a place of - if we're *doing* this,
> then let's do this the *best* that we possibly can,
> right? Cos' this *matters*.

Even without structured feedback or judging criteria, live performance is a space for *live drafting*, a place where we can gain a feel for edits that need to take place. Slam gives some form and measure to this process.

Redmond continues:

> If you're a stand-up comedian, there is a really
> clear gauge of whether you are doing your
> job well, cos' people laugh. And if you're a
> performance poet...what's the measure?[37]

If slam 'makes judgement public, and publicizes the diversity of judgement within a public', then the act of making judgement explicit (even if it is reduced to numbers) does at least provoke an argument. This dispute can make audiences better audiences and poets better poets. As poet Lucy English remembers, 'you can't win a slam now with a poem that would win you a slam in the nineties.'[38]

The assessment of live poetry is contested because people care deeply about getting it right, and 'right' is the topic of endless debate. In opening poetry up to public scrutiny, slam has knocked the scab off an old tension in poetry—that between the 'popular' and the 'cultivated'. Of course, what qualifies as 'cultivated' is itself open to debate. Thanks to slam, that debate is happening in the audience.

Summary

Over the last quarter of a century, UK slam has become a diverse and vital feature in the poetry landscape. Rooted in play and experimentation it is (in the UK at least) less a *destination* than a *beginning*. Slam gives us rituals that allow for new voices to sidestep less-accessible routes of publication and become certified as audience-worthy. At the heart of the game is an insistence on invoking the crowd. This audience focus helps sharpen the performance qualities of verse, rewarding the music, theatrics and humour of those who may not have a background in English 'literature'. It also offers a carnivalesque dynamic, a remedy to 'play deprivation' in society and literature alike.

The desire to make poets accountable to the crowd tussles ceaselessly with the complications of handing poetic judgement to groups of random people. It remains to be seen if an increas-

ingly mature live poetry circuit will remain content with au-
dience-judged slams. It also remains to be seen whether slam's
game of *deliberative democracy* will continue to entice audiences to
take part in poetry and the arguments around it.

What we can say, however, is that slam is not the 'death of art',
but an evolution of it, a continual process of re-becoming. Indeed,
as we will now see, it belongs to a family tree that is larger than
we might think.

Part 3: How Big is the Slam Family?
The Tradition of Verbal Duels

Slam is not new, nor is it a departure from what poetry is or
should be. Though it is rarely recognised in the discussion
surrounding slam, adversarial poetry belongs to a long and
multifarious tradition. This section will place slam in the context
of its history, and of the extended family of verbal contest genres
around the world.

Slam's (documented) history dates back to the beginning
of written records and encompasses a vast variety of styles and
formats. Whereas most modern slams bestow a symbolic title of
'Slam Champion', past poetic tournaments might involve prize
money, goods, or even spiritual benediction. Bouts could be
funny, informative, or philosophical, and they were often deadly
serious.[39] The satirical verse of ancient Arabic poet-magicians,
for example, were believed to induce anything from blisters to
death.[40] Throughout history, such practices have belonged to
commoners or aristocrats alike. In the Japanese courts (9–15th
century CE) lengthy and elaborate tournaments forged new
ground in poetic theory and practice. They were the main
outlet of publication and the most important feature of Japanese
literature for over half a millennium.[41]

The Ancient Greeks had a genre of *invective poetry* (poetry
that denounces or insults) called *iambos*, (*iamboi* in the plural).[42]
These frenzied and impassioned performances are believed to
have been highly sexual and were sung and danced at festivals
that honoured Dionysius (the god of wine and ecstasy). *Iamboi*

used rhythms that were considered closest to everyday speech. Because of this association, the genre lent its name to the metrical system that has been elemental to the poetry of Western civilisation ever since—the iambic.[43]

In the modern world, verbal duels open the door to 'a rich and complex universe of verbal art that has been insufficiently explored or understood' argues Valentina Pagliai.[44] They can range from the duels of Sardinian shepherds, alone with each other for months in the hills, to the song duels of Inuit people, or even large multimedia events replete with music, dance, and costume (as we will see below). Scholarship, she argues, has too often generalised them as combative and primitive. Looked at closely, however, verbal contests merit attention for their 'eloquence, cleverness and beautiful imagery'.[45]

Let's look at some examples that help illustrate this variety. The following contests cover four separate continents, drawn from both history and the modern world:

Flyting

Flyting was the verbal jousting of medieval Celtic, Norse, and Anglo Saxon feast halls and courts. Competitors hurled rhyming couplets at each other in bouts that could be either serious or funny. The winner, who was decided by the audience, was often presented with a large cup of mead, though bouts were also known to end in sword fights. In Scotland, *flyting* served as a forum of identity politics, frequently playing on rivalries between highlanders and lowlanders as well as those between English and Gaelic speakers.[46] It continued there until the eighteenth century, even though participants could face fines, or even whipping, for public profanities.[47] Since the 1980s scholarship has revised our understanding of this 'base' activity as a battleground of 'astonishing dexterity'.[48] Practitioners would experiment with literary and rhetorical techniques to gain status, wealth, and respect in their communities. Below is an excerpt of Scottish *flyting* from the 1580s court of King James VI. Patrick Hume of Polwarth ridicules Montgomerie for his drunken verse:

Thy raggit roundaillis, reifand royt,
Sum schort, sum lang and out of lyne
With skabrous collouris, fowsome floyt
Proceiding from ane pynt of wyne

Your irregular roundels, thieving fiddler
Some short, some long, and out of line
With harsh, unpolished metres, nauseating flute[-player]
Proceeding from a pint of wine[49]

Aitysh

In modern day Kazakhstan and Kyrgyzstan *aitysh* (or *aitys*) competitions host the verbal artistry of singer-poets who sling witty and satirical improvisations at each other to the accompaniment of stringed instruments or accordions. Winners are decided by the audience. Throughout its thousand year history (including times of Soviet occupation when it survived underground), the art form has served as a vehicle of Islamic Sufi mysticism, current affairs, and cultural identity.[50] Today, many practitioners enjoy celebrity status through televised competitions that win them anything from cars and apartments to large cash prizes. *Aitysh* poets, who can be male or female, train in their craft for many years and are revered as the 'historical memory' of their people. *Aitysh* is not just an art form but a 'way of thinking' and a vehicle for the 'cultural code' of the land.[51] In 2015 *aitysh* was listed as a UNESCO representative of the Intangible Cultural Heritage of Humanity.[52]

The Dozens

The Dozens, also known as 'sounding', 'signifying', 'woofing', 'wolfing', and 'sigging' (among other names), was a comic battle of improvised insults (and frequent 'your momma' jokes) that was popular among black American adolescents up until the late 1970s.[53] The practice, which emerged from the same 'cultural-historical matrix' that gave birth to rap battles of the hip hop era,[54] has often been pathologised as an 'infantile', or even 'neurotic' release of masculine aggression and sexuality.[55] Comparisons have also been made between *the dozens* and the verbal combat of 'primitive' societies.[56] Recent research has reappraised this tradition for its complex interactivity that forces contestants to involve, monitor, and respond to the audience and their opponents.[57] In his autobiography of the late 1960s, H. Rap Brown recalls playing *the dozens* in his childhood:

> Hell, we exercised our minds by playing the dozens. And the teacher expected me to sit up in class and study poetry after I could run down shit like that. If anybody needed to study poetry, she needed to study mine... Sometimes I wonder why I even bothered to go to school. Practically everything I know I learned on the corner.[58]

Haló

Haló events are serious business. In modern-day Ghana, the Anlo-Ewe people use these elaborately staged multimedia contests to settle disputes between villages. Spoken word performances combine with music, costume, and visual icons.[59] Groups can spend years in secret rehearsals preparing for a single show. In *haló*, the human voice is in close dialogue with a chorus of singers as well as drum patterns that imitate the rhythms of the poet's speech. Mime and specially produced wooden carvings are used to emphasise particular verbal attacks. In case the opponent doesn't get the message, singers periodically stop to explain the insults hidden in the metaphors.[60] Unlike *the dozens*, *haló* events are *meant* to cause insult. Each target of the abuse must be present and made known so that the accuracy of the lampoons can be judged by the audience (who are separated from performers by a rope to prevent attacks). Bouts frequently end in violence. After the village chief has declared the winners, he symbolically 'buries the song' in the ground and warns the warring parties to cease.[61]

Summary

Considered within the family of verbal contest genres, slams are relatively uncompetitive. Unlike the above examples, poets are not pitched face-to-face, nor do they react with witty invectives against opponents. These samples only scratch the surface of what competitive verse has contributed to poetry. Yet the format is so recurrent that it can well be assumed as simply part of what human societies do.[62] It is also a central aspect of *oral* culture. For Walter Ong, orality is inherently more combative, or *agonistic* than literacy. The spoken word is a provocation that lives in the contested conversation of 'us' and 'here', and the very presence of the performers creates an arena well suited to proving selfhood and establishing identity.[63] Mouth-to-mouth combat, then, is intrinsic to poetry in performance.

Notes

1   Wheeler, *Voicing American Poetry* (2008), p.127; Johnson, *Killing Poetry* (2017), p.1; Novak, *Live Poetry* (2011), p.181.

2   Thick Richard now performs solo. In 2005 he was part of a double act with Bob Moyler who now performs in Scotland as a Morris dancer with a sex robot. See interview with Thick Richard, Stage Invasion, Vimeo.

3   Oliver, *Rules for the Dance* (1998).

4   Johnson also foregrounds the roles of black poets in the genesis of slam (as well as its continued development) and challenges Somers-Willett's idea that slam has 'white working-class' roots. See Johnson, *Killing Poetry* (2017), p.23.

5   Smith & Eleveld, *The Spoken Word Revolution* (2003).

6   Smith & Eleveld, as above.

7   Clare, 'Slam: A Poetic Dialogue' (2010), p.137.

8   Smith & Eleveld, as above, p.116.

9   Aptowicz, *Words in Your Face* (2007), p.35.

10   See Chapter 5 of Wheeler, *Voicing American Poetry* (2008).

11   For a fuller comparison of UK and US slam see Gregory, 'Texts in Performance' (2009); Gregory, '(Re)presenting Ourselves' (2008); Wilson, 'Edinburgh versus Austin' (2018).

12   Gregory (2008); Gregory (2009), as above.

13   Diggs & Smith, 'Why Poetry Is The Best Medium For Kids Who Want To Change The World', 19 Jul. 2016, https://www.huffingtonpost.co.uk/entry/why-poetry-is-the-best-medium-for-kids-who-want-to-change-the-world_us_578c0c57e4b03fc3ee5146d3?guc-counter=1.

14   Bailey, 'Poets Vs MCs 2018 Review', 24 Jan. 2018, *Brighton Source*, https://brightonsource.co.uk/reviews/poets-vs-mcs-2018-review/.

15   Holloway, 'Flash-Slam – National Flash-Fiction Day', https://nationalflashfictionday.co.uk/index.php/category/flash-slam/ ; Monologue Slam, http://monologueslamuk.com/.

16   Hammer & Tongue, http://hammerandtongue.com.

17   See Bakhtin, *The Dialogic Imagination* (1982); and, for application

to spoken word, Hoffman, 'Treacherous Laughter' (2001).

18   Quoted in Glazner, *Poetry Slam* (2000), p.16.

19   Davies, 'Orality, Literacy, Popular Culture' (2010).

20   Davies, as above, p.308.

21   Fleming, *Surviving the Future* (2006), p.64.

22   Read-Brown, 'Crowd Pleaser', unpublished poem.

23   Hoffman, 'Treacherous Laughter' (2001), p.49.

24   Sissay, 'Lemn Sissay Interview', Apples and Snakes, 20 Dec. 2017, https://www.youtube.com/watch?v=RqgWjwLDHE0.

25   Joelle Taylor Interview, Stage Invasion, Vimeo.

26   Gräbner, 'Is Performance Poetry Dead?' (2007), p.82.

27   Somers-Willett, 'Can Slam Poetry Matter?', https://www.rattle.com/rattle27/somerswillett.htm.

28   Foley, *How to Read an Oral Poem* (2002), p.164–165.

29   McDaniel, 'Slam and the Academy' (2000), p.36.

30   Theresa Lola Interview, Stage Invasion, Vimeo.

31   McDaniel, as above.

32   Harrington, *Poetry and the Public* (2002), p.184.

33   Harrington, as above, p.176.

34   Harrington, as above, p.174.

35   Donaldson, 'This Is Why You Probably Hate Slam Poetry, According to a Linguistic Scholar', Feb. 2017, https://www.vice.com/en_uk/article/aejne8/this-is-why-you-probably-hate-slam-poetry-according-to-a-linguistic-scholar.

36   Marc Smith, 5 Apr. 2013, https://www.youtube.com/watch?v=M-mH_ePoYCOM.

37   Chris Redmond Interview, Stage Invasion, Vimeo.

38   Lucy English email to Peter Bearder, 1 Aug. 2018.

39   Reinink & Vanstiphout, *Dispute Poems and Dialogues in the Ancient and Mediaeval Near East* (1991), p.2–3.

40   Miner, 'Poetic Contests' (1993).

41   Miner, as above.

42   Brogan, 'Invective' (1993), p.627.

43   Brogan, 'Iambic' (1993), p.548.

44   Pagliai, 'The Art of Dueling with Words' (2009), p.82.

45   Pagliai, as above.

46   Flynn & Mitchell, '"It may be verifyit that thy wit is thin"' (2014).

47   Hughes, *An Encyclopedia of Swearing* (2006), p.175.

48   Flynn & Mitchell, as above, p.72.

49   Quoted in Flynn & Mitchell, as above, p.73.

50   Shatayeva, 'Aitys: Gem of Kazakh Spoken Literary Tradition, Platform for Human Rights', 6 Jan. 2017, https://astanatimes. com/2017/01/aitys-gem-of-kazakh-spoken-literary-tradition-plat-form-for-human-rights/.

51   UNESCO, 'Aitysh/Aitys, Art of Improvisation - YouTube', 2 Dec. 2015, https://www.youtube.com/watch?v=hKBG6JmJK0k.

52   UNESCO, 'Aitysh/Aitys, Art of Improvisation - Intangible Heritage - Culture Sector', 2015, https://ich.unesco.org/en/RL/ aitysh-aitys-art-of-improvisation-00997.

53   Lefever, '"Playing the Dozens": A Mechanism for Social Control' (1981), p.73.

54   Pagliai, as above.

55   Abrahams, '"Playing the Dozens"' (1962).

56   Lefever, as above.

57   Samy Alim, & Mason Carris, 'Moving the Crowd', "Crowding" the Emcee' (2011).

58   Lefever, as above, p.75.

59   Pagliai, as above.

60   Avorgbedor, 'Freedom to Sing, License to Insult' (1994), p.92.

61   Avorgbedor, as above, p.95.

62   Parks, 'Flyting, Sounding, Debate' (1986), p.439.

63   Ong, *Orality and Literacy* (1982), p.44.

Chapter 2:
What is Spoken Word Poetry?

Throughout this book I will be using a variety of terms interchangeably: *spoken word, poetry, performance poetry, live poetry, oral poetry* and *live literature*. The best synthesis in a single name is *spoken word poetry*. All of these terms are, in part, social constructs. That is to say, they are made up *by,* and made up *of,* people. Among these people are differing groups, agendas, and trends that form a complex and evolving ecosystem. To speak of this ecosystem, we must first explore the territory. To that end, this chapter will look at:

Part 1: **The Medium**
(the media through which it speaks)
Part 2: **The Style**
(some broad stylistic trends)
Part 3: **The Social Form**
(the community and its process, beliefs, and values)
Part 4: **Towards a Genre of Spoken Word Poetry**
(summary and definition)

Spoken word has not been widely examined as a genre in its own right, but (as we will see in this chapter) it deserves to be. Genres come into existence through the work of communities that interpret, and speak them into being.[1] In that spirit, let's begin.

Part 1: The Medium of Spoken Word Poetry

First to the *medium,* or the *form of delivery*; on one level this may seem obvious—spoken word is an *oral* art form, it is about the *spoken, performed* word. We will start here by looking at the ancient practice of oral poetry (or *orature*) then look at modern names for oral poetry in the UK, notably *spoken word, performance poetry* and *live literature,* to unpack some assumptions around this often misunderstood art form

1.1 The 'Oral Tradition'

'Spoken word reignites the ancient fireside tradition' I was once told by the poet Richard 'Dreadlock Alien' Grant backstage at Glastonbury festival. I have heard this sentiment frequently expressed in the spoken word movement, and rightly so. It is hard to underestimate the importance of *spoken* artistry to humanity as its lineage is as far-reaching as our chromosomes.

A lack of recorded evidence makes it impossible to trace the development of the verbal arts fully. Nevertheless, human language is believed to have evolved from a kind of 'musi-language' that was spoken by our early hominid ancestors. This form of expressive utterance (that we can find today in many of our animal cousins) most likely used musical-poetic elements such as melody, timbre, metre, tone, and onomatopoeia.[2]

We have been fully-developed as modern humans for 300,000 years, while literacy only arrived to (some) human societies from 10,000 years ago. For most of that history, it has been the preserve of small groups (such as scribes, priests, and ruling officials), and 'mass literacy' started only within the last few hundred years.[3] If we were to condense human history into the last twenty-four hours, the appearance of societies with widespread literacy will have occurred only in the last forty-three seconds.[4]

Humanity has always reverberated with oral poems, chants, and songs; verbal patterning to lull us to sleep, learn, work, wed, drink, march, battle, and bury. In modern times, this body of lore has come to be known as the *oral tradition*. This tradition encompasses a spectrum of spells, charms, curses, incantations, proverbs, and riddles, as well as nursery rhymes, genealogies, recipe poems, and funeral laments, to scratch but the surface.

A bird's eye view of the 'tradition' necessarily makes modern categories, like 'poetry', 'prose' and 'rhetoric' defunct. In any case, such terms are arbitrary constructs that are culturally relative to particular places and moments in history. The Yoruba people of West Africa, for example, have separate names for praise poetry, hunting poetry, and festival poetry, but no overarching word for *poetry*.[5]

Not only is the oral tradition diverse, but it is also, very often, a high art. Scholar of orature Paul Zumthor explains:

> oral poetry generally has more rules, and more
> complex ones than the written form: in pre-
> dominantly oral societies, oral poetry is often a
> much more elaborate art than are the majority
> of our written productions [6]

In pre-Roman times, Druids were reported to have trained for twenty years, maintaining sacred knowledge in the form of verse.[7] Later, in medieval Ireland, special bardic schools would teach highly prized poets in the lauding of praise and curse. Their words were believed to have magical properties with which to shape reality, and the chief poet had a status equivalent to the king (as well as a special chair in court).[8] Indeed, the poets of oral cultures are often the bearers of societies' history and knowledge. (W)rapped in rhyme, story and song, they purvey genealogies, property deeds, and even juridical knowledge. They are, in the words of David Abram, 'living encyclopedias'.[9]

Deeply embedded in society, oral poetry has been an age-old 'equipment for living' in a way not generally associated with the 'high art' of poetry today.[10] For scholar of medieval poetry John Niles the idea of poetry as 'a separate realm empty of social function' is an aberration of modern industrial societies.[11]

Spoken word, then, is a return to what poetry has been for the overwhelming majority of its history. To recognise this is not to reduce it to the status of primitive or uncivilised, but to understand it as an often complex craft, that can be a vital part of how society functions. What is more, spoken word's willingness to expert itself in what is popular and accessible helps to *de-privatise* poetry. Key to all this is a focus on the intrinsically *social* medium of the *spoken* voice. In the words of James Foley:

> Oral poetry is a crucial cog in the revolving
> wheel of culture, a verbal support system for
> social activity and identification, a partner to
> effective cultural citizenship.[12]

1.2 Not the 'Oral Tradition'

Beyond these broad similarities, spoken word should not be con-
flated too directly with the 'oral tradition'. This is both because it
is the product of a literate society and because the tradition con-
tains so much variety that it can stretch comparisons to breaking
point. It is this variety that I will turn to now.

Oral poetry is a vast and nebulous concept whose definition
shifts according to its situation in time and space. Oral poets
may sing, chant, or have instruments such as a lyre or drum.
They may recount the stories of ancestors or spin tales of their
own. They may poem for love, for money, or only to (or from)
the gods.[13] Oral poetry might be memorised or improvised.[14] It
might 'belong' to a family, village, ancestor, or even some magico-religious entity.[15] Perhaps the most significant similarity between spoken word and the oral tradition is that it is so hard to
define.

One aspect that illuminates this diversity is that of status. Orature may well be practiced by revolutionaries, buskers, and outlaws, but it is also the property of courtiers, shamans, healers, and oracles. Spoken word's current identity as a
grass-roots poetic then, is at odds with many of the more cere-
monious masks the tradition has worn in the past. In sixteenth
century England, for example, a 'minstrel' was a licensed po-
et-musician who was entitled to practice the revered art form.
Unlicensed poets, on the other hand, were persecuted as beggars
and vagabonds.[16]

The difficulty in defining spoken word by the oral tradition
doesn't stop there. Scholar of oral poetry Zumthor (backed up by
Finnegan) points to the remarkable fact that 'most poetic performances, in all civilisations, have always been sung'.[17] Of course,
'sung' is often difficult to distinguish from 'chanted' or 'shouted'
and oral poetry lives on a continuum of various registers. Nevertheless, the use of a quiet, spoken voice we might associate with
the 'reading' or 'recital' is very much a product of a literate society. In the absence of microphones, or books to carry the word,
the resonant music of the human voice takes on new importance.

It is also noteworthy that societies without close contact with writing rarely use full-rhymes, preferring instead to thread their verse with things like partial rhymes, alliteration, and assonance.[18] While it is true that the European ballad tradition has ended its 'lines' with full rhymes since medieval times, this was *not* the poetry of a 'pristine oral society', but a partially literate one. This finding refutes the tempting assumption that, if we cannot see a poem written down, we need to rhyme it to remember it.

Since entirely oral cultures have no written records, it is impossible for them to learn a version of a poem that is fixed or 'definitive' in the modern sense of the word. The development of *oral-formulaic theory* has shown how oral cultures use story to memorise poems of epic length. Repeated clichés (the textbook taboo of modern poetry) are skilfully deployed to aid memorisation in oral verse (see the 'wine dark sea' and 'rosy-fingered dawn' used by 'Homer'). Oral epics are also relatively elastic affairs that are retold in part-improvised form.[19] Today's Nepalese shaman, for example, can recount performances equivalent to over ten thousand lines in length, delivered with expert embellishments, and tailored to the audience at hand.[20]

Though many spoken word poets don't come from a 'literary' background, our poetry is, inextricably, the product of a literate society. As Finnegan points out, oral poems don't usually have titles.[21] Nor do they, argues Walter Ong, tend towards *lists*. This fact is significant because one of the most common forms we hear in spoken word is the 'list poem'. While the use of repetition and refrains are regular features of oral poetics, the very idea of a list (which, along with so much else, came to humanity through text) would be inconceivable to a member of a pristine oral (or non-literate) society.[22] Much of our culture's proclivity toward abstract thinking, and our ability to index vast quantities of information, was given to us by writing. Literacy gave birth to academia and, in part, civilisation itself.[23] Indeed the very notion and study of the 'oral tradition' is a product of our classificatory, literate culture.

A romantic identification between 'spoken word' and the oral tradition can also overlook considerable differences in the production and reception of differing poetries. With their writing process, books, and online presence, the spoken word artist may have more in common with James Joyce than the bard of old.

What is more, the prevalence of confessional poetry and first-person narrative that is so familiar to modern spoken word is a relatively recent phenomenon in Britain. Ernst Fischer argues that the rapid social change and the increased individualism of post-tribal, post-feudal societies enabled the *individual experience* to 'hold its own by the side of the tribal chronicle, the heroic epic, the sacred chant and the war song'.[24]

In post-Renaissance Europe, mythology's ancient grip on culture gave way to the 'self-seeking' pursuits of travel, scientific discovery and 'enlightenment'.[25] This change set in motion a path that, by the early nineteenth century, would lead to (among other things) the world's first artist-celebrity, the Romantic poet Lord Byron.[26]

Such developments in creative autonomy are at odds with the often *conservative* nature of the oral tradition. The necessities of memorisation and the importance of preserving ancient knowledge in verse often creates hostility to re-stylisations. This is not to say that individual creativity is absent. As Albert B. Lord points out, the composition of oral poetry is in the (part improvised) performance. In this way the oral poet achieves 'the preservation of tradition by the constant re-creation of it.'[27] Nevertheless, there is a greater tendency in the oral tradition to stay within stock narratives and mythological themes rather than details of the poet's own life. In this sense, spoken word diverges from oral culture which, argues Haun Saussy, is 'engineered by censorship', locked in a closed feedback loop of collective design.[28]

To summarise, British spoken word both is, and isn't, a continuation of the 'oral tradition'. The statement 'spoken word is part of the oral tradition' begs the question 'which traditions, and which parts of them?'

Nevertheless, spoken word is one of the most recent permutations of a vast heritage. Its popularity offers permission to an oral discipline that is often wrongly perceived as beneath 'high culture'. As we will see in Part 2, it draws from (and evolves) a wealth of different oralities. For these reasons, we must speak of contemporary orature on its own terms, and it is those I will analyse now.

1.3 'Spoken' Word, 'Live' Literature and 'Performance' Poetry

The inheritance of this dual citizenship, as both a written and spoken craft, has given modern spoken word an identity crisis. Spoken word is about live, spoken performance, right? The answer to that is—not quite.

First, there is the growth in 'spoken word publishing'. One such publisher, Burning Eye Books, make it their stated aim to print 'the book of the show', which suggests a two-way conversation: page to stage, and stage to page.[29] Even when a spoken word artist is speaking in front of you, they are usually relaying a pre-written text. For this reason, founder of the *Oral Tradition* journal, James Foley, classifies spoken word as 'voiced text'.[30] We could also apply the term *oral literature*, which implies cross-fertilisation of the two mediums.

The label *live literature* is often used to capture this crossover, but this also comes with problems. Philip Auslander attacks the fetishisation of 'liveness', arguing that there is no pure un-mediated (or '*im-mediate*') performance. Instead, the live and the mediated co-exist and co-evolve in a mutual dependence.[31] I once did a TEDx talk in Brixton that was 'live', yet two-thirds of the audience were looking at my face on large screens and few of them could have heard me without the mediation of amplification. My words were then reproduced digitally as film footage on social media. The whole event was made possible by months of web design, promotional graphics, and the prolific literary output of social media.

Any atavistic preoccupation with liveness, while entirely valid in one sense, also risks implying a hierarchy between an *original* and *embodied* spoken word, and a *secondary*, *de-natured* derivative of it on the page. The philosopher Jacques Derrida famously deconstructs the perceived hierarchy of (i) thought, (ii) the spoken word (a *sign* of thought), and (iii) the written word (a *sign* of a *sign*). He argues instead that the world writes (or languages itself) across many mediums: from body language, binary code, to even the algorithms of DNA. For Derrida, each medium of writing has different capabilities and restrictions. None can be said to be closer to the pure *im-mediate* present. Our psyche, for example, mediates sound through the act of listening.[32] By this analysis, we could say the performed poem is a *re-mediation* of the text. Similarly, the individual poet could be said to be a *re-mediation* of societal and artistic patternings. According to Derrida, the idea of a 'pure present' that belongs to an unadulterated 'live' is unstable, bordering on myth.

If the concept of liveness is controversial, surely *performance poetry* describes what we are looking at? The principal method of publication for spoken word poets is performance (whether live or digitally mediated by video or recording). What's more, many poets give and attend performance workshops. As we will see later in this chapter (Part 2.2), a culture of performance does exist in spoken word, making the *medium* part of the *craft* of the art form.

Nowhere is this truer than in spoken word theatre, consisting of theatre shows (usually lasting an hour) performed through spoken word poetry. Spoken word theatre blends theatrical staging with the conversational and intimate delivery of spoken word. Typically, these shows are low-tech though they are now evolving into more complex multimedia orchestrations. The shows are almost always one-person shows that break the fourth wall to address audiences directly with stories told in the first-person or in character, by the authors themselves.[33]

Werner Wolf captures this shift in theatrical approach: 'playwrights and actors were cogs in the wheel; in spoken word, the writer/performer was the wheel'.[34] This type of theatre has become so popular that it appears to have been appropriated by the theatre world under the name 'gig theatre'. Playwright John Farndon argues that 'this is what spoken word has given theatre'.[35] But it is also what 'performance poetry' has given to 'poetry'—linking it back to the theatrical and highly physical origins of its ancient (spoken) history.

Spoken word artists, however, may emphasise or downplay the 'performance' of their texts. As we will see in Part 2.2, there are as many performance styles as there are personalities and some performance poets have performance styles that are purposefully *un-performative* (see Chapter 5). To add to the confusion, some performance poets are not even performance poets. One of the UK's most famous 'performance poets', Hollie McNish, expresses a strong allegiance to the scene but also rejects the label: 'It's not like I'm a performance poet: at my gigs I'm basically reading my poems from the page.'[36]

In short, we are not looking at poetry that is either 'page' or 'stage'. We could even argue that there is no such thing as performance poetry. In the words of Steve Larkin:

> There is only poetry. Some of it is badly written and well performed. Some of it is well written and badly performed. Some of it is well written and well performed. Some of it is just shite.[37]

Summary

In this section we have seen how the vocality of spoken word links it to the broad diaspora of the oral tradition. The title 'spoken word', then, represents a re-centring of contemporary poetry to the ancient influence of the spoken voice. Today, this voice is always in close consultation with the written word (as well as the typed word and a variety of other media). Defining spoken word by its name alone is not sufficient to describe it in the fullest sense. As we will now see, the name 'spoken word' is a large umbrella of character traits.

Part 2: The Style of Spoken Word Poetry

Can spoken word be explained as a style of poetry? In the words of Julia Novak, 'I think what most people understand when they hear "spoken word" is the accessible, politically engaged, often humorous work, that is very popular'.[38] This section will try to find out if it is possible, or even reasonable, to amalgamate spoken word into a definable style. We will do this by looking at some of the significant trends shaping oral poetics in the UK, and testing the validity of the stereotypes pinned to it.

2.1 Is Slam a Style?

Slammy (adjective): Crowd-pleasing poetry that uses excessive theatrics to perform humour, political rhetoric or extremes of emotion (usually relating to the performer's own life), crafted with little attention to writing techniques traditionally associated with poetry.

'Slammy' isn't in the English dictionary, but it is used in the spoken word community (as well as outside it) and usually disparagingly.[1] For some, there should be no such thing as 'slam poetry', which wrongly conflates a poetic *format* (a timed poetry competition judged by the audience) with an *aesthetic*. Yet the old slam maxim: 'there is no such thing as slam poetry, there is only a poetry slam', is widely ignored. The terms 'slam poetry' and 'spoken word' are often used interchangeably. In Germany, for example, I was once asked to perform at a 'poetry slam' that is just a succession of poets doing sets.

In his article 'Slam Poetry Does Not Exist: How a Movement Has Been Misconstrued as a Genre', the Canadian poetry activist Chris Gilpin attacks the 'genre-izing' of slam. The result, he argues, is to exclude different styles and voices from what was founded as a democratic and inclusive movement. Genre, says

Gilpin, leads to imitation, and imitation leads to cliché:

> yelling, speed, tones of distress, waving their
> arms – believing that they are correctly recre-
> ating a cool, new poetic style. In this way, the
> idea of slam poetry has crushed a great deal of
> artistic self-expression.

He goes on to claim that there is nothing in the slam rules that should create this:

> They only compel the artist to focus solely on
> words, voice and gesture in conveying their
> poem, which are the performative requirements
> in any form of orature.[3940]

Susan Somers-Willett's landmark book, *The Cultural Politics of Slam Poetry*, identifies a number of performance tropes (such as extremes of anger, or stories of victimisation) that have become 'formulaic' to American slam. She also notes the use of the *volta* or 'break it down moment': a shift in tone towards the end of the poem 'to reveal an epiphany or sense of truth'.[41] These devices, she argues, make up a repertoire of 'authentic slam techniques' alongside 'call-and-response, repetition, sampling, rapping, beatboxing and effusive rhyme.'[42]

For Somers-Willett, slam is a 'representational practice'; an arena where poetry about leftist politics and racial identity scores highly. These poems, she continues, can sometimes be self-validating for the mostly white and politically liberal audience members who are judging the slam. The book has since been criticised by Javon Johnson, who argues that the book doesn't offer the possibility that black poets can win slams by virtue of their art.[43]

The 'founder' of the slam competition, Marc Smith (See Chapter 1, Part 2), is disparaging of what he sees as having developed into narcissistic virtue signalling and careerism. For Smith, these indulgences diverge from the original aim of the competition:

> At the beginning, this was really a grass-roots thing about people who were writing poetry for years and years and years and had no audience…Now there's an audience, and people just want to write what the last guy wrote so they can get their face on TV. Well, O.K., but that's not what people in this country, from Marc's point of view, need. We've got too much of that. This show wasn't started to crank out that kind of thing.[44]

For poet and scholar of the movement Katie Ailes the *counter cultural* positioning that Marc Smith laid down also created the conditions for 'underdog' poetry to become successful and marketable in slam. She goes on to argue that the slam rule which requires poets to perform their own material has led to an emphasis on poetry about the Self. What Catherine Wilson calls the 'bizarre and unique ethical policy of honesty' sets spoken word apart from more fictionalized art forms like theatre or novel writing and may be endemic to slam (see also Part 3.3).[45]

On top of this, slam's emphasis on audience engagement (see Chapter 1) creates a prevalence of *accessible* poetry. Ultimately, however, the idea of 'slam poetry' like that of 'open mic music' says Ailes, is an unreliable stylistic marker for a plethora of slam scene micro-environments around the world.[46]

To sum up, there is undoubtedly a risk of spoken word creating a pastiche of itself through slam; one that indulges in bathos at the expense of art and pyrotechnics at the expense of subtlety. Part of this is to do with the culture that it has grown from, which makes it, to borrow a phrase from Keith Jarrett, 'inclusive with a big I'.[47] Yet, while a *slammy* archetype undeniably exists it is, like all archetypes, more reliable as an idea than a stable reality in the real world. It is the instability of *slammy* that I will turn to now.

2.2 Is 'Urban Poetry' a Style?

Slam, especially as it was popularised in the US, is closely associated with hip hop and, by proxy, 'urban' cultural production.

Somers-Willett evidences a 'ghetto fetish' in the portrayal US slam as it has moved closer to the mainstream media. The phenomenon of 'blacksploitation' that stereotypes black gender roles and urban criminality, has already been well-documented in the evolution of hip hop.[48] When applied to spoken word, well-trodden media archetypes of gritty, real, and edgy urban poetry can serve to perpetuate the idea of what Lewis R. Gordon calls 'hip hop poetry'.[49]

Spoken word certainly owes much to the aesthetic of hip hop. Many UK poets, notably Kate Tempest, George the Poet, and Dizraeli have a poetic that is influenced by the hip hop scene to which they owe allegiance. The same debt is owed to the UK's rap poetic of grime by poets like Deborah 'Debris' Stevenson and Sabrina Mahfouz.

Yet, for all of these artists the real import of these genres is not their style of dress or anything reducible to a marketable cliché of urban culture. Through rap, spoken word has gained flow, rhythmic vitality, and complex syncopated rhyme schemes. In one sense, spoken word is the mid-point in a continuum between the precision, ambiguity, and conceptual density associated with 'poetry', and the play, music, and fluidity of 'rap'. They also share a history of grass-roots expression that often (though not always) speaks out against mainstream culture. What UK rapper Carpetface calls 'the Hip Hop values of peace, love, unity, fun and knowledge' could also be applied to spoken word.[50]

However, even in the US where poetry began its relationship with hip hop, spoken word shares its family tree with a diverse family of poetics. These include everything from Dadaism, cabaret, and beat poetry, to Chicanx (or Latinx) poetry, and even cowboy poetry. It also draws on the black church and cultural movements such as the Harlem Renaissance of the 1920s and the Black Arts Movement of the 1960s and 70s (see Chapter 3). What's more, the influence of Motown, blues, RnB, and Jazz show us that hip hop is only *one* musical genre to have fed into US spoken word.[51]

For the uninitiated, it might be tempting to equate spoken word with urban culture. Indeed, the movement as a whole should be wary of lazy journalism which may perpetuate a two-dimensional depiction. Wherever you look in spoken word, you find more and more variety.

2.3 Is UK Spoken Word a Style?

The UK has a history that co-evolved alongside the above. Popular performed verse has been growing in the UK since the Second World War.[52] Its first superstar was the 'Welsh Bard' Dylan Thomas who popularised the image of the travelling performance poet with high-profile tours of the US. Since then, we have had a crop of beat poets, Mersey poets, punk poets, dub poets, and more (see Chapter 3). While slam is a cultural import, British performance poetry is not an Americanism.

'Spoken word' on the other hand, may well be an Americanism. In Britain, over the last ten years, the term 'performance poet' has gradually been superseded by 'spoken word artist'. The term spoken word was used in the UK before this, but connoted other things beyond just performance poetry, including non-poetic forms (such as lectures, book readings, or speaker tours). Jonny 'Fluffypunk' Seagrave remembers a typical 'spoken word' act of the nineties might be a 'hip' journalist reading a column he or she wrote for an underground magazine.[53] The current sense of the term is apparently adopted from the US, which points to an influence of the larger North American scene. It can be no coincidence that this process happened alongside the growth of popular US YouTube channels such as Button Poetry and Speakeasy NYC.

This influence may have changed UK spoken word for the better. As an American poet once told me at the Edinburgh Fringe festival, American verse has 'a wider emotional spectrum' than its British counterpart. If we British are 'mildly culturally autistic' and in possession of a 'social disease' (as the cultural anthropologist Kate Fox argues),[54] then the emotionally candid and unapologetically expressive American way might offer a healthy balance.

Could a globalised 'McPoetry' kill the diversity of UK spoken word? At the turn of the century, performance poet SuAndi lamented that 'in the past two years the poetry performance circuit [in the UK] has died a death'. One of the culprits, she argues, is the American import of slam which did 'tremendous harm'.[55] Criticisms such as these are based on the idea that US spoken word has a history and cultural context that cannot be reproduced elsewhere.

Two decades on, the same criticisms are frequently made. As one of the coordinators of the annual UniSlam (an inter-university slam) pointed out to me, the influence of the American voice can be heard in many of the younger poets rising through the scene.[56] The complaint of unoriginality is frequently leveled at the confessional and highly personal 'trauma poems' more closely associated with North American spoken word. YouTube and slam then, may well be Trojan Horses for the import of US poetics to the UK.

Yet significant differences remain. In her 2017 comparison of the slam scenes of Edinburgh and Austin, Texas, Scottish poet Catherine Wilson found the CUPSI national student slam to be worlds away from what she was familiar with at home. The main difference is just how seriously competition is taken Stateside, with team coaches scribbling scores on hand made charts and calculating averages as the bouts progressed. 'Unfair' judging decisions had long and complex appeal process and numerous poets cried to the point of breakdown during their pieces. For Wilson, this 'breaches an unspoken ethical understanding in Scottish spoken word'. If a poem is that triggering, she argues, it is not ready to share and it raises suspicion that the poet is faking it for competitive impact.[57] Perhaps more than anything, it is the degree of *sincerity* (or perhaps *insincerity*) that separates the poetics on either side of the pond. Taking oneself too seriously breaks what Fox calls the 'oh come off it' rule of British social intercourse.[58]

What differences, then, between the styles of vocal delivery? Hannah Silva cracks the genome of the 'British spoken word voice', distilling it as:

A   Consistent use of falling tones at the
         end of every phrase.

B   A narrow range of pitch, clustering around high tones.

C   The placement of pauses or in breaths in a way that disrupts the usual formation of sentences: after, rather than before the word that separates clauses.[59]

From her interviews with poets, Silva finds evidence that this has been steadily converging towards 'American spoken word voice' since slam began in the mid-eighties. American spoken word voice differs only in one respect: a rise in intonation (or pitch) at the end of phrases.[60] I should note here that Silva does recognise that 'poetry voices' are constantly changing and it is impossible not to vastly generalise on this matter.

Many older poets I have spoken to have lamented the loss of diversity in British performance poetry that was previously known for its humour and cabaret quirk.[61] Would a younger version of a top-hatted gentleman eccentric like A.F. Harrold, or drag acts such as Rachel Pantechnicon or Chloe Poems (now Gerry Potter), fare as well in today's world of spoken word? As Seagrave put it to me, 'it all seems to be gritty urban realism these days.'[62]

In an influential blog post of 2014, Niall O'Sullivan, the host of one of London's longest running open mics, Poetry Unplugged, remembered 'The Death of Performance Poetry'. Performance poetry, he argues, ran from the 1970s through to the late nineties / early noughties This 'distinctive style and approach to poetry' was carried by punk poets like John Cooper Clarke, John Hegley, and Attila the Stockbroker; as well as dub poets like Linton Kwesi Johnson, Jean 'Binta' Breeze, and Benjamin Zephaniah. These poets were superseded by 'later phase' performance poets such as Patience Agbabi, Lemn Sissay, and Murray Lachlan Young:

It was this breadth of performative style as well as a literary style that signified performance

poetry as a mature art form…individuals that
were truly married to their craft.[63]

After this came 'spoken word', a new phase exemplified by names
such as Polarbear and Scroobius Pip who often quoted 'hip hop
artists as their immediate influences rather than poets'. O'Sullivan ends by softening his criticism, noting that, as spoken
word entered the maturity of its second decade, innovation was
bubbling up through all the initial excitement.

O'Sullivan's blog doesn't pretend to be an in-depth analysis of
the history of spoken word, and his distinction between performance poetry and spoken word should not be taken too literally.
If there ever was a point of transition, the nights, organisers, and
poets blurred between the two 'eras', and many just adopted the
new name.

2.4 'Dear America': the Slamming of Slammy in Slam

There are strong reasons to suspect that the 'slamminess' of the
US spoken word archetype has not successfully cloned itself in
the UK. We can find evidence of this at the Anti-Slam Apocalypse (a slam where the most cringe-inducing poem wins), held
at the Hackney Attic, London, on 9 December 2016. Here the
slammy caricature became the object of satire in a team performance by spoken word artists Sarah Hirsch and Ben Fagan.

The poets (going under the name #TeamTrending) stand before two microphones in thick-rimmed glasses, beanies, and fun-
damentalist, monochrome black. Their postures are stiff, their
expressions are grave and defiant, and their eyes fix on the back
of the room. Each of them holds a selfie stick so they can live-
stream their performance. In bad American accents, they perform the following poem, 'Dear America':

Both:	He called me baby
Male:	because fuck you.
Female:	Dear America -
Both:	ONE

Male:	The first time I saw my father cry
	his tears were your blood
	and your blood was stained
	with the ancestry too white,
	blood, too red
Both:	TWO
Male:	...red...period.

[...]

Female:	I am metaphor.
Male:	Fuck you.

[...]

Female:	My body is not an apology.
Male:	My tongue is not an excuse.
Female:	My womb is not an accident.
Both:	FIVE
Female:	They told me my pretty was just
	sleeping
	like Jesus, when he slept
	and dreamed about America.
Both:	If this is the American dream,
	pinch me,
	because I need to wake up.

The piece caricatures the now overused 'letter poem' form, and not without reason. A search for the word 'Dear' on the Button Poetry YouTube channel returns an amusing litany of correspondences: 'Dear Straight People', 'Dear Privilege', 'Dear White America', 'Dear Creationists', 'Dear Beyonce', etc. It also takes a shot at the clichéd 'number poem'; perhaps from Guante's viral piece 'Ten Responses to the Phrase "Man Up"' which opens with: 'Number one: Fuck you'. It also pays homage to Taylor Mali's famous spoof slam piece, 'How to Write a Political Poem' with its line 'somewhere in Florida, votes are STILL BEING COUNTED'.

[…]

Female:	Somewhere in America, all the children are taking drugs.
Male:	Somewhere in the world, other children are making drugs.
Female:	Somewhere in this room, some drugs are making children. Sex.
Both:	SIX
Female:	sex is a beautiful car crash.

[…]

Female:	My eyes are Twitter blue.
Male:	I am simile
Female:	like….me on Facebook.[64]

The self-streaming antics of the #TeamTrending twitterati poke fun at the digital literacy of hipster chic and the famously inflated ego of the poet-preacher-freedom-fighter. The piece also brings to life the US archetype of the hyper-sincere and politically charged spoken word artist, declaiming in a tone of righteous anger.

'Dear America', then, is an example of what Urayoán Noel calls the 'post slam era', where the confessional pathos, 'vocal histrionics', and 'programmatically celebratory or denunciatory', are recognised as the clichés that they are.[65] Nowhere is this more apparent than in the reaction of the Anti-Slam audience (drawn from the UK spoken word scene) falling over itself in cathartic laughter.

The poem also shows that slam is an evolving historical phenomenon, with a culture engaging in a self-reflexive critical conversation. If it did become too stylish for its own good, #TeamTrending suggests it may be getting over itself. More proof is needed, however, before 'slam style' can be put to bed. Let's see now if that can be done.

2.5 Is UK Slam Statistically 'Slammy' in Style?

At the 2018 Hammer & Tongue Nation Slam Final, I collected data on 140 poems from sixty-one spoken word artists. From this snapshot I will investigate if there is such a thing as a *slam style* in the UK. Below is a summary of the findings; a more detailed breakdown can be found in full in the Appendix at the back of the book.

To recap, *slammy* can be described as: 'crowd-pleasing poetry that uses excessive theatrics to perform humour, political rhetoric or extremes of emotion (usually relating to the performer's own life) crafted with little attention to writing techniques often associated with poetry.'

From all the data collected, the characteristic that stood out most noticeably was that an unignorable 80 per cent of poems made 'medium' to 'heavy' use of humour; that is to say that they had many jokes, or were primarily funny poems. The near monocultural use of humour does conform to the *slammy* stereotype. We could attribute this to the famous British sense of humour or even a specific culture within Hammer & Tongue events. It might also be because this was a slam, and poets want to please the audience, which is also valid thing to want to do.

Concerning subject matter, most of the poetry was pretty 'woke' and 'conscious' of the issues of the day; a fact that also fits with the slammy stereotype. For a full breakdown of subject matters see Part 3.1. The majority of the poems also used accessible, everyday language. Depending on your viewpoint, you could see this as populist dumbing-down or democratic and audience friendly.

Beyond this, the slammy archetype begins to break down. I estimated that only around 50 per cent of poems were explicitly about the poets' own lives, or people in their lives. This figure challenges the idea that 'realness' and 'me me poetry' are central pillars of slam and spoken word. Poems were imaginatively theatrical, with a fifth of all poems inhabiting the voice of a persona. What's more, the range and quantity of poetic devices used dispels the notion of slam as artless soapboxing. It was also interesting that a piece from Brenda Read-Brown made a gag about 'blank verse' which got laughs from the crowd, suggesting that poets are competing in the context of a relatively 'literary' audience.

Regarding performance, only a fifth of pieces were committed to memory. Nevertheless, there was attention to the delivery of texts read from the page, which shows an apparent culture of performance. There was, however, no 'typical' slam performance. Performance styles varied between performers, and between different poems from the same performer.

Somers-Willett's 'authentic slam techniques' of 'call-and-response, repetition, sampling, rapping, beatboxing and effusive rhyme' were almost non-existent. Poets mostly didn't over-perform their material but used a range of performance registers appropriate to their pieces.

In summary, the poems were mostly funny, 'conscious', and accessible—which you might expect from slam. Yet page-craft interanimated with this and there was not an excess of theatrics or gimmickry. These statistics indicate, then, that UK poetry slams are not *slammy*, neither is there a uniform style of UK slam poetry nor perhaps, by extension, of spoken word.

Summary

At the beginning of this section, I asked if it is possible to define spoken word as one particular style. The short answer to this is no. Though we have only looked at broad stylistic trends here, we can say that the influence of US spoken word has been *the* dominant theme—and controversy—in making the current UK scene. Beyond that, stereotypes betray what is a diverse family of styles in the 'post slam era'. This diversity is not just because the divisions between page and stage are blurring, but because many of the tropes that characterise slam have become hackneyed and been abandoned. One thing that isn't abandoned, as we will now see, is an undeniable streak of red.

Part 3: The Social Form of Spoken Word

> *"'poetry" is not reducible to "poems"'*
> —Joseph Harrington

If spoken word poetry is more than a *medium*, and cannot be reliably described as a *style*; perhaps its most salient feature is its *social form*: its shape as a sphere of *human action*. This section will unpack the idea of spoken word as a *democratic literary movement*, an art form that is open to non-'literary' disciplines, and is defined by a *people* and the *ethos* that animates them.

Who then are the 'people' of spoken word? Cristin O'Keefe Aptowicz describes spoken word as a 'Noah's Ark, with persons of every ethnicity, every political view, shouting and whispering onstage',[66] yet very little concrete information exists on the people who make up spoken word. This section will start by looking at the *art worlds* that feed into it. I will then touch on the theme of diversity by analysing the role of poets of colour. From these findings, it will be possible to identify some ethics and ways-of-doing that have emerged from spoken word as a *social form*.

3.1 The Art World(s) of Spoken Word

Poet and slam scholar Helen Gregory describes spoken word as many interlocking *art worlds* (a phrase she borrows from sociologist Howard Becker).[67] As a performance arena, spoken word draws on worlds beyond 'literature' alone and this openness is a defining feature of the genre.

Though some arrive in spoken word through rap (see Part 2.2), many start as actors. Kat François, for example, has a theatrical background that still peppers her spoken word sets with dramatic monologues. Others, such as Rachel Rose Reid, came from the world of storytelling, while many begin as musicians (including myself as a singer-songwriter). Chris Redmond started in the pantomimes his dad put on when he was a child:

> I grew up with this feeling of *this is what we do,*
> we *get people together*…we sing, there's jokes…
> we go for the experience… So from a performance
> sense, I have a very strong impulse to gather people.[68]

Spoken word lives in a 'triangle between theatre, live music and comedy' argues stand-up poet Thick Richard. He remembers his route to poetry through cabaret and band nights:

> It opened us up to different criticisms, really.
> The expectations of a band night and that kind of thing
> are very different to the poetry…You have to grab their
> attention…You have to grab em' with one hand and beat
> em' around the head with the other… [With poetry]
> people have turned up to sit down quietly and listen, and
> then I start blabbering on this horrible stuff and calling
> them a bunch of cunts and they're like, '*why are you shout-
> ing at us*!?' [laughs] [69]

The differing routes to the spoken word stage have fed what Cornelia Gräbner calls a 'critical, marginal or even outsider position towards the poetic establishment'.[70] This position is fast being abandoned, especially among the more established (and published) spoken word artists. In growing closer to the platforms, funds, and festivities of the 'literary establishment' poets often begin to reject the designations 'spoken word artist' or 'performance poet' as 'label[s] they put to tell us we're not proper poets.'[71]

This journey back to 'poetry' may also be a symptom of the art becoming more 'respectable'. Poet Jem Rolls calls this 'the revenge of the normal', a regression to a more genteel and safe 'literary' standard.[72] In the nineties his Big Word night in London brandished the tagline 'this is not books, this is raw word'.

The diversity of *social forms* that have fed into spoken word results in a variety of *critical expectations*. To understand it as a genre, then, we must look at the communities and the people in it. Who are these people? I will now look to poets of colour to help explore this.

3.2 Poets of Colour and UK Spoken Word

British poetry has had problems when it comes to racial diversity. In 2017, The Complete Works' report damned the poetry publishing industry's 'tradition of whiteness', pointing to the fact that Faber & Faber has published three poets of colour in its eighty-eight year history.[73] As late as 2005, less than 1 per cent of poets published by major UK presses were black or Asian.[74]

Spoken word has been an arena of poetry in which this has changed in recent years. For spoken word poet Salena Godden the increase in diversity has been significant since she started:

> I'm not the only girl one, or the only brown one
> in the village any more, whereas in the old days it
> was a kind of toss-up between me and Francesca
> Beard in 1994… and Patience Agbabi.[75]

At the 2018 Hammer & Tongue Slam Final, I estimated around 10–13 per cent of competitors to be poets 'of colour', a figure that roughly matches the 13 per cent of the British population from black and minority ethnic backgrounds.[76] It is important to note that this figure doesn't account for how the poets self-identified. It also doesn't tell us about spoken word more generally, or about Hammer & Tongue slam finals across different years.

What can be said is that Hammer & Tongue actively seeks to reflect diversity when programming guest performers and this is typical among spoken word organisations. Tobi Kyeremateng, a producer at England's largest spoken word agency Apples and Snakes, outlines her motivations for representing poets of colour:

> For me, living in London – as diverse a city as
> it is – predominately Black spaces are few and
> far between, and this isn't a coincidence. Black
> spaces are known to have been targeted and
> attacked by authorities and racist communities,
> meaning there are few consistent spaces for
> Black people to congregate in without being
> seen as threatening.[77]

Apples and Snakes have booked over 2000 poets for 1700 gigs since 1982. Of their top ten most booked artists, seven are poets of colour.[78] Again, such figures can't be held up as representative of the scene as a whole, yet we cannot deny the role of poets of colour in UK spoken word and it is not without reason that Lucy English says that they have been 'the chief engines of the popularity of spoken word.'[79]

In *Moving Voices: Black Performance Poetry*, Asher and Martin Hoyles show how black oral traditions have been a Gulf Stream that has changed the British poetry climate permanently. In the eighties and nineties, for example, Caribbean poets like John Agard, James Berry, and Valerie Bloom MBE, started in the performance poetry circuit and ended up all over the GCSE syllabus.[80]

Hannah Silva points to the 'black sermonic tradition' as a principal source of 'British spoken word voice'. The 'grand, preacher-like declamatory style' of Kate Tempest, for example, can be traced to the African-American and Caribbean techniques of political oratory (see Martin Luther King) and the oral practices of black worship. Evidence of the 'longstanding relationship' between the two types of 'cultural performance' can be found in the call-and-response familiar to many spoken word and hip hop spaces.[81] Silva even argues that the phrasing and delivery of British spoken word voice, as well as its strong musicality, has descended directly from Afro-diasporic orature (see also Part 2.3).

True though this inheritance is, there are dangers in labelling spoken word as 'diverse' and 'accessible'. For one, it can emphasise a sense of difference between the poetry of privileged and unprivileged groups. This risks patronising poets from disadvantaged backgrounds as participating in a 'poetry for people who don't like poetry'.[82] Many poets of colour reject the terms 'spoken word artist' or 'performance poet' because of their associations as a lesser art form than page poetry.[83] Such titles can serve to enforce the 'literary ghettoization' of belonging to an art world of black writers. This is understandable given the history of discrimination, tokenism, and exoticism that has been used to depict poets based on their colour, or their class, gender, nationality, or region.[84]

I once heard someone refer to 'black poetry', which is not a genre of poetry any more than 'black clothes' is a type of clothing. While almost nobody, at least publicly, uses this term, it reveals an attitude that, while seeking to be inclusive, can ultimately enforce otherness. The equation of spoken word with ethnic diversity then, risks racialising how the art form is depicted.

Nevertheless, the fact that spoken word has become more diverse is to its credit. Since 2002, the number of black and Asian poets published by major UK presses rose from 1 per cent to 20 per cent, and many of these have grown out of the spoken word art world (including Bernardine Evaristo, Roger Robinson, Nick Makoha, Malika Booker and Inua Ellams). In the last few years, 50 per cent of those shortlisted for the esteemed Forward Prize and Ted Hughes Award have been non-white.[85]

Spoken Word has played a big role in this. As a hybrid art form, it has embraced the oral tradition of places like the Caribbean and the poetics of popular culture (like dub and hip hop). Black performance poets who started as outsiders to the literary world in the eighties and nineties, like Linton Kwesi Johnson and Nick Makoha, are now judges in the prestigious Ted Hughes Award (2019) and T.S. Eliot Prize (2019) respectively. Spoken word poets are now regular nominees and winners of the Ted Hughes Award (see Introduction) and, in 2018, the black American spoken word artist Danez Smith won the Forward Prize. At the award ceremony they performed their viral poem from the Button Poetry YouTube channel 'Dinosaurs in the Hood'. 'Not bad for a slam poet, huh?' they tweeted after the event.

If spoken word is motivated by a drive to foreground marginalised voices, we cannot understand the art form without understanding its politics. It is those I will move to now.

3.3 Spoken Word as a Leftist Ethos

What are the political opinions of spoken word? To label it with a single political ideology would be as reductive as giving it an

individual style. And yet, as a movement of people, it is undoubtedly 'progressive', and *implicitly leftist*.

At the 2018 Hammer & Tongue National Slam Final, none
of the poetry was right wing, though much of it was 'right-on'. It
is likely that Conservative voters in the audience (if there were
any) would have felt pretty uncomfortable. This fact in itself challenges the idea of spoken word as all-inclusive 'Noah's Ark'.

The most visited subject matters related to *social and economic
justice* (including gentrification, housing, education, class, and
treatment of the elderly). Other issues (in order of quantity) were:
sexuality/gender identity, *feminist issues* (including discrimination and
perceptions of beauty), *racial and national identity*, and *mental health*.
The remaining subjects of note were: *poetry*, *religion*, and *royalty*, as
well as *social media*, *vegetarianism*, and *terrorism*. Massive hippies.

If this data sounds like a bunch of people reading *The Guardian*
at you for twelve hours, don't worry. Many of these topics were
carried in personal stories, like this short poem from an emerging young poet from Brighton, Sebastian Causton:

Who I am

I bath in the dark,

but by the flickering candle light I can see my body.
The bubbles have betrayed me,

dispersed into little islands leaving my flesh exposed.

I see my curves,
my hips,
my cunt,
my tits.

I bring the slightly damp joint to my lips,
plant them tightly,
like receiving my lover's last kiss.
I close my eyes and think, but I know who I am.
For the first time I can say with some clarity;

I'm a man.
One with curves,
and hips,
and a cunt,
and tits.

It's taken nearly 25 years to understand,

but this is it.

Causton's poem is a living testimony, straight from the lips of the author-performer. Unlike the artist who hangs a painting in a gallery, Causton *is* the art, 'an animate subject rather than an inanimate object'.[86] This *authenticity* has become a central concept to spoken word and it has everything to do with 'Who I Am'.[87] We cannot disentangle the poem from the fact of him standing on stage, making an intensely private picture visible. While he is first-and-foremost a person sharing a poem about his life, the performance is *implicitly leftist*, an act of 'visibility politics' that re-presents an identity, and challenges the hegemony of the heteronormative.

'We have to read poetry as cultural practice' writes Gräbner. The performed word cannot be separated from other cultural markers, such as accent, background, and dress (or artefactual communication). All of these things and more come together in the body of the performer which makes spoken word, to borrow from Gräbner, 'an intersection of social, political and literary spheres'.[88]

Spoken word, then, is a discussion; a forum for people to gather and share stories. In the words of Matt 'Monkey Poet' Panesh: 'You can't call yourself civilised unless people have got the access to the tools of self-expression, and poetry is the first step on that road.'[89]

Poet and promoter Sam Berkson was drawn into spoken word because, as a 'radical democratic space', it was both *implicitly* and *explicitly* political. While a student at Oxford University he was put off by the readings of the University Poetry Society which he found to be 'very dry' and 'deathly boring', partly because they were closed social environments. Outside the college walls, he found an 'inclusive space' in the Hammer & Tongue 'community events'.

> There's a vibe that is created by the fact that it
> is run by people with those sort of politics. Even
> though there is nothing explicitly political about
> running a poetry night, it informs the way in
> which the night is organised, the way people are
> welcomed, the relationship between performer
> and audience and also the political viewpoints
> of the poetry that is coming out.[90]

Spoken word is undoubtedly a cultural territory of the left. This trait is both explicit (in its stated belief systems) and implicit (in the way that it functions as a community and a live art). However, we must make an important distinction: this is not *political discourse* so much as *poetic discourse*, where the global and the public mix with the personal and the intimate. As we will now see, this intimacy is another defining feature of spoken word as a social form.

3.4 Spoken Word's Ethos of Sociality

'This is not a mic; it's a baton. You pass it on.'
—Joelle Taylor

In light of what we know of the people and the beliefs of UK spoken word, it is possible to identify some characteristics that can be said to be its *ethos*: the spirit, attitudes, and aspirations through which it manifests itself. By looking to what surrounds the text, spoken word becomes a genre based on *sociality;* possessing a method that is intrinsically sociable and based on cooperation and mutual support.

In his book *The Spell of the Sensuous,* David Abram argues that the spoken utterance feeds, and is fed by, the 'pulse of the place'. It weaves into an embodied interaction with the living fabric of life in a way that the written word does not. According to Abram, the phenomenon of the silent reader, alone with the page, is a symptom of literate societies that are characterised by *interiority* and divorced from the rituals and interactions that encircle the work of the oral poet. [91]

Indeed, *asocial reading* (the practice of reading silently from the page) only came about in the few hundred years since literacy became widespread, and with it the practice of reading for private leisure. Before this, reading mostly occurred as a social activity that happened—aloud—in places like monasteries, taverns, and barns.[92]

Since then, the idea of poetry surrounded by people in this way has become a distinct ideological position. For some, poetry should be a contemplative affair that not only dwells in silence but thrives on it. Performance, they argue, should be approached with great caution, and it should certainly not be loud and entertaining. In the words of Richard Howard:

> If we are to save poetry, which means if we are
> to savor it, we must restore poetry to that status
> of seclusion and even secrecy that characterizes
> our authentic pleasures.[93]

By this philosophy, our relationship to the page is a séance with the imaginary, the distant, and the dead. Ralph Waldo Emerson once said that a library is 'a kind of magic cavern which is full of dead men. And those dead men can be reborn, and brought to life when you open their pages'.[94] This séance with the unseen continues when we write. As Mary Oliver puts it 'when you write a poem, you write it for anybody and everybody.'[95]

When we perform a poem, however, we perform it for whoever is in front of us. This is where the *sociality* of spoken word begins. Raymond Antrobus, a poet whose work lives on both the page and the stage, believes that the world of page craft comes with its own distinct psychodynamics. Live performance offers the poet an instant and accessible gratification that can't be found through publishing on the page:

> You write in private (unless you're one of the lucky
> people with a trusted writing community) and you
> submit your work blindly into the sphere and hope
> for the best. If you're seeking validation from the
> mainstream publishing industry, this is a slow
> anxiety-riddled process.[96]

'Being able to speak offers control and ownership' argues Leicester's poetry activist Emma Lee. Lee uses spoken word to open up spaces for healing among those who have suffered trauma such as asylum seekers or victims of abuse. The standardised rejection slips of literary magazines don't encourage poets to retry, she argues, 'the more rejections they get the harder it becomes to keep submitting poems for possible publication.'[97] Indeed, acceptance rates for these magazines are often under 1 per cent and many accomplished poets with online submission management systems have similar success rates.[98] Of course, not all forms of publication need to be easily accessible, but if poets want isolation and discouragement, publishing in litmags can be a great way to get it.

In contrast, spoken word finds 'authentic pleasures' of sociality. Nowhere is this more so than in poetry education, which has been transformed over the last thirty years by the initiative of spoken word poets. Spoken word education is a fun and performative form of 'dialogic learning'; a horizontal and emancipatory educational philosophy based on sharing experiences and getting involved (rather than being taught, or analysing the work of 'the greats').[99]

Since 2014, the Spoken Word Education Programme has worked to embed full-time, trained spoken word educators in London secondary schools. The programme (which I was lucky enough to take part in) was founded in collaboration with Goldsmiths, University of London by the world's first full-time spoken word educator on a school payroll, Chicago's Peter Khan. The programme created artistic communities in class and at after-school spoken word clubs. Here, young people shared stories—through performance—in a way that developed social-emotional skills as well as an understanding of literature.[100]

Students prepared team performances over periods of several months for showcases that were attended by classmates, families, and teachers. It was here that the *social form* of spoken word worked its magic. The day after the showcases the 'Poets', consecrated by human attention, walked taller around the school.

In schools, as elsewhere, spoken word is driven by a desire to enable voices. I will now turn my attention to the manner in which I have found this done.

The title 'poetry activist' was coined by New York 'slam master' Bob Holman to capture the idea of poetry as *social action:* a way of changing both society and poetry from the bottom up.[101] This grass-roots approach is *rhizomatic*. Rhizomes (like crabgrass or ginger) are horizontal root stalks. Unlike vertical root networks (such as those of trees), a rhizome can give rise to a new plant from any piece of itself, even if separated. The symbol of the rhizome (developed by philosophers Gilles Deleuze and Felix Guattari) has become popular in anarchist political theory as a metaphor to describe leaderless organisation.[102]

Spoken word, like a rhizome, is not a *hierarchy*, but a *heterarchy*. As we will explore in Chapter 4, it owes its existence to its horizontal connections as much as its vertical ones. In its most basic form, it needs no financial root network and can happen without institutional support, venue, or even amplification.

We can see this in the story of spoken word artist James McKay, who recalls visiting Berlin for the Millennium celebrations:

> It absolutely blew my mind. Here was this decaying
> city in which people were throwing parties, opening
> night clubs, squatting buildings, opening up galleries...

Berlin's rhizomatic DIY ethos had created a vibrant cultural scene with little-to-no money. Inspired, McKay put on a living room gig in the spring of 2000 which served as the genesis of a spoken word scene and his life as poetry activist:

> In Newcastle upon Tyne there was (I think it was
> fair to say) not much to do... the bars had all discovered
> DJs (which are cheaper than bands), all the musicians
> were out of work and moaning about not having any-

where to play. There *just* wasn't anything that wasn't mainstream, short sleeve shirt and violent. So we stayed in creatively and started a living room cabaret.[103]

Like all poetry activists, McKay helped improvise a micro-environment within a movement that would go on to support him as a poet, an educator, and an organiser.

All of this is at odds with the notion of the secluded, contemplative art of poetry. Intrinsically social, spoken word is threaded with a culture of human contact, a sociality that can be said to make up an ethos of the movement as a social form.

Summary

There has not been space to give a full rundown of diversity in UK spoken word, and I have focused here on poets of colour. Much more could be written on gender, age, disability, and sexuality, and the Appendix has more statistics on some of these from my research. But given the absence, and arguably the impossibility, of a precise definition of *who* spoken word is, it is better to look at the values and processes that hold it together as a *social form*.

Of this, we can say that spoken word's identity grows from its background as a *grass-roots aesthetic* that has given a platform to 'non-literary' strands of verbal arts, and to artists who didn't have a voice elsewhere. As a conversational arena of sharing, togetherness, and mutual support, spoken word is *implicitly progressive*, and very often it is *explicitly* so as well. Like it or not, spoken word is *structurally leftist*, and even if we believe that art should be above ideology, we cannot deny that it exists.

Part 4: Toward a Genre of Spoken Word Poetry?

This broad investigation cannot capture the movement in its entirety. I have given no attention to the forms of spoken word that mirror the sonnets, villanelles, or haikus of the page.[104] There is also no account of UK spoken word's many organisations, events, and activities.

Nevertheless, spoken word has enough *generic* traits to qualify it as a genre in its own right. I am using the word *genre* here in the broad sense as a *category* rather than as a *style* because the latter (as we have seen in Part 2) is too unstable.

Spoken word poetry possesses:

- A name that both betrays and re-presents a history of verbal arts that has existed under many names and many forms throughout humanity.

- An emphasis on the spoken (or occasionally sung) performance of written texts.

- A recognition of the role of 'audiotext' and 'bodytext' in the meaning-making potential of poetry.[105]

- A heightened recognition of the audience's role in the reception, ritual, and community of performance.

- A multidisciplinary artistic heritage that incorporates 'stand-up comedy', 'dramatic monologue', 'storytelling', and 'rap' alongside 'literature'.

- An emphasis on reading the poet's own work, with value placed on identity and authenticity.

- A predominance of accessible language and vernacular speech.

- A salience of politically conscious & 'progressive' content.

- A rhizomatic, grass-roots organisational structure, based on the do-it-yourself ethos that consciously seeks to widen access to the verbal arts.

- An innovative engagement with new technologies in the production, publication, and dissemination of poetry.

Since many of the above bullet points could be attributed to poetry more generally, it is tempting to simply call this 'poetry', partly as an act of reclamation, and partly as an act of consensual plurality. However, doing this overlooks many important trends, one of which is the fact that people *identify* as spoken word poets. This fact, I believe, deserves to be recognised.

Yet spoken word is not a solid entity, but a constellation of 'art worlds'. This porosity could even be said to be spoken word's main feature. Indeed, any attempt to build too solid a wall around it creates a territory of meaning as false as that of 'a nation' or 'a people'. Where does 'dramatic monologue' end, and 'persona poem' begin? Is there really a difference between 'the skilful use of tone to effect irony and surprise' and 'a joke'?

The fact that we are still struggling with names and definitions is proof of how successful it has been at bending genres and (re) incorporating things not often associated with 'poetry'. Given the history, it is surprising that the *social, interactive* and *spoken* elements are often dissociated from that word. Spoken word is a renaissance of orature, with all of the skill and technique that word entails.

Yet this renaissance is taking place in a literate society. Its activities are spread across media and a growing *digital literacy* is making it increasingly globalised. The influence of North America on UK spoken word shows how it is part of a *global* conversation that cross-fertilises and risks (but perhaps does not critically endanger) local diversity.

Of all the three sections we have looked at (*Medium, Style* and *Social Form*), the third gives the most reliable measure. With so many spoken word artists writing for the page, it is impossible to define it by the *medium* of live performance alone. Regarding *style,* spoken word is now so large and diverse that it is impossible to reduce it to a single aesthetic. What we can be more certain of is its status as a network, held together by certain values and conventions.

For many poetry activists, spoken word is social and artistic activism. This almost missionary zeal makes it *structurally,* or at least *implicitly progressive* and its success in honouring new voices and new poetics is a democratic victory, a 'devolution' of British culture. This devolution has created an interpretive community that is big enough to claim 'cultural property rights' for itself.[106]

I'm not arguing here that spoken word *belongs* to any one group. A better way to see it is as a *social algorithm,* a replicating formula that patterns itself in art, as well as society at large. Like all social processes, it is continually evolving, and the anatomy I have sketched here is not something fixed. Indeed, the algorithm has changed before, patterning itself into many forms through history. It is these that we will look to next.

Notes

1   For a good take on genres (and how arbitrary they are)
           see Bennett, *Outside Literature* (1990), specifically Chapter 4
           'The Sociology of Genres', p.107.

2   Nussbaum, *The Musical Representation: Meaning, Ontology, and Emotion* (2012).

3   Nunberg, 'The Rise of Mass Literacy in History of Information',
           2 Mar. 2017, https://bcourses.berkeley.edu/courses/1457197/
           files/70812767/download?verifier=jwPo16PWNuIxNi8FVkWlx0BA-
           UUeGjUytlzfm2oAK

4   This figure is calculated from the arrival of mass literacy to the
           British working class through the 1870 Education Act. Fossil records
           for anatomically developed humans date back 300,000 years,
           see Hublin et al, 'New Fossils from Jebel Irhoud, Morocco and the
           Pan-African Origin of Homo Sapiens' (2017).

5   Finnegan, *Oral Poetry* (1977), p.26.

6   Zumthor, *Oral Poetry: An Introduction* (1990), p.60.

7   Saussy, *The Ethnography of Rhythm* (2016), ix.

8   Kinney, *Welsh Traditional Music* (2011), p.2.

9   Abram, *The Spell of the Sensuous* (1996), p.104.

10   Nealon quotes Kenneth Burke here in his argument that late
           twentieth-century literature has syphoned itself off from the
           conversation in society through its taste for obscurity and its
           post-modernist rejection of 'truth' or 'meaning'. See Nealon,
           Post-Postmodernism (2012), p.46.

11   Niles, *Homo Narrans* (2010), p.67.

12   Foley, *How to Read an Oral Poem* (2002), p.189.

13   Finnegan, as above, p.202–205.

14   Foley, as above, p.49.

15   Finnegan, as above, p.270.

16   Kinney, as above, p.7.

17   Zumthor, as above, p.142; Finnegan, as above, p.13.

18   Zumthor, as above, p.139; Finnegan, as above, p.96.

19   Lord, *The Singer of Tales* (1960).

20   Sales, 'The Sources of Authority for Shamanic Speech' (2016), p.246.

21   Finnegan, as above, p.107.

22   Ong, *Orality and Literacy* (1982).

23   McGilchrist, *The Master and His Emissary* (2012).

24   Fischer, *The Necessity of Art* (2010), p.56

25   Mahood, *Poetry and Humanism* (1950).

26   Fischer, as above, p.65–74.

27   Lord, as above, p.29.

28   Saussy, as above, p.54.

29   Melia, 25 Oct. 2017, https://www.bristol247.com/culture/books/
        burning-eye-books-bristol

30   Foley, as above.

31   Auslander, *Liveness: Performance in a Mediatized Culture* (2008).

32   Derrida, *Of Grammatology* (1967).

33   There are exceptions to the one-person show format. UK examples
        include the shows of the Harry & Chris double act, as well as Byron
        Vincent & Dave McGinn. In the US there have even been spoken
        word operas.

34   Quoted in Novak, *Live Poetry* (2011), p.59.

35   John Farndon email to Peter Bearder, 18 Dec. 2018.

36   O'Keeffe, 'Hollie McNish: The Politics and Poetry of Boyfriends,
        Babies and Breastfeeding', 16 Jun. 2017, https://www.theguardian.
        com/books/2017/jun/16/hollie-mcnish-politics-of-poetry-ted-
        hughes-prize-winner

37   Steve Larkin email to Peter Bearder, 12 April 2019.

38   Interview with Julia Novak, Stage Invasion, Vimeo, (00:08:20).

39   Behrle, 'How to Write a Love Poem', https://www.utne.com/arts/
        how-to-write-a-love-poem

40   Gilpin, 'Slam Poetry Does Not Exist', 2015,
        http://www.litlive.ca/story/602

41   Somers-Willett, *The Cultural Politics of Slam Poetry* (2009), p.85.

42   See chapter 'I Sing the Body Authentic' in Somers-Willett, as above.

43   Johnson, *Killing Poetry* (2017), p.22.

44   Rohter, 'Is Slam in Danger of Going Soft', 2 Jun. 2009,
        https://www.nytimes.com/2009/06/03/books/03slam.html.

45   Wilson, 'Edinburgh versus Austin' (2018).

46   Ailes, 'Why "Slam Poetry" Is Not a Genre', 9 Feb. 2016,
        https://katieailes.com/2016/02/09/why-slam-poetry-is-not-a-genre/

47   Keith Jarrett Interview, Stage Invasion, Vimeo, (00:23:00).

48   Rose, *Black Noise: Rap Music and Black Culture in Contemporary America*
        (1994).

49   Gordon, 'The Problem of Maturity in Hip Hop' (2005).

50   Carpetface email to Peter Bearder, 12 Jan. 2019.

51   Schmid, 'Performance, Poetics and Place' (2000), p78–79;
        for a look at cowboy poetry see Gioia, *Disappearing Ink* (2004).

52   Marsh, Middleton & Sheppard, '"Blasts of Language"' (2006), 44–67.

53   John Seagrave Interview, Stage Invasion, Vimeo.

54   Fox, *Watching the English* (2004).

55   Munden & Wade, *Reading the Applause* (1999), p.45.

56   Dan Simpson email to Peter Bearder, 15 Mar. 2019.

57   Wilson, as above.

58   Fox, as above.

59   Silva, 'Live Writing' (2018), p.107.

60   Silva, as above, p.106.

61   Russell Thompson Interview, Stage Invasion, Vimeo.

62   John Seagrave, email to Peter Bearder, 12 Sept. 2018.

63   O'Sullivan, 'Remembering the Death of the Performance
        Poet', 2014, http://niallosullivan.co.uk/index/remember-
        ing-the-death-of-performance-poetry

64   Anti-Slam Apocalypse, 6 Feb. 2017, https://www.youtube.com/
        watch?v=CZsdfk68I1I

65   Noel, 'The Body's Territories' (2011), p.92.

66   Aptowicz, *Words in Your Face* (2007), xiv.

67   Gregory, 'Texts in Performance' (2009), p.60.

68   Chris Redmond Interview, Stage Invasion, Vimeo, (00:06:00).

69   Thick Richard Interview, Stage Invasion, Vimeo, (00:05:50).

70   Gräbner & Casas, *Performing Poetry* (2011), p.10.

71   This quote from Tim Wells is a sentiment that appears frequently
        in interviews with established artists. Wells, who has been on the
        scene since the 1980s has always rejected the label performance
        poet and spoken word artist, see Tim Wells Interview, Stage Inva-
        sion, Vimeo, (00:01:40).

72   Jem Rolls Interview, Stage Invasion, Vimeo.

73   Teitler, *Freed Verse: Diversity in British Poetry 2015 – 2017* (2017), p.15.

74   Teitler, as above, p.2.

75   Salena Godden Interview, Stage Invasion, Vimeo, (00:02:00)

76   'Ethnicity in the UK', https://www.ethnicity-facts-figures.service.
        gov.uk/ethnicity-in-the-uk

77   Apples and Snakes, 'Producers Reflect on Some Recent Decisions'

https://applesandsnakes.org/producers_blog/

78   Apples and Snakes, 'The Apples and Snakes Story', https://www.spokenwordarchive.org.uk/content/new-contributions/apples-snakes-story

79   Lucy English email to Peter Bearder, 20 Oct. 2018.

80   Hoyles & Hoyles, *Moving Voices* (2002).

81   Silva, as above.

82   'Poetry for people who don't like poetry' is the tagline of the Bang Said the Gun spoken word night.

83   Nick Makoha Interview, Stage Invasion, Vimeo, (00:27:00).

84   Fowler, 'Publishing Manchester's Black and Asian Writers' (2013).

85   The percentage of poets published by major UK presses who were black and Asian had increased to 17% by 2017, see Teitler, as above. I am told by the same author that the figure now stands at 20%, Nathalie Teitler, email to Peter Bearder, 14 May 2019.

86   Stiles, 'Performance' (2003), p.73.

87   Katie Ailes looks at the fascinating fetish of the 'authentic' in spoken word, highlighting the distinction between honesty (which is something the artist may practice) and authenticity (a heavily constructed, subjective quality the audience may perceive). See her forthcoming book on the subject, or Ailes, 'What Cult? A Critical Engagement with Watts', 2018, http://sabotagereviews.com/2018/03/06/what-cult-a-critical-engagement-with-watts-essay/. See also the chapter 'I Sing the Body Authentic' in Somers-Willett, as above; Wilson, as above; and Damon, 'Was That "Different," "Dissident" or "Dissonant"?' (1998), p.329.

88   Gräbner, 'Performance Poetry and Academic Theory in the Trenches' (2008), https://poeticsofresistance.wordpress.com/2019/04/07/performance-poetry-and-academic-theory-in-the-trenches-suggestions-for-a-new-dialogue/

89   Monkey Poet Interview, Stage Invasion, Vimeo.

90   Sam Berkson Interview, Stage Invasion, Vimeo, (00:05:00)

91   see Chapter 7 of Abram, as above, p.182.

92   Accompanying the rise of asocial reading was the practice of reading silently (un-vocalised) from the page. This was aided by the introduction of written punctuation and spaces between words (by monks in the medieval period) that helped people read more fluently. In her review of scholarship on this subject

Thu-Huong Ha says that the spread of silent reading is believed to be linked to an increasingly introspective modern culture. See Ha, Thu-Huong, 'History of Reading: The Beginning of Silent Reading Changed Humans' Interior Life', 19 Nov. 2017, https://qz.com/quartzy/1118580/the-beginning-of-silent-reading-was-also-the-beginning-of-an-interior-life

93   Quoted in Groff, 'The Perils of the Poetry Reading', 26 Jan. 2005, https://www.poets.org/poetsorg/text/peril-poetry-reading-page-versus-performance

94   Quoted in Madera, 'Magic and Music Steer This Vessel', 29 Oct. 2009, https://fictionwritersreview.com/essay/magic-and-music-steer-this-vessel-jorge-luis-borges-this-craft-of-verse/

95   Oliver, 'Mary Oliver "Listening to the World"', 17 Jan. 2019, https://onbeing.org/series/podcast/

96   Raymond Antrobus email to Peter Bearder, 22 Feb. 2019.

97   Lee, 'Spoken Word as a Way of Dismantling Barriers and Creating Space for Healing' (2018).

98   Michel, 'Lit Mag Submissions 101', 1 Dec. 2016, https://electricliterature.com/lit-mag-submissions-101-how-when-and-where-to-send-your-work/

99   For some excellent texts on dialogic learning see Freire's classic thesis *Pedagogy of the Oppressed* (1970) as well as Rogers, *Freedom to Learn* (1969) and Claxton, *What's the Point in School* (2008). For a practical application of this philosophy to spoken word see: Weiss, Herndon & Morris, *Brave New Voices* (2001).

100   Bearder, 'Communities of Words' (2015).

101   Schmid, as above, p.108

102   Clinton, 'Annotation of Deleuze', 2003, http://csmt.uchicago.edu/annotations/deleuzerhizome.htm

103   James McKay Interview, Stage Invasion, Vimeo, (00:01:15).

104   I have found little discussion on stage forms, though I am sure that structural conventions do exist and that 'free verse' is not as free as one might think. As I understand them, these forms are less spatial (constructed as lines on the page) and more temporal (constructed through stretches of time). More research can be done to identify conventions of poem length and structure in popular oral poetics. For a brief look at conventions in the US, see Somers-Willett, as above, p86.

105   'Audiotext' is a term used by Julia Novak to explore the potential for
        meaning in 'rhythm, pitch, volume, articulation and timbre'. These
        elements are, she argues, inextricable to live poetry in a way that
        'reveals the inadequacies of page-bound concepts (such as metre)
        for the analysis of live poetry.' see Novak, as above, p.13. 'Bodytext'
        refers to body language.

106   I am borrowing the term 'cultural property rights' from
        Bauman & Briggs, 'Poetics and Performance' (1990).

Chapter 3:
A Brief History of Democratic Literary Movements

'We inherit not "what really happened" to the dead but what lives on from that happening, what is conjured from it, how past generations and events occupy the force field of the present'
—Wendy Brown

Introduction

Breaking with poetic tradition is itself a long tradition. Each generation has had its own things to say, places to say them, and ways of saying it. Each has attempted to redefine the 'centre' and the 'periphery' of culture, with new stories, testimonies, and canons of cultural heritage. Each has recognised poetry's ability to change the conversation and innovated new ways of doing it. These attempts to rebuild 'The People's Republic of Poetry', have elevated many of the ideas and movements that have shaped history.[1]

This chapter will take a two-hundred-year sprint through a (necessarily incomplete) selection of poetic movements that I believe have fed into British spoken word poetry as a *countercultural* movement. It will focus heavily on some older movements (Romantic, Chartist, Modernist, and the Harlem Renaissance) as these have received relatively little attention in the few existing histories of spoken word.[2] We will then pass through some poetic movements in the US and the UK that co-evolved, and coalesced into UK spoken word.

First, let's situate them as *democratic literary movements*. Since all the movements in this chapter were composed (overwhelmingly) of *literate* poets, they can own the term '*literary*' movements. That said, they were movements which often said yes to 'non-literary' ways of speaking, and moved beyond the demands of the publishing house to make their voices heard. They are *'democratic'* because they expanded the verbal arts: who gets to do them, where they are done, and what they can be. They then used this poetry to challenge taboos, attitudes, and the social architecture of power itself. Lastly, they are *'movements'* of poetry, peoples, and ideas that were carried on tides of migration, conflict, and sheer exuberance.

1. Poets of the Romantic Era   c.1790s–1850s

The Romantic period was a revolutionary cultural, philosophical, and intellectual movement of the late eighteenth to the mid-nineteenth centuries which gave Britain some of its most celebrated poets, including Wordsworth, Coleridge, Shelley, and Keats. The Romantic poets championed the right-brained qualities of feeling, passion, and irrationality. They also rejected much of what they saw as the ornate and pretentious language of the aristocracy, as well as the poetic rules and forms of the day.

Around this time, British cities were exploding in size with what Blake called the 'dark satanic mills' of industrialisation. With these mills came a new concentration of 'people power' and the birth of modern democracy. The success of the American and French revolutions enflamed hopes of freedom and equality for the common man and woman, as well as a half-century-long 'age of revolutions' in Europe. Romantic poets were heavily involved in these ideals, and everywhere they were breaking the rules.

William Blake (who was no friend of royalty) once appeared before magistrates for, allegedly, throwing a soldier out of his garden and uttering an incitement to rebellion.[3] In 1780, he took part in the Gordon Riots which attacked Newgate Prison with shovels and pickaxes, released its prisoners, and set it on fire.[4] Percy Bysshe Shelley was kicked out of Oxford for writing an essay called *The Necessity of Atheism*. Lord Byron (who led a debauched lifestyle and had scandalous affairs with numerous men and women) is remembered as a hero of Greek independence after he died of a fever while fighting the Ottoman Empire. William Wordsworth participated in the French Revolution. While he and Samuel Taylor Coleridge wrote *The Lyrical Ballads* they were spied on by the authorities. The informant recorded them saying the words 'spy nosy' after he misheard them talking about the philosopher Spinoza.[5]

Yet the Romantic period was also notable for the increased visibility it offered those authors who were often denied participation in public affairs—women. Mary Wollstonecraft, who wrote the groundbreaking *A Vindication of the Rights of Woman*, is widely considered the world's first feminist philosopher. The literary achievements of writers like Mary Robinson and Mary Shelley were all the more pronounced in the context of a fiercely patriarchal society. Women writers had to struggle to carve a space for poetry in the face of intense legal disadvantages, domestic servitude, and financial dependence on inescapable marriages.[6] In a move that was risqué by the standards of the day, the poet Charlotte Smith separated from her husband, whose frivolous lifestyle broke the family finances. In the face of impoverishing legal battles with publishers, she sustained a career as a writer and twelve children for over twenty years. Charlotte Smith revived the English sonnet, was a big influence on Wordsworth and Keats, and is believed by some to be the 'first Romantic poet'.[7]

In 1819, it was women, men, and children that were sabered, trampled, and injured by government troops, during a pro-democracy demonstration at St Peter's Field, Manchester (the Peterloo Massacre). In response, Percy Bysshe Shelley penned 'The Masque of Anarchy', whose closing lines were to become anthemic to the British left:

> Rise like lions after slumber
> In unvanquishable number,
> Shake your chains to earth like dew
> Which in sleep had fallen on you —
> Ye are many — they are few.

Due to censorship and political suppression, the poem circulated underground for thirteen years until it was safe to publish in 1832. Publishers often refused to print 'blasphemous' and 'seditious' poetry for fear of reprisals and Byron was one of many poets who were forced to publish some of their work anonymously.[8] On the death of Prime Minister Castlereagh, he wrote:

> Posterity will ne'er survey
> A nobler grave than this
> Here lie the bones of Castlereagh
> Stop, traveller, and piss.

But Romantic poetry was more than a political battle, it was an ideological assault on the scientific rationality of the age and the steam-powered brutality of industry. The industrial revolution was one of the most significant and fast-moving social upheavals the world had experienced. In one sense, the poetry of Romanticism was the linguistic expression of humanity's psychic reaction to this. Their poetry expressed a nostalgia for a folk culture and reacted against the alienation of modern life.

Though Romantic poetry drew on 'folk culture', it was not always genuinely the culture of ordinary 'folk'. Appreciation of the 'oral ballad' among the well-to-do (and literate) was a form of 'ventriloquized' folk culture, re-mediated to print.[9] While the ballad was admitted to literature in 'a fit of gothic enthusiasm', folktales, legends, folk plays, and folk songs were left out.[10]

Still, Romantic poets did hold a belief in the wealth of 'non-literary' language in a way that resonates with the spirit of spoken word. Wordsworth's *Preface to Lyrical Ballads,* published in 1800, became a manifesto for the Romantic movement. In it he championed 'the real language of men in a state of vivid sensation' that came from people 'less under the influence of social vanity':

> The principal object, then, proposed in these
> Poems was to choose incidents and situations
> from common life, and to relate or describe
> them, throughout, as far as was possible in a
> selection of language really used by men.[11]

Over two hundred years later, spoken word poet Gerry Potter continues:

> Sometimes you go to a poetry gig, and people
> are waffling on in very beautiful language about
> something that is very *hard*. I think language
> needs to be harder…you have to get into the
> actual language of the event…the blast of the
> event…and decorate it…but give it your voice…
> let's critique more from *within*…within the
> confines even of our own language, rather than,
> quite often the florid, blustery language of old
> yore, or perhaps modern times.[12]

Yet Romanticism was not *performance* poetry as we now understand it. Performance was important to Romantic poets. Samuel Taylor Coleridge, for example, would often read his poems at the performance lectures he gave in opposition to the slave trade. Yet Romantic poetry was principally a literary phenomenon and such gentlemanly activities were a far cry from that of the street corner ballad singers of the day.[13] Nor was Romanticism (in the context of a still widely illiterate society) a grass-roots artistic practice. For historian Simon Rennie, their legacy to spoken word was their emphasis on the Self (see Chapter 2 Part 1.2), which brought together an expression of the poet's innermost feelings with the political struggles of the day.[14]

Indeed, Romantic poetry has been of lasting influence on democratic movements of poetry. In December 2017 a group of British spoken word poets met, through Utter! Spoken Word in Luton, to start work on a book commemorating Shelley's 'Masque of Anarchy' ahead of the 2019 bicentenary of the Peterloo Massacre. Shelley's poem was recited by Labour leader Jeremy Corbyn that year on the Pyramid Stage of Glastonbury festival. Whether the revolutionary incitements of Shelley and Wollstonecraft, the philosophical musings of Blake, or the nature worship of Wordsworth, British counterculture has a particular fetish for Romantic poetry.

2. The Chartist Poets   1830s–1850s

Though the early nineteenth century is remembered for its Romantic poets, there was a groundswell of poetic activity emanating from a new phenomenon of human society: the industrial working class. Britain was the world's first industrial country and no sooner did a working class exist than it began to use poetry to express a new consciousness — that of 'the people'.[15] Nowhere was this more apparent than in the world's first mass workers movement, Chartism. Though Chartism was principally a *political* movement, poetry was so central to it that it deserves attention here.

First, a little about why Chartism existed. Chartism was a movement for democratic reforms between 1838 and 1858. Among the Chartist demands were: votes for all men (regardless of whether they owned property or not) and more frequent, and fairer, elections. The Chartists demanded pay for elected representatives, so that working people could afford to take part in the political conversation. They also called for a shorter, ten-hour working day and better working conditions.[16]

While some of this may seem fairly moderate, it should be remembered that 'democracy' and 'free speech' were relatively new concepts in Victorian England. Political creativity often took place under the watch of informers, and radicals could expect reprisals from employers and magistrates. Because of this fear, many Chartist poets are known to us by their initials alone. As several Chartist leaders found out in 1848, a strongly worded speech in public could get you imprisoned. That year, revolution swept across Europe, and many thought Britain to be on the brink of an uprising.

Chartist poetry spoke of freedom and the dream of a more equitable world. To be working class in Victorian England was to suffer the cultural dislocation of urbanisation, the grinding discipline of work, and the genuine prospect of famine and destitution. Chartist poetry gave voice to these complaints and helped circulate ideas of resistance. In often very colloquial language, poets wrote about early (pre-socialist) notions of 'solidarity', as well as revolution, anti-imperialism, and the abolition of slavery, to name just four.

This poem came from 'A.W':

> How comes it that ye toil and sweat
> And bear the oppressor's rod
> For cruel man who dare to change
> The equal laws of God?
> How come that man with tyrant heart
> Is caused to rule another,
> To rob, oppress and, leech-like, suck
> The life's blood of a brother? [17]

Most Chartist poetry was not in books or poetry collections, but in the growing DIY economy of pamphlets and newspapers—the social media of its day. It is believed that, at its peak, the Chartist's *Northern Star* paper alone had a readership in excess of one million and published almost 1,500 poems from at least 390 Chartist poets between 1839 and 1852.[18] By 1840, its editor asked his contributors to be patient. 'The Poets must really give us a little breathing time. We have heaps upon heaps accumulating which we cannot find room for.'[19]

Culture was right at the centre of Chartism. This is significant because, at this time, few leisure activities were available to the urban poor who were often forced to work up to sixteen hours a day.[20] Music was occasionally available (in its live form only) and team sports became commonplace only in the latter part of the century.[21] Chartism helped open up an ecology of meetings and clubs for self-education and recreation.[22] Alongside choral societies and rambling clubs,[23] poetry was part of the cultural and expressive tide that helped carry the joys and aspirations of 'the people'.

It also lived inside a protest culture of communal singing and speech-making that took place at mass public meetings.[24] Chartist leader Ernest Jones (who was quoted by Jeremy Corbyn at the 2018 Labour Party Conference) was a firebrand orator and a (Shelley-inspired) poet of much fame. When he died, thousands attended his funeral in Manchester.[25] This is an extract from his poem 'Our Summons':

No! no! we cry united by our suffering's mighty length:
Ye—ye have ruled for ages—now we will rule as well!
No! no! we cry triumphant in our right's resistless strength;
We—we will share your heaven—or ye shall share
our hell!

Spoken word fans will recognise the music and the fight of this verse. Unapologetically rhetorical (bordering on sermonic), the poem is surrounded by people and swims in the current of the times.

It was not uncommon for 'gentleman radical' poets like Ernest Jones and Feargus O'Connor to rise to the top of radical groups. In the nineteenth century, formal political activities were often deemed illegal by the authorities and this hindered transparency and accountability in activist organisations. In practice, this frequently meant that leadership fell to the most 'well-spoken'.[26] Nevertheless, the bulk of Chartist leadership at both national and regional level was drawn from the working class.[27]

Women were excluded from Chartist leadership, as from so much of Victorian public life. Historian E.P. Thompson says that radical leaders of the time were frequently marred by the very masculine pitfalls of personal vanity, in-fighting, and 'demagogic' tendencies.[28] Chartism, in part, bucked this trend. Women, who were able to be members, spoke at public meetings, contributed to the Chartist press and often formed Female Chartist Associations.[29] Scholar Florence Boos argues that their verse expressed a high degree of political consciousness, and poets like Eliza Cook used poetry to tell-it-like-it-is, on many social problems like education, violence, and the effects of alcohol.[30]

To sum up, the Chartist poets deserve their place in the canon of democratic literary movements. In the face of social exclusion, they told their story, articulated their peoplehood, and proved their sophistication in creating culture. In the words of Mike Sanders:

> Composing poetry was an affirmation of work-
> ing-class creativity in the face of the dehuman-
> ising grind of industrial capitalism – a reminder
> that the 'hands' who worked the machines
> themselves possessed hands capable of produc-
> ing beauty as well as profit.[31]

Chartism was not just about political and economic rights, but 'cultural enfranchisement'.[32] But this surge of working-class po-etry did not survive into the twentieth century intact. Popular verse became absorbed by the mass media and popular enter-tainment in a way that prefigured the commercialisation of mod-ern spoken word.[33] For poet and historian of grass-roots poetry Tim Wells, the Chartist legacy is an important one. He links the 1980s punks and 'ranters' (see sections 10 & 11, below) to a 'work-ing class poetry tradition that dates back to the Chartists and which sadly we seem to have forgotten.'[34] Thankfully, Chartist poets are beginning to receive the attention they deserve.

3. Modernism   1900s to 1940s

With the following century still young, the world erupted into the First World War. The upheaval wrought by the machinery of modern times engendered a search for a poetic language that adequately reflected this rupture. Modernist poetry ditched the genteel vocabulary of the Victorian era for ordinary language, subject matters, and rhythms of speech.[35] Like the Romantics before them, the Modernists abandoned traditional forms to experiment with what became known as *free verse*. Poets like the North American E.E. Cummings burnt the rule book of capitalisation, syntax, and line breaks (seriously revolutionary by poetic standards).

This is his poem 'l(a':

> l(a
>
> le
> af
> fa
>
> ll
>
> s)
> one
> l
>
> iness

Despite its democratic beginnings, Modernism today is usually associated with the *high modernist literature* taught in universities: dense, unsentimental, and hard work.[36] For many Modernists, it was an ideological principle that poetry should not *do* anything; it was above being useful for mass culture or the market, and was better off *difficult* than popular. Ezra Pound captured this chauvinistic sentiment when he wrote 'we're in such a beautiful position to save the public's soul by punching its face that it seems a crime not to do so.'[37] In this respect, Modernism splinters its evolutionary line to the more populist spoken word poetry of today.

*

Yet there was a curiously forgotten poetic renaissance in 1930s Britain that reclaimed Modernist poetry for the people. In this 'period of revolutionary opportunity' a large movement called The Popular Front grew in solidarity with the Spanish struggle against fascism.[38] This was a broad-based political and cultural alliance, which married the work of 'respectable' poets like W.H. Auden with the hymn sheet of organised labour.

The scale of the cultural activism that accompanied The Popular Front was staggering. By 1939, the anti-fascist Left Book

Club alone had around 57,000 members, 1500 reading groups, and was a significant development in the publishing industry nationally.[39] As form of grass-roots education, it also helped lay the foundations for the post-Second World War Labour Party victory.

Poets like Jack Lindsay worked for a 'reconciliation of poetry and people'. They believed that Modernist poetry had calcified into a specialist academic pursuit that had grown out of class exploitation. By forcing 'the people' into the factory work of cities, Lindsay argued that capitalism had severed them from their own social life, traditions, and culture. Through verse, songs, and folk plays, Lindsay and others sought to rekindle a lost folk heritage in the service of political revival.[40]

It was also through live performance that the poets of The Popular Front helped overturn what they saw as the specialist and individualistic page craft of 'high modernism'. The Popular Front would recite poems in unison from pamphlets at meetings, demos, and rallies. These 'mass declamations', like that of Lindsay's 'On Guard for Spain' in Trafalgar Square, were fascinating experiments in a collective poetic consciousness. They were grounded in a belief that poetry, when performed en masse, could be a conduit of human solidarity.[41]

> [...]
> if you but understand, if your bodies flow
> into this steel of resistance, this welded mass,
> making you one with us, and making us
> unconquerable.
> Workers,
> drive off the fascist vultures gathering
> to pick the bones of Spanish cities,
> to leave the Spanish fields
> dunged with peasant dead
> that greed may reap the fattened crops.
> Fuse your unity in the furnace of our pain.
> Enter this compact of steel,
> and then we shall not complain.
> On guard for the human future!
> On guard for the people of Spain![42]

Popular Front poetry was also accompanied by large theatrical productions at festivals and pageants. The following poetry of Randall Swingler was staged with choreographed dance, choirs, orchestras, and processions in an extravagant 'aesthetic validation' of the people's struggle:[43]

> [...]
> Our world is life. Our theme is man,
> Whose music since the world began
> Like tributaried river runs
> Through villages and swarming towns
> And whose original springs arise
> Deep down in man's necessities.[44]

These were impressive events. One pageant in the Royal Albert Hall in 1939 fetched an audience of ten thousand. Another in Lancashire in 1932 involved 12,000 performers, 1500 singers, 500 dancers, 5 bands, and 18 months of preparation. Here, poetry was harnessed in the service of 'imaging a community to itself' and rallying anti-fascist organisation through mass spectacle.[45]

*

This was not the first performance culture of Modernism. During the First World War, artists, radicals, and peace-loving proto-hippies ('conscientious objectors') gathered in Zürich. As a neutral country, Switzerland offered refuge and freedom for avant-garde (vanguard or experimental) poetry. The Dadaist movement, for example, rejected the logic and reason of the modern world in favour of nonsense and irrationality. In perhaps the most iconic moment in the history of performed verse, Dada founder and sound poet Hugo Ball was carried onto the stage of the legendary Cabaret Voltaire in a giant cardboard priest costume that covered everything but his face. He then launched into the opening lines of his 'sound poem': 'gadi beri bimba / glandridi lauli lonni cadori...' He recalled of the experience:

I noticed that my voice had no choice but to take
on the ancient cadence of priestly lamentation,
that style of liturgical singing that wails in all the
catholic Churches of East and West [...] For a
moment it seemed as if there were a pale bewildered
face in my cubist mask, that half fright, half curious
face of a ten-year-old boy, trembling and hanging
avidly on the priest's words in the requiems and high
masses in his home parish. Then the lights went out
as I had ordered, and bathed in sweat I was carried
down from the stage like a magical bishop.[46]

Poetry here existed as the realm of the *carnivalesque*, attempting to break through the staid conventions of bourgeois morality and taste. Hans Arp described one of the Cabaret Voltaire performances as:

Total pandemonium. The people around us
are shouting, laughing and gesticulating...
Tzara is wriggling his behind like the belly of
an Oriental dancer [...] Madame Hennings,
with a famous Madonna face, is doing the splits.
Huelsenbeck is banging away nonstop on the
great drum.[47]

Such descriptions bring to mind the early days of slam in the UK. Here Jonny 'Fluffypunk' Seagrave recalls his first ever poetry slam in the nineties:

There was a guy dressed as a fish. And there
was someone else who did a wordless poem
about international relations just with noises
and cardboard spaceships.[48]

In 2002, Joelle Taylor regularly lost her voice at youth poetry slams in the London Assembly Rooms, which she remembers as 'anarchic' and 'absolute madness'.[49] The events helped break new territories of poetic sensibility, with DJs, banners, claxons, streamers, and male 'bikini girls' brandishing scorecards. All of this was in keeping with the experimental tradition of avant-garde cabaret.

The radical experimentation of sound poets continued to be a peripheral, but no less important part of twentieth-century British 'performance poetry'. Sound poet Michael Horovitz was a mainstay of the scene from the 1960s onwards and the sound and visual poetry of Bob Cobbing was frequently booked by Apples and Snakes until his death in the 1980s. Spoken word archivist Russell Thompson describes Cobbing's act:

> having ululated for a couple of minutes, he
> would say, 'Well the poem I've just read is
> this one', and he would pick up this piece of
> paper...with patterns on it like you get from a
> photocopier with a faulty drum.[50]

More recently, we see avant-garde experimentation in the poetry of David J, whose collages of vocal sound effects and impersonations mimic the streaming digital consciousness of modern media. Hannah Silva, a regular on the spoken word scene, also takes sound poetry into the twenty-first century, with loop stations and delay effects to create entire voice-worlds within a single poem (see Chapter 5). Cabaret Voltaire's particular brand of the avant-garde, as well as its performance spirit, lives on in spoken word.

We will now continue our journey on the other side of the pond. It is here we can find the tap roots of a countercultural American poetic that would find its way over to Europe, coalescing with poetic traditions here to become what we now know as spoken word.

4. The Harlem Renaissance   1920s to early 1930s

Evolving alongside Modernism in the interwar years was a flowering of African-American art and thought that came to be known as the Harlem Renaissance.

The Harlem Renaissance emerged from 'The Great Migration' when 1.5 million black people of the rural South headed for jobs in North Eastern cities over the space of two decades.[51] In Harlem, New York, the growing jazz culture of the 'roaring twenties' was met with white interest (and money) as something new and 'exotic'. Its poetry swung with jazz rhythms and lilted with the sigh of the blues (itself a folk poetic). It also drew on a rich vocal heritage of the black church which, through a history of segregated worship, had given space and freedom for innovative black artistry.[52]

'I, too, sing America', wrote Langston Hughes, the poet at the forefront of the movement. A charismatic performer, he wrote skilfully in everyday language. Hughes was the hero of the ordinary man and woman and toured nationally to sold-out audiences.[53] It is hard to overplay the importance of Hughes to the lineage we are exploring here. Hughes was the first African American to earn a living from writing and performing alone and opened the door for future generations of black performance poets.[54] He was a key influence on the Beat poets (whom we will look to next) and, over half a century on, remains a significant influence on American spoken word.[55]

Alongside its gritty depictions of black urban America, the Renaissance was *romantic* in that it rekindled an African 'folk' heritage.[56] Scholar and linguist of the movement Paul Robeson found a 'kinship of rhythm and intonation' between black American and West African dialects in what would come to be known as *retention theory*.[57]

For most of the previous century, minstrelsy had been a constant feature of popular entertainment in the US, with white performers in blackface mocking black people as slapstick layabouts and happy-go-lucky buffoons. In the white-owned media and entertainment industries, such stereotypes mingled with narratives of black people as passive victims.[58] Renaissance poets asserted a proud identity that altered these images. This is from Gwendolyn Bennett's 1923 poem 'Heritage':

> I want to hear the chanting
> Around a heathen fire
> Of a strange black race.
>
> I want to breathe the Lotus flow'r,
> Sighing to the stars
> With tendrils drinking at the Nile...
>
> I want to feel the surging
> Of my sad people's soul
> Hidden by a minstrel-smile.[59]

This expression of peoplehood emerged in the context of fierce discrimination and racial violence. The 'whitelash' that followed the abolition of slavery in 1865 was still in full swing, with lynch mobs like the Ku Klux Klan reviving their membership and spreading north. By 1924 they had four and a half million members.[60] In the words of Robert E. Washington, the Harlem poets saw themselves 'not simply as a new generation of black writers but as the juggernaut of a race relations revolution'.[61]

One prominent writer of the Renaissance, Claude McKay, had already written the first collection of poems to be published in Patois (*Songs of Jamaica*, 1912). Throughout the 'Black Atlantic' of Jamaica, New York and London, McKay wrote and campaigned against racism.[62] In 1919, his poem 'If We Must Die' was read out in Congress by Senator Henry Cabot Lodge.

> If we must die, let it not be like hogs
> Hunted and penned in an inglorious spot. [...]
> Like men we'll face the murderous cowardly pack,
> Pressed to the wall, dying, but fighting back!

The Harlem heyday came to an end with the Great Depression of the 1930s. But the sanctuary that it opened up for African-American culture and aspiration, helped sow the seeds for the civil rights struggles of the 1950s and 1960s, a movement threaded with the oratory of black transcendence (including that of Maya Angelou and Langston Hughes). In his poem 'Harlem', Hughes asks:

What happens to a dream deferred?

Does it dry up
like a raisin in the sun?
Or fester like a sore—
And then run?
Does it stink like rotten meat?
Or crust and sugar over—
like a syrupy sweet?

Maybe it just sags
like a heavy load.
Or does it explode? [63]

Strands of the Harlem Renaissance's pan-African philosophy still motivate spoken word communities in the US[64] and on the other side of the 'Black Atlantic', the UK. Though the UK has its own distinct post-colonial history, the achievements and ideas of the Renaissance still resonate with a commitment to foregrounding historically marginalised voices.[65] In May 2018, for example, Apples and Snakes provided a line-up of black spoken word artists to the Afropunk festival in an effort to give an 'intergenerational Black poetry space'.[66] Poets of colour today work in a society that is radically different to that of the 1920s. What distinguishes the Harlem Renaissance, is that it happened in a world of formalised racial segregation, over three decades before the Civil Rights Act of 1964. By the 1950s this situation was beginning to thaw. The post-war generations had arrived and intended to break all the rules.

5. The Beat Poets   mid 1950s to mid 1960s

The poetry of the Beat generation grew out of cultural mixing in American cities. Poet Lorenzo Thomas describes the Beats as 'probably the first group of so-called white people who—past the age of puberty—actually knew some black people as individuals, equals, and sometimes even lovers.'[67] The Beats drew heavily on the Jazz poetry of the Harlem Renaissance. Their poetic was performative, using everyday speech and rhythms, and embracing *the breath* as a structuring principle of the writing process.[68]

The 'San Francisco Poetry Renaissance' kicked off in the mid-1950s when City Lights Books started publishing poets in paperback (a format considered trashy at the time). Beat poets reacted against the academic poetry they saw as dry and irrelevant. The publication of Allen Ginsberg's *Howl and Other Poems* by City Lights in 1956, led to a whirlwind court case over 'obscene' homosexual content. The case propelled Ginsberg to fame, and he became one of the great stylists of sixties counterculture, even coining the phrase 'flower power'.[69]

Ginsberg often performed his poetry at protests, like those that blocked trains carrying nuclear weapons, and he was not alone. Poets in the sixties were on the frontline of struggles for peace, civil rights, gay rights, women's liberation, and the environment. Through into the seventies, 'Poetry Be-Ins' (poetic university occupations) were part of a student protest movement that politicised a generation and helped bring an end to the Vietnam War.[70] This was a time when laws, as well as taboos, needed to be broken by poets.

But the Beats were also, in the words of Gregory Corso, 'revolutionaries of spirit', a feature that aligns them with the Romantics of a century before. Blake's spiritual ecstasy, as well as his advocacy of 'free love' (see 'Visions of the Daughters of Albion'), appealed to a hippie movement rebelling against the sexual repression and sterile consumerism of suburban life. Ginsberg was particularly obsessed by Blake, even (during the summer of 1948) claiming to have been visited by him in a vision just after masturbating.[71] Now *that's* an orgasm. Blake's nemeses—the mechanical values of reason and science—had tumoured into the military industrial complex of Ginsberg's America. What linked both writers was an opposition to the establishment and a concern for the *consciousness* of the people. For Ginsberg, psychedelic drugs could free us from the 'mind-forged manacles' that Blake had heralded at the birth of industrial civilisation. While studying Blake's work in 1969, Ginsberg scrawled in his notes:

> the soul of the planet is wakening, the time of dis-
> solution of material forms is here, our generation's
> trapped in imperial satanic cities and nations, and
> only the prophetic priestly consciousness of the
> bard—Blake, Whitman or our own new selves—can
> steady our gaze into the fiery eyes of the tygers of the
> wrath to come.[72]

Ginsberg would chant Buddhist mantras at his performances in an attempt to summon psychological insight in his listeners[73] (he would also induce other insights by frequently getting naked on stage).

Yet the history of this movement, known so often for its men, is increasingly being remembered for its women. Poets such as Hettie Jones and Diane di Prima broke many of the rules constraining women in the 1950s: they left home, got jobs, and even pursued their creative visions.[74] Their poetry often touched on such 'improper' subjects as the female body, menstruation, and (god forbid) sex. This was revolutionary in a society that was still unready for birth control and abortion. In the words of Beat scholar Regina Weinreich, 'you were not even supposed to be having sex unless you were married…In fact, you weren't supposed to be living in any situation other than either your father's house or your husband's'.[75] The Beat women, then, had further to fall when 'dropping out'. They are remembered as the avant-garde of the sexual revolution, and the new attitudes of 1960s America.[76]

To summarise, the Beat poets were the philosophical godfathers and godmothers of the sixties. They pioneered youth culture, activism, and altered states of consciousness and their words (and deeds) helped catalyse a sea change in cultural values to which we owe many of our rights and freedoms.

American slammer and academic Jeff McDaniel compares spoken word unfavourably with the Beats:

> The Beats flourished in a far more conservative era
> and were more intellectual, more anti-establishment,
> whereas slammers, despite their countercultural

> pose, are often eager to be a$$imilated into the
> mainstream culture through MTV, commercials,
> movies, even electronic poetry billboards.[77]

Yet there can be no doubting the legacy of Beats to spoken word. Both have been countercultural and politicised movements, founded on the providence of pleasure, performance, and revelrous joy.

6. British Beats and the Liverpool Poets 1960s

In 1965, seven thousand flocked to London's Royal Albert Hall for The International Poetry Incarnation. Big attractions on the bill included North American Beat infamies Allen Ginsberg, Gregory Corso, and Lawrence Ferlinghetti. The line-up was overwhelmingly male, white, and on acid. Audience members danced, smoked weed, heckled, and waited (in vain) for Ginsberg to take his clothes off. The event marked a springtime of British 'flower power' and performance poetry. It launched the careers of Pete Brown, Adrian Mitchell, and Michael Horovitz (the 'UK's first professional performance poets'), who would become prominent voices on the scene for decades to come.[78] In the words of Mitchell:

> It led to readings all over the country. You suddenly
> got more women reading and publishing poems, as
> well as gay guys and poets from all over the world.
> Until that time, published poetry had been very
> university-based: white, male, middle-class. We were
> trying to break poetry out of its academic confines.[79]

The Beat aesthetic was, however, already evolving in the UK before this event. From 1961, the Poetry and Jazz in Concert series pulled in audiences of over two hundred to London's Royal Festival Hall, where 'you can take your girlfriend without embarrassment'.[80] Nevertheless, The International Poetry Incarnation stands as one of the world's most notorious poetry events to date and helped kickstart a wave of countercultural poetry in the sixties and seventies often referred to as the 'British Poetry Revival'.

On the more popular end of this revival, the 'Liverpool Poets' gave voice to the 'Merseybeat' scene in the riptide caused by pop icons The Beatles. For a brief moment in history, through poets like Adrian Henri, Roger McGough, and Brian Patten, poetry was rock 'n' roll.

True to the Scouse sensibility, the Liverpool poets wrote (and spoke) with a bloody-minded sense of humour (and frequently about their home town). In his poem 'I Want to Paint' Adrian Henri called for 'The Installation of Roger McGough to the Chair of Poetry at Oxford', 'the assassination of the entire Royal Family', 'The Beatles composing a new National Anthem', and 'Brian Patten writing poems with a flame thrower on disused ferryboats'.[81]

The Liverpool poets grew from a scene of live performance event-gatherings called 'happenings', where different art forms mingled with each other and the audience. As part of the free and spontaneous ethos of the happening, these audiences were really participants, and the events *were* the art. At Liverpool happenings, Henri (who was also a painter) performed live on canvas alongside dance, poetry, and recorded jazz music. Within this scene, stagecraft and crowd engagement became a big part of the poetic. In his 1967 book on the scene, Edward Lucie-Smith characterised the poetry as 'an agent rather than an artifact' and a 'service' rather than a 'commodity'. [82]

But what a commodity it was. *The Mersey Sound* anthology (1967) is one of the best-selling British poetry anthologies of all time, selling over half a million copies(!)[83] Perhaps unsurprisingly, the Liverpool poets were criticised for their 'pop fashionability' in ways that foretold the later controversies of spoken word. In his history of the phenomenon, spoken word artist Nathan Penlington defends their legacy to British poetry:

> the main innovation that The Liverpool Poets
> collectively introduced to a wider audience was
> something that would affect people's conception
> of poetry for the decades to follow: the use of the
> voice, and images from life, that were natural to
> the performer.[84]

7. The Black Arts Movement   late 1960s & 1970s

The Black Arts Movement ('BAM') of the 1960s and 1970s had unfinished business to deal with. Many poets felt that the Harlem Renaissance had pandered to the paternalist benevolence of white patrons. They split with the Beats for a more radical, and *racial*, politics of liberation.[85] In 1965 Malcolm X was assassinated and many other black civil rights leaders met the same fate at the hands of the CIA who flooded their communities with drugs and guns to prevent neighbourhood organisation.[86] Galvanised, BAM armed itself with culture and sought to validate and elevate black talent and testimonies. In an explosion of defiant innovation, the movement worked to raise consciousness and build resistance.

Poets were right at the front of this. In 1965, a former associate of the Beats, the poet Amiri Baraka, moved to Harlem and started organising. Baraka recalls:

> For eight weeks, we brought Drama, Poetry, Paint-
> ing, Music, Dance, night after night all across Har-
> lem. We had a fleet of five trucks and stages created
> with banquet tables. And each night our five units
> would go out in playgrounds, street corners, vacant
> lots, play streets, parks, bringing Black Art directly
> to the people.[87]

In the New York riots of 1967, Baraka was beaten almost to death by police. On his death in 2014, fellow Black Arts poet Sonia Sanchez gave this tribute:

> he stood tall as lightning…his tongue caught fire…
> his poems exploded from clouds and intestines…he
> sewed himself into the sleeves of history and change
> and said…'Hey, I've got some words…you've got to
> learn from these words…you've got to *do* this thing
> called language, *do* this thing called freedom, do this
> thing called *change*'.[88][89]

Sanchez and other female poets of BAM (like Gwendolyn Brooks, Nikki Giovanni, and Ntozake Shange) were loud voices in the movement (often known for its misogyny) and served to prevent it from being taken over by men.[90]

Shange pioneered the 'choreopoem', a form of poetic theatre that foreshadowed hip hop theatre and spoken word theatre. It abandoned traditional methods of storytelling, and used performance poetry, alongside dance, to provoke emotion and political indignation from audiences.[91] In the words of David Colón, it 'syncretized poetry, theatre and black consciousness into a new subgenre of live performance'.[92]

Indeed, much of what would later come from hip hop was seeded in BAM. Proto-rapper Gil Scott-Heron bought revolutionary passion to the ears and hearts of millions with his defiant jazz, blues, and soul-inspired spoken word which is most famously remembered in 'The Revolution Will Not Be Televised'. Also dedicating their lyrics to black consciousness were The Last Poets trio. Their name was taken from a poem by the South African revolutionary poet Keorapetse Kgositsile who heralded the last generation of poetry before the guns took over.[93] The Last Poets' success in the American charts was considered such a threat that they became targets of FBI surveillance.[94]

BAM gave a direct inheritance to American spoken word. In the words of Yeezy, a young poet of a spoken word education programme in LA:

> These voices of literary artists encourage and moti-
> vate us to stand up and fight against oppression by
> following their footsteps…[T]he artists of the Black
> Arts Movement served as messengers, politicians,
> spokesmen, role models and counselors[95]

This is not to suggest that US spoken word belongs to a primarily *black* artistic tradition, or that the politics of BAM is shared by all spoken word poets of colour. Today, many spoken word artists of colour disagree with its depictions of black 'authenticity', as well as its oppositional politics.[96] Nevertheless, it did help build poetry as a space for black and minority ethnic voices and a discussion about colour. The Nuyorican Poets Café, famous today for slam, was established in the early seventies. Its success then, as today, was built on the poetry and politics of black and Latinx poets.[97]

8. Dub Poetry   late 1970s onwards

By the osmosis of transatlantic immigration, British poetry inherited a new way of speaking in the reggae folk poetic—dub poetry. As with The Last Poets, Gil Scott-Heron, and the wordsmiths of hip hop, dub poetry spread on the trade winds of a musical movement, spinning onto the turntables in the form of vinyl.

Its style of delivery drew on the Caribbean vocal tradition of *toasting:* a part-spoken, part-chanted incantation that accompanied reggae, ska, dancehall, and dub music. Loretta Collins captures it well as 'rudie slang delivered in sardonic lighthearted patter or somber monotonous voice-as-drum',[98] The *riddims* of dub poetry broke the mould of British verse. As Barbadian poet and historian Edward Kamau Brathwaite points out, 'the hurricane does not roar in pentameters'.[99] This is from Jamaica's Linton Kwesi Johnson's 'Reggae Sounds':

> Shock, black double down-beat bouncin'
> Rock-wize tumble doun sound music
> Foot drop, find drum blood story
> Bass his'try is a-movin' is a-hurtin' black story
>
> [...]
>
> Ridim of a tropical, electrical storm
> Cool doun to de base of struggle

> Flame ridim of historical yearnin'
> Flame ridim of de time of turnin'
> Measurin' de time for bombs and for burnin'

Key voices of the dub movement were Louise Bennett, Mikey Smith, Mutabaruka and Oku Onuora. Onuora (considered by some to be the founder of the poetic) was a figurehead in the struggle against police oppression. In prison his performances were considered so inflammatory that the wardens confiscated his writing book. Onuora continued to write and his verse was smuggled out of captivity to earn him the status of a political prisoner and a prominent voice of Black Power politics. In the face of popular support for his work, the Jamaican government released him with an official pardon.[100]

Christian Habekost distils dub poetry as 'Word, Sound, and Power'; the written and spoken word, synced with reggae and the politics of its people.[101] Reggae's 'syncopated, apocalyptic preaching' called forth the *'fyah!'* (a metaphor for rapid social change) and from 1962, the fyah of Jamaican independence spread as revolutionary art and DIY musical mobilisation. The reggae 'sound system' was nothing less than a form of cultural, social, and political organisation, or to quote Dick Hebdige, 'a black heart beating back to Africa on a steady pulse of dub.'[102]

Before moving to the UK, Jean 'Binta' Breeze performed poetry to large crowds at Jamaican plantations that had been turned into communal farms in the wake of Jamaican freedom. Johnson, a former member of the militant Black Panthers, also crossed the Atlantic to help translate dub's postcolonial anti-racism to inner-city Britain. His poetry called for solidarity against the inequality wrought by 'Maggi Tatcha' with poems like 'Ingan Is A Bitch' and 'Di Great Insoreckshan' which chronicled the Brixton Uprising of 1981.

Benjamin Zephaniah on the other hand, grew up in Birmingham before moving to London to help bring poetry to underground cabarets, dance floors, and demos. His poem 'Knowing Me' was written at a time when punks and Rastas were fighting the racism of far-right thugs, and police were targeting black communities with new stop and search laws. This extract from 'Knowing Me' confronts lazy stereotypes of black identity:

> With my Jamaican hand on my Ethiopian heart
> The African heart deep in my Brummie chest,
> And I chant, Aston Villa, Aston Villa, Aston Villa,
> Believe me I know my stuff.
> I am not wandering drunk into the rootless future
> Nor am I going back in time to find somewhere to live.
> I just don't want to live in a field with my past [103]

Zephaniah and other dub poets got the hurricane of Jamaican patois into the school curriculum and made it part of the cultural conversation. Though few poets today label themselves as dub poets, its influence on UK spoken word was formative. For Lemn Sissay (a poet of Ethiopian heritage who started performing in the mid-eighties) they opened poetry up to a new generation of African descended poets, 'it was the Caribbean poets who laid the groundwork for my entire career'.[104]

9. Hip Hop late 1970s onwards

Back in New York, a scene was emerging in the impoverished neighbourhoods of the Bronx. The jazz poetry of the Harlem Renaissance had evolved into a new street corner poetic, freestyling. Jazz's vocal percussion (scatting) and the vocal percussion of acapella blues singers, reappeared as beatboxing.[105] Rapping combined with breakdancing, deejaying, and graffiti to articulate a culture, an attitude, and an urban consciousness. Hip hop had arrived, and it was to become one of the most popular cultural phenomena of the modern world.

The initial catalyst for hip hop was a peace treaty between gangs, brokered by the warlord Afrika Bambaataa. In the wake of this, his gang (Black Spades) repurposed itself as a hip hop collective, Zulu Nation, which incorporated the once warring Puerto Ricans and black people. The streets and parks of the Bronx became safe for young people to party and it was here that the hip hop party scene ignited.[106] Hip hop historian Jeff Chang argues that hip hop succeeded in *de-segregating* those who had previously been *re-segregated* by deprivation and violence.

For Chang, the movement carried the 'prophetic tradition' of black liberation, and offered a cultural cement of dialogue and self-expression for black (as well as latinx and white) working class Americans.[107] Reporting on a gang truce meeting after the Los Angeles riots of 1992, writer Mike Davis witnessed calls for unity and political action:

> These guys were very eloquent, and they
> spoke in a rap rhythm and with rap eloquence,
> which I think kind of shook up the white
> television crews.[108]

Perhaps the greatest achievement of hip hop, at least in the early years, was to *socially* empower political struggles for change.[109] It was, to borrow from historian Eugene Lunn, a 'democratically controlled technology', an open 'social process' that conveyed the culture of a people.[110]

Spoken word, especially in the US, is a sister movement to hip hop. It inherits and shares much of this grass-roots politics, as well as its mode of address: the voice of personal experience, with the rapper taking on the identity of an observer or narrator.[111] In her history of slam in New York, Cristin O'Keefe Aptowicz correlates the rise of slam with the arrival of gangsta rap, which she identifies as a mainstream and co-opted form of hip hop. Spoken word, she argues, provided a stage for MCs to communicate more 'conscious' lyrics, or at least lyrics that were not about gangsta themes.[112] When spoken word went big it arrived to the HBO TV network as Def Poetry Jam, hosted by political rapper Mos Def. American spoken word, and by extension UK spoken word, has deep roots in hip hop. From the early eighties, rap increasingly became the principal art form for kids with something to say. Poet and slam organiser, Sam Berkson even goes so far as saying 'If we're talking about spoken word, we are really talking about hip hop poetry... hip hop's influence over live poetry is so great that spoken word is almost a sub-genre of hip hop'.[113]

10. Punk Poetry   late 1970s & 1980s

Though the influence of hip hop on spoken word is well known, the musical movement that came before it is often forgotten. 'A lot of what is attributed to hip hop in our scene *isn't* hip hop. It's punk', remembers Joelle Taylor.[114] In the seventies and eighties punk was *the* street culture in the UK and poetry was part of its articulation. Like hip hop, it wasn't just a music trend, but a philosophy and a way of life, drawing heavily on anarcho-syndicalist values of DIY, squatting, and riotous joy. Punk said *fuck you* to the canon; if you had something to say and wanted to say it, that was enough.

The godfather of British punk poetry, John Cooper Clarke, hybridised poetry with the dry, sardonic wit of punk bravado and his own gritty Northern realism: 'the fucking scene is fucking sad / the fucking news is fucking bad / the fucking weed is fucking turf / the fucking speed is fucking surf', he writes in 'Evidently Chicken Town'.[115]

Another key figure, Attila the Stockbroker, has done over three thousand gigs since the early eighties. In the first years, his shows often involved fist fights with fascists in the back rooms of pubs. As Attila and fellow ranter Seething Wells would say, 'If we mention cherry blossom in our poetry, we're talking about boot polish'. Attila has since taken his fighting talk to campaigns such as Rock Against Racism, Anti Nazi League, the Miners' Strike, the Poll Tax demos, and protests against a string of Middle Eastern wars.

Punk poetry evolved in a soundscape of distorted guitars and pounded snare drums. Kinetic, raw, and interactive, it dealt with boisterous audiences the same way it dealt with Tory politics—with fist-shaking defiance and a sardonic sense of humour. Often taking the mic on band changeovers, punk poets did not have the luxury of silent audiences or even audiences with an interest in poetry. If they didn't grab the crowd's attention (and keep it), they risked having a bottle launched at them. In this way, says Taylor, 'form dictated content'.[116] This was the era of the *ranter*, wielding poems that were, as Andrew Darlington recalls, 'lethal devices with short fuses'.[117] Punk poet (turned novelist) Joolz Denby remembers the risks poets took to get their poetry out there:

I had no fear, which in those days, especially as a
woman, you needed to have no fear ...They would
throw lighted cigarettes at you, they'd throw full
cans of beer, they'd spit at you, throw glasses at you.
I remember standing up at Bogies in Cardiff and it
was so bad the bouncers had to come on the stage
behind me... I remember standing up in Scotland
and literally looking at a hail of glass coming towards
me. You could see it glinting and it was smashing and
exploding on the floor around my feet. One glass hit
me in the face... and I thought 'this is gonna be a
tough gig' [laughs].[118]

Though they are not considered punk poets, John Hegley and
Joelle Taylor also started their poetic lives climbing on stage between punk bands. Though not the phenomenon it was, punk
still informs spoken word's DIY method of organising and 'having a go'. Many poets today, such as Henry Raby, Bridget Hart,
Furious George, and Paul 'Captain of the Rant' Case proudly
bear the punk philosophy.

11. UK Alternative Cabaret   1980s & 1990s

Throughout the eighties, punk and dub poets found a common
home in the bawdy alternative cabaret scene, where poetry and
radical politics mixed with variety performance.

As with spoken word today, this scene grew in response to
Tory 'austerity', as this 1984 article from *Marxism Today* reports:

The public role of the new generation of radical poets
is, oddly enough, aided by the current recession. As
theatre companies close for lack of funds and grants,
so the actors involved have re-formed into variety
acts performing at the many cabarets which have
sprung up across London.[119]

New venues meant new audiences and new expectations. Swearing until that time was rare among variety acts as it was banned in theatres. By contrast, the pub gigs offered what comedian Oliver Double called a 'beery intimacy' that was 'somewhere between a fringe theatre show and a drink with some friends.'[120]

Here, poetry existed alongside drag acts, comedians, musicians, and pretty much anything else. The cabarets were a place where 'anything goes', with costumes, props and manic creativity that was closer to *performance* art than *performing* art, as Jonny 'Fluffypunk' Seagrave remembers:

> You'd have things like Ian Saville, the socialist
> magician...and Randolph the Remarkable who
> used to pick up a washing up bowl with his stomach...
> and poetry was part of that...and it certainly wasn't
> coming from the canon.[121]

'Stand-up poetry' took root in this scene, with quirky acts like the bespectacled John Hegley taking the stage with his ukulele (very cabaret). Hegley developed a mastery of comic wordplay, audience participation, and cleverly timed pauses, which he absorbed (in part) from the comedians around him. This poem, 'Amen', is from his first book, a short run of which was originally printed by his own press, Down the Publishing Company:

> surely it should be A man
> or some men
> and if its some men
> how many?
> is it just the big two
> the father and son
> or is it one or two men more
> or is it many more men
> or is it just no women
> (eh men?)[122]

The cabarets were fiercely left wing, rejecting the Pakistani gags and misogyny of the working men's club comedy circuit. In the context of rocketing unemployment and an impending cold war apocalypse, the new crop delivered anti-racist, anti-sexist, and anti-Tory material with punk enthusiasm.

Since 'performance poetry' was surging in popularity, acts like Benjamin Zephaniah, John Hegley, and Attila the Stockbroker were often bigger names than the comedians they shared the bill with. Many of those comics, like Stewart Lee, Alexei Sayle, and Phil 'Porky the Poet' Jupitus, would become household names. In the nineties, stand-up comedy became the big business it is today. Most of the poets of alternative cabaret, including Joolz Denby, Tim Wells, and Steven 'Seething' Wells remained underground.

The poetry of alternative cabaret had less emotional range and sincerity than the spoken word of today. Yet its spirit continued into the nineties and noughties with acts like Rachel Pantechnicon—the comic surrealist drag act of Russell Thompson—who served as an Apples and Snakes London Programme Coordinator for eleven years. Reflecting on the scene he grew out of, Thompson now believes it has, for all its greatness, 'lost some of its experimental edge'.[123] The back-room cabaret poetic lives on, however, in he continued work of its poets (many of whom are the elders of the scene) as well as more recent stand-up poets like Kate Fox, Thick Richard, and the absurdist, prop-wielding Rob Auton.

Assessing the Canon

Throughout the last two centuries we have used poetry to accumulate cultural momentum and challenge power. This cultural activism has enabled us to build communities, as well the ideas that propel them. In short, poetry has helped us create power itself, and deserves recognition as a catalyst of historical change.

I cannot claim here to speak of all the grass-roots poetics that have fed this multicultural society. For the sake of space, I've focused on some notable ones, most of which are *performative* and drawn from the UK and US. This re-canonisation is a strangely new conversation, and more celebration, elaboration, and disagreement deserves to take place. To return to the words of Wendy Brown, history is 'less what we dwell in… or are determined by, than we fight over, fight for, and aspire to honour'.[124] As new people and influences come into spoken word, the 'force field of the present' becomes populated anew.

Of those movements I have discussed, none of them (with the exception of the Black Arts Movement and the Popular Front poetry) need to be defined as principally *political*. There were a myriad of motivations and themes that informed their poetry. Still, progressive ideologies were distinguishing features of all of them.

In different ways, each movement sought to honour and vocalise the wisdom of ordinary folk and draw on the *linguistic capital* of those not usually associated with the 'high art' of poetry.[125] This is as true of the Romantics, as it was with the poetry of blues, jazz, rock 'n' roll, hip hop, and punk. In absorbing these songs, poetry drew new reservoirs of culture.

Each movement was avant-garde, improvising new styles, and new relationships between poetry, technology, and society. Yet they were not all avant-garde in the same way. Some embraced popular culture (such as hip hop, punk and the Liverpool poets), while others (such as the Avant-Garde Modernists) rejected accessible verse as part of their countercultural stance. Some groups pioneered poetry into new spaces and new performance disciplines (such as alternative cabaret), while the Romantics (for all their radical beliefs and non-conformist poetics) were a small group of relatively privileged poets who wrote mostly for the page and for each other.

One of the most significant changes to British poetry over this period has been an undeniable surge of melanin. British spoken word cannot be considered outside of the history of race relations in the UK and, by extension, the US. Spoken word is part of a long lineage of black and minority literary practices that have sought to redefine power, place, and purpose.

Today, spoken word continues the struggle for social visibility. It continues to refuse poetic 'value' as defined by cultural elites and to claim new territory for the People's Republic of Poetry. In the next chapter, we will see how they do it.

Notes

1   I have borrowed the name The People's Republic of Poetry from Yorkshire's Firm of Poets collective who did shows and workshops under the name in recent years.

2   It is fashionable (and manageably short) to date spoken word back to the era of the Beats (1950s onwards), for some histories that look at this in depth see Brady, Cleary & Willey, 'British Poetry in Performance, 1960-2008' http://projects.beyondtext.ac.uk/poetry-inperformance/index.php. See also Marsh, Middleton & Sheppard, '"Blasts of Language"' (2006). For some histories that link spoken word to earlier decades and centuries, see Hoffman, *American Poetry in Performance: From Walt Whitman to Hip Hop* (2013); Wheeler, *Voicing American Poetry* (2008); Harrington, *Poetry and the Public* (2002).

3   Mee & Crosby, '"This Soldierlike Danger"' (2016), p.113.

4   Gilchrist, *The Life of William Blake* (2008), p.36.

5   De Quincey, *Recollections Of The Lakes And The Lake Poets* (1863), p.178.

6   Alexander, *Women in Romanticism* (1989).

7   'BBC - Radio 4 Woman's Hour -Charlotte Smith', 28 Dec. 2006, http://www.bbc.co.uk/radio4/womanshour/04/2006_52_thu.shtml

8   Boyle, 'Lord Byron' (2015).

9   McLane, 'On the Use and Abuse of "Orality" for Art' (2002), p.145.

10   Pettitt, 'Ballads and Bad Quartos' (2003).

11   Wordsworth, *Preface to the Lyrical Ballads* (1800).

12   Potter, 'How Do You Respect Fuck All?', 3 Aug. 2012, http://indiefeedpp.libsyn.com/gerry-potter-how-do-you-respect-fuck-all.

13   Pike, 'History of Poetry in Bristol', lecture at Lyra Poetry Festival, 20 Mar. 2019.

14   Simon Rennie, email to Peter Bearder, 14 Mar. 2019.

15   Scholars of Chartist poetry frequently link this cultural development to 'The Making of the English Working Class', see Thompson (1963). Thompson's landmark book has fascinating insights into clandestine publishing and oratory in the nineteenth century, see pages: 782, 820, 833.

16   Walton, *Chartism* (2001).

17   Cited in Scheckner, *An Anthology of Chartist Poetry* (1989), p.88–89.

18   Sanders, 'Making Better Rhymes', 22 Jan. 2016, https://culturema
        ters.org.uk/index.php/culture/festivals/item/2209-making-better-
        rhymes-chartist-poetry-and-working-class-struggle

19   Quoted in Ward, 'Lost Voices of Victorian Working Class Un-
        covered in Political Protest Poems', 15 Mar. 2007, https://www.
        theguardian.com/uk/2007/mar/15/books.booksnews1

20   Hastings, *Chartism in the North* (2004), p.2.

21   Vicinus, 'The Study of Nineteenth-Century British Working Class
        Poetry' (1971).

22   Historical Association, https://www.history.org.uk/student/
        categories/495/module/4701/podcast-series-politics-re-
        form-and-war/4703/the-chartists

23   Riley, 20 Dec. 2012, http://fortnightlyreview.co.uk/2012/12/work-
        ing-class-poetry

24   Sanders, *The Poetry of Chartism* (2009), p.63.

25   Rennie, 'The Poetic Negotiations of a Gentleman Radical' (2015).

26   Thompson, *The Making of the English Working Class* (1963), p.682–683.

27   Mike Sanders email to Peter Bearder, 20 Feb. 2019.

28   Thompson, as above, p.682–683.

29   Mike Sanders, as above.

30   Boos, *Working-Class Women Poets in Victorian Britain* (2008), p.220.

31   Sanders, 'Making Better Rhymes', 22 Jan. 2016, https://culture-
        matters.org.uk/index.php/culture/festivals/item/2209-making-
        better-rhymes-chartist-poetry-and-working-class-struggle.

32   Samuel Laycock quoted in Boos, 'The Poetics of the Working
        Classes' (2001).

33   Vicinus, 'The Study of Nineteenth-Century British Working Class
        Poetry' (1971).

34   Wells, 'Oi the Poetry – Garry Bushell', https://standupandspit
        wordpress.com/2014/07/08/oi-the-poetry-garry-bushell/

35   Harrington, *Poetry and the Public* (2002), p.33.

36   Diepeveen, *The Difficulties of Modernism* (2002).

37   Quoted in Harrington, as above, p.44.

38   Harker, '"Communism is English"' (2011).

39   Harker, as above.

40   Harker, as above.

41   Harker, as above.

42   Lindsay, *Who are the English* (2014), p.52–53.

43   Wallis, 'Pageantry and the Popular Front' (1994), p.147.

44   Cited in Wallis, as above.

45   Wallis, as above, see p.148; p.134.

46   Kahn, 'Noises of the Avant-Garde' (2012), p.431.

47   Taylor, *Left-Wing Nietzscheans* (2012), p.178.

48   Jonny Fluffypunk Interview, Stage Invasion, Vimeo, (00:26:45).

49   Joelle Taylor Interview, Stage Invasion, Vimeo.

50   Russell Thompson Interview, Stage Invasion, Vimeo, (00:26:00).

51   C Q Researcher, *Issues for Debate in American Public Policy* (2013), p.13

52   Hoyles & Hoyles, *Moving Voices* (2002), p.23.

53   Thomas, 'Neon Griot' (1998), p.304.

54   'Langston Hughes', https://www.poetryfoundation.org/poets/
      langston-hughes

55   Aptowicz, *Words in Your Face* (2007), p.5.

56   Primeau, 'Frank Horne and the Second Echelon Poets of the
      Harlem Renaissance' (1996), p.265.

57   Hoyles, as above.

58   Hoyles, as above, p.24.

59   Gwendolyn Bennett's poem 'Heritage' was published in The Crisis,
      magazine of the NAACP, during November 1923.

60   Zinn, *A People's History of the United States* (1980), p.373.

61   Washington, *The Ideologies of African American Literature* (2001), p.14.

62   Maxwell, 'Claude McKay' (2014), 466–476.

63   Hughes, L., 'Harlem', Reprinted by permission of Harold Ober
      Associates. Copyright 1994 by the Langston Hughes Estate.

64   Johnson, *Killing Poetry* (2017), p.39–41.

65   Evaristo, Bernardine, 'Amiri Baraka: My Fiery Inspiration', 10
      Jan. 2014, https://www.theguardian.com/books/booksblog/2014/
      jan/10/amil-baraka-inspiration-bernardine-evaristo

66   The Apples and Snakes collaboration with the Afropunk festival was
      surrounded by controversy when it became apparent that the poets
      would be crossing the picket line of striking workers at Brixton's
      Ritzy Cinema. Apples and Snakes moved venues, but hit back at
      opponents online, arguing for the need to protect venues that still
      supported black art in a city in which has 'targeted and attacked'
      black spaces. See Apples and Snakes, 'Producers Reflect on Some
      Recent Decisions' https://applesandsnakes.org/producers_blog/

67   Thomas, 'Neon Griot' (1998), p.305.

68   Charles Olson's article 'Projective Verse' written in 1950 influenced many poets of this era. It advocated the breath as a structuring principle for poetry see Chapter 5 for more on this.

69   Pinsker, 'An Appreciation: Allen Ginsberg Defined His Age - And its Attitude' (1997), p. 9.

70   Wheeler, *Voicing American Poetry* (2008), p.134.

71   Schmidgall, 'Triangulating Blake, Whitman, and Ginsberg' (2015), p.136.

72   Schmidgall, as above, p133.

73   Wheeler, as above, p.132.

74   Barton, 'The Beat Women', https://www.bbc.co.uk/sounds/play/b06084ks (00:03:00).

75   Barton, as above.

76   Lee, 'Avant-Garde Poetry as Subcultural Practice' (2010).

77   McDaniel, 'Slam and the Academy' (2000), p.35.

78   Pete Brown, email to Peter Bearder, 10 Feb. 2019.

79   Quoted in Morrison, 'The International Poetry Incarnation', 22 Sept. 2005, https://www.independent.co.uk/arts-entertainment/books/features/the-international-poetry-incarnation-the-beat-goes-on-314324.html

80   Robson, *Poetry and Jazz in Concert* (1969), p.13.

81   Henri, 'I Want to Paint', in Henri, McGough & Patten, *The Mersey Sound* (1967), 24–25.

82   See Introduction and p.8 of Lucie-Smith, *The Liverpool Scene* (1967).

83   Monson, *British Prose Poetry* (2018), p.62.

84   Penlington, 'Don't Need English Lessons to Learn Our Lines', 1999, http://nathanpenlington.com/post/157016614067/dont-need-english-lessons-to-learn-our-lines, p.8–9.

85   Thomas, 'Neon Griot' (1998), p.311.

86   Potash, *Drugs as Weapons Against Us* (2015).

87   Thomas, as above, p.312.

88   Democracy Now, 'Remembering Amiri Baraka', 10 Jan. 2014, https://www.democracynow.org/2014/1/10/remembering_amiri_baraka_part_2_featuring

89   Baraka's legacy is a controversial one. Early in his career, he was accused of advocating the rape of white women in the script of a play which dramatised black revolutionary struggles. Later in life, he performed work that suggested a Jewish conspiracy in the 9/11 attacks. Baraka refused to resign from his post of New Jersey Poet Laureate. When it turned out there was no constitutional way to remove him, New Jersey dissolved the position. See Battle, *Free at Last* (2006), p.211.

90   Mitchell & Davis, *An Encyclopedia of the Black Arts Movement* (2019), p.196–198.

91   Effiong, *In Search of a Model for African-American Drama* (2000), p.134.

92   Colón, 'Siempre Pa'l Arte' (2016), p.152.

93   Anonymous, 'In Memoriam' (2018), p.1–3.

94   Otten, 'The Last Poets', 21 Nov. 2016, https://www.theguardian.com/books/2016/nov/21/the-last-poets-america-in-poetry-from-black-power-to-black-lives-matter

95   Quoted in Camangian, 'Untempered Tongues' (2008), p.41.

96   Johnson, *Killing Poetry* (2017), p.42.

97   Akbar-Williams, 'Poetry Jams' (2010), p.1103.

98   Collins, 'Rude Bwoys, Riddim, Rub-a-Dub, and Rastas' (1997), p.197.

99   Quoted in Gräbner, 'Hurricanes don't Roar in Pentameters' (2011), p.75.

100   Miller, *Writing Down the Visions: Essays & Prophesies* (2013), p.80–83.

101   Habekost, *Verbal Riddim* (1993).

102   Collins, as above, p.173–176.

103   Zephaniah, 'Knowing Me', in *Too Black, Too Strong* (2001).

104   Caribbean poets are not synonymous with dub poets, but the history of UK 'Caribbean poetry' cannot be considered without reference to dub poetry. Sissay's quote can be found at: Apples and Snakes, 'Lemn Sissay: FULL INTERVIEW, 20 Dec. 2017, https://www.youtube.com/watch?v=RqgWjwLDHE0&t=1374s

105   TyTe & Defenitial, 'Part 1: The Pre-History of Beatboxing', 28 Feb. 2005, https://www.humanbeatbox.com/articles/history-of-beatboxing-part-1/

106   Chang, *Can't Stop, Won't Stop (2006)*, p.382.

107   Chang, as above.

108   Quoted in Rose, *Black Noise* (1994).

109 Rose, as above.

110 Quoted in Maher, 'Brechtian Hip Hop' (2005).

111 Rose, as above.

112 Aptowicz, *Words in Your Face* (2007), p.9.

113 Sam Berkson email to Peter Bearder, 22 Apr. 2019.

114 Joelle Taylor Interview, Stage Invasion, Vimeo, (00.13:00)

115 'John Cooper Clarke – Evidently Chicken Town',
   https://www.youtube.com/watch?v=3KgB-sI2H-c

116 Taylor, as above.

117 Darlington, 'The Ranters, 18 years on' (1999).

118 What is remarkable about Denby's work was that, in spite of these
   conditions, she refused to write crowd pleasers, instead delivering
   'difficult dark material'. These quotes are taken from the Apples
   and Snakes archive: 'Joolz Denby Has NO FEAR | Spoken Word
   Archive - YouTube', 2. Jan. 2018, https://www.youtube.com/
   watch?v=vMZxI9Lbq_M&t=2s

119 Wells, 'Radical Poetry In The 80s', https://standupandspit.word-
   press.com/2017/04/14/radical-poetry-in-the-80s/

120 Double, *Stand Up* (1997), p.193.

121 Jonny Fluffypunk Interview, Stage Invasion, Vimeo, (00:22:00).

122 From Hegley, *The Family Pack* (1996), p.21.

123 Russell Thompson Interview, Stage Invasion, Vimeo, (00:26:00).

124 Quoted in Burgum, *Occupying London* (2018), p.148.

125 The term *linguistic capital* was coined by sociologist Pierre Bourdieu
   to describe how the currency of language (a source of power
   and wealth) relates to the formation and interaction of different
   social groups. See Bourdieu, 'The Economics of Linguistic
   Exchanges' (1977).

Chapter 4:
The DIY Renewal of Poetry

'Forms of oppression rob a people of its right to poetry—and the crisis for poetry is to create a space for poetry again and again.'
—Charles Bernstein

'Community is culture's habitat. Culture is the centre of the community's life, its essence and DNA.'
—David Fleming

If spoken word is a *do-it-yourself* movement, how does it *do* and how does it *self*? This chapter is about the *how* of poetry, not as an aesthetic, but as a *social form*. Poetry, from Ancient Greek *poiein* (meaning 'to make') is an act of creating *communities*, as well as the words that gather around them. This act of *autopoiesis* ('self-creation') has generated and sustained a thriving ecology of art and, perhaps more importantly, people. This ecology is enabling many of its participants to escape 'the man' to do work that stretches its tendrils far beyond poetry alone. What follows is a cultural geography of spoken word, and a road map for *cultural renewal* in an age of economic collapse and growing inequality.

For sociologist Pierre Bourdieu, art arises from a 'field of cultural production'. This *field* is a network of relationships that elects, enables, and elevates the art, which would, he says:

> be nothing but a crazy gesture without the universe
> of celebrants and believers who are ready to produce
> it as endowed with meaning and value by reference
> to the entire tradition which produced their catego-
> ries of perception and appreciation.[1]

The creation of 'categories of perception', the definition of taste, and the legitimation of particular poetics is an act of social power. Bourdieu called this power *social capital* (a counter-concept to economic capital). Organisers, audiences, and commentators all have agency in co-authoring spoken word. This chapter will look at a number of *horizontal* links (between peers) and *vertical* links (between the grass roots and institutions) through which this network negotiates and cultivates its power.

*

As an 'event-based art practice', spoken word exists in a lived relationship between art and life.[2] This relationship italicises the role of the audience (a group traditionally understudied in poetry).[3] Audiences detect cliché, demand novelty, and reward risk. When we share a video online, invite a friend to a gig, and argue over the poetry we like and dislike, we are ordaining and propagating poetry. When we buy a poet's book or CD, or pay to see them perform, we are collaborating in the production of more poetry and live performance.

In developing a live economy around poetry, spoken word has inherited a vocabulary of 'gigs' and 'punters' from the world of comedy and music. Indeed, the musical, performative, and interactive features of spoken word are likely to be both the *cause* and the *product* of this new relationship.

Responding to audiences does not have to mean 'pandering', but recognising them as a unique coalescence of historical circumstance. In orchestrating their set, the poet asks 'what does the occasion demand?' In this way, the audience shapes, completes, and, in Bourdieu's words 'consecrates' the art.[4] The revolutionary poet Vladimir Mayakovsky called this the 'social command' of poetry. He was writing at a time when peasant illiteracy was being eradicated in early twentieth century Russia. In response to the historical moment, he rejected poetry's 'religio-artistic aura of sanctity' in favour of verse that reflected everyday life.[5] Today, poets have their favourite audiences, just as audiences have their favourite poets. From them we draw feedback, support, inspiration, and a sense of purpose. In short, good poets need good audiences.

Salena Godden, a poet I will return to a number of times in this chapter, has been finding ways to serve these audiences for a quarter of a century. In the mid-nineties she would hunt down friends who had jobs so she could borrow the franking machine to steal postage and send out flyers.[6] Her early publications were printed in home-made, 'roll your sleeves up' chapbooks and, when she found a publisher, she continued her struggle from the peripheries of the literary world:

> When *Springfield Road* came out I walked around the city to all the shops asking them to stock it, going in person to bookshops all over London. I tried so hard to get it distributed and stocked like a real book…It's amazing how far I have got without my books and albums even being properly stocked in shops or on lists like everyone else's.[7]

Beyond the bookshop, spoken word's relationship with live audiences has enabled the work of Godden and many others. Let's now take a closer look at the mechanisms by which spoken word poets receive the *consecration* of their audiences.

*

Audiences must be cultivated over time, and poets cannot do this alone. Promoters, programmers, and those unflatteringly called 'arts administrators', are social facilitators of the highest order. Across the country these people commission hundreds of live performances every night via an endless stream of communicative transactions: emails, text messages, meetings, web shots, and social media posts. These words, perhaps far more numerous than the poetry itself, are how the ecosystem of spoken word metabolises. Weaving poetry into moments, places, and people is a complex and dynamic creative act.

Of all the actors in the *field*, the promoter is in the greatest position of risk. In the context of funding cutbacks[8] and the closure of live venues,[9] the promoter gambles budgets that are often fronted from their own back pockets. In this context, spoken word gives us a relatively low-cost and low-tech way to mobilise live entertainment. Building on the success of poets like Kate

Fox and Matt Harvey, Inn Crowd found a space for poets in *rural touring*, putting poets in informal venues (like pubs and village halls) across the country. Here, The National Rural Touring Forum describes a formula that could have come straight out of a manual for spoken word:

> performers need to be much more self-sufficient,
> they need to be able to get there, be flexible with
> get-ins and have minimal or easy set ups... They
> will probably arrive with the audience, perform near
> the audience and then have a drink and a chat with
> them after. They may even be staying with one.[10]

Using this formula, the 'poetry activist' builds scenes, and even institutions, out of ideas, enthusiasm, and tireless work. Putting on a night not only involves programming poets, but compèring events, and designing flyers and banners. Other tasks include social media work, covering the door, hosting poets on couches, and covering childcare on the night of the gig. Like many poets, I have promoted events to help pay the rent, and have learned the hard way that this works better as a *collective* endeavour. In sharing risks, rewards, and skills, I built a bank of *social capital* (though they prefer to be called *friends*).

Building on this capital, a professional network of gigs has emerged that is now proliferating into a wide spectrum of activities. Hammer & Tongue, for example, has built up a national touring network of ticketed slam events over fifteen years with only occasional splashes of funding. Similarly, Tongue Fu has run gigs since 2007 that place poets, rappers, storytellers, and comedians alongside improvised jazz. Parallel to this, the spoken word record label Nymphs and Thugs emerged out of a collaboration in Leeds with indie music label Heist or Hit Records. The new label (whose tagline is 'proudly DIY since 2015') combines national live tours with sales of CDs, vinyl, zines, and t-shirts. One of its albums (*LIVEwire* by Salena Godden) was nominated for the Ted Hughes Award in 2017.[11]

Feeding these more ambitious initiatives are countless 'nights' that have become small institutions in their towns, cities, and villages. In staging touring poets, and propelling new poets into touring activities, these nights widen the cultural orbit of poets and audiences alike. In the words of 'slam papi' Marc 'So What' Smith, 'the most important thing about slam is the organisers'.[12]

*

In order to evolve, art also needs *informed critics*. While an abundance of literature exists about 'the canon', very little discusses poetry as a performance discipline—with distinct genres and sub-genres. Without the words to describe spoken word there can be no discussion, and without a discussion there can be no progress. This deficit, however, is not down to wilful ignorance. Research shows that there is a strong demand for a critical discussion among poets and organisers. As poet and researcher Katie Ailes explains:

> in the interviews I conducted with spoken word artists in the UK, the grand majority of artists bemoaned the lack of a rigorous critical culture around our art form. They expressed a wish for spoken word to be taken seriously and criticised within a framework befitting it (i.e. taking into account the fact it is composed for live performance, etc.).[13]

Most poetry criticism, in print and online, is a closed conversation. A damning academic report published in 2018 found that the 'overwhelming majority' of British and Irish poetry magazines are 'failing to meet even the most basic standards of inclusivity'. While 12.9 per cent of Britons identify as BAME, and 50.9 per cent as female or non-binary, these groups comprise a mere 4.9 per cent and 46.5 per cent of poetry critics, respectively.[14]

The difficulty of penetrating this is compounded by a number of factors. Traditionally, much of the conversation around poetry has been inaccessible to those outside of universities due to the densely analytical and academic culture that has grown around it (see 'A Little Existing Literature' in the Introduction to this book). There is also friction between spoken word's DIY ethos and the need to cultivate a craft of writing and performance which, like anything, requires years of research, practice, and often tuition fees. To exacerbate the problem, high-quality documentation of the scene requires specialist (and expensive) skills in graphic design, web development, and videography.

The spoken word *ethos of sociality* (see Chapter 2, Part 3.4) also complicates things. Those who have published in the emerging field of spoken word criticism report difficulties in finding critics who are not unhelpfully friendly. In scenes where everyone knows each other, and are in the same room, a review of a live performance is often less critical than that of a written publication.[15] Rebecca Watts's scathing critique of Hollie McNish and Kate Tempest in the (relatively 'highbrow' and 'literary') *PN Review*, drew considerable outcry from the spoken word community. The conflict suggests a tension between a cultivated and specialist elite on one side and a cosy and uncritical community on the other.[16]

For poet Raymond Antrobus binary distinctions like this are discriminatory and unhelpful. Antrobus grew out of the spoken word scene, but has gone on to become a celebrated member of the 'literati' for his work on the page. While he reports 'toxicities, jealousies' and 'cliques' in a variety of poetry spaces, he concludes that the establishment's 'promises of major cultural influence and power' can lead to 'more potential for snobbish and undemocratic behaviour.' He continues:

> Literature is a major part of England's cultural
> legacy, a lot of authors pride themselves on self-
> perceived excellence but, as Shakespeare puts it,
> 'There is thy gold, worse *poison* to men's souls'.[17]

There is evidence that spoken word is finding ways to administer safe amounts of such poison to inoculate against ill-crafted poetry. Sabotage Reviews have worked to create a reviewing culture by making open calls for reviews, and offering support and training.[18] Workshops at their 2018 gathering included 'Writing a Live Literature Review' and 'The Perilous Art of Poetry Reviewing'. Their live literature reviews try to pay attention to the strength of language and phrasing, as well as the way that the writing interacts with things like props or music. This review of Andy Craven-Griffiths' show *Joygernaut* recounts the audience's experience in a way that understands spoken word as an *event* of literature:

> Craven-Griffiths is a skilled performer and storyteller, dynamic and engaging throughout. The space is used well, performance pace is just right, and day and scene changes are marked with effective lighting design... Audience participation is also used to good effect with a handful of individuals used briefly as characters, and whilst this story is very much contemporary, the charisma of Andy's performance keeps the diverse audience on side and engaged.[19]

Since 2011, Sabotage Reviews' annual Saboteur Awards have provided a space for the spoken word community to celebrate and assess its constituents with workshops, live showcases, and a much-anticipated award ceremony. The spoken word community, it seems, is finding ways to give shape to Bourdieu's 'categories of perception'.

*

The growth of this grass-roots infrastructure has even extended into a territory once perceived as outside the spoken word community's remit—the publishing industry. Flagship 'punk publishers' Burning Eye Books, confronted the drought of publishing opportunities in spoken word and succeeded. This is no small achievement. Poetry represents a fraction of the income for publishing, an industry in which it is notoriously difficult to succeed. In the words of John Calder, 'you can make a small fortune in publishing, as long as you start out with a big one.'[20] Without any funding or personal finance, Burning Eye has pioneered a path taken up by newer publishers. In 2018 alone they published thirty books. The press is founded on an ethos of encouraging emerging poets to break through, and curating a repertoire that reflects the diversity of the scene.[21]

The groundswell of poetry publishing has opened up a new field of poetic expression that is independent of the large players in 'the industry'. Burning Eye's online sales figures, for example, show that seventy-five to eighty per cent of purchases come from first-time buyers. This poetic 'welcome tent' (to quote Birnie) is the *autopoiesis* of a poetry readership.[22]

On a more human level, the work of these 'alternative institutions' has deepened connections within the community.[23] Travelling the land, with bags stacked full of small incendiary devices, spoken word poets are now reverberating back into audiences in time lag, through bookshelves, back pockets, and bedside tables.

It remains to be seen if this new stream of publishing will stay indigenous to the scene. In recent years, publishers that have hitherto not associated themselves with spoken word like Picador Poetry and Carcanet have started publishing poets from the scene, evidence perhaps that the vultures are circling. Grass-roots poetry publishing is, however, on the rise. This book, for example, is published by Out-Spoken Press, which has grown a team to disseminate the work of writers outside of the established publishing world. Since its inception in 2015, it has established a distribution network of bookshops, and ventured into audiobooks and live touring. Similarly, Unbound Press has capitalised on crowdsourced funding which, since 2006, has exploded into social media to mobilise the support of audiences.[24] The press, 'funded by the people, powered by the people' has platformed the work of many poets from the scene, including George Chopping, Inua Ellams and Musa Okwonga, and won a string of awards for its crowd-funded response to media hysteria over immigration, *The Good Immigrant*.[25]

*

Online, emerging poetries have spearheaded new poetic ecosystems. The 'digisphere' offers a direct and (relatively) unmediated interface for poets to find new audiences. In doing so, they have innovated new techniques of publishing on YouTube, Twitter, Instagram, and Tumblr. So successful have these linkages become, that it has enabled poets such as Suli Breaks and George the Poet to leapfrog the scene, and reach audiences of millions, without having worked their way up through it as live performers. Sensations like these, as well as the growth of YouTube channels with multi-million hit counts (see Button Poetry), show how social media can offer rags-to-riches ascendency which, ironically, bypasses poetry's grass-root networks of gigs.

In the *PN Review* article mentioned above, Watts attacks the use of social media to spread poetry. The 'floodgates have been opened' she complains, 'the reader is dead: long live consumer-driven content and the "instant gratification" this affords'. In her treatment of these media, however, Watts doesn't allow the possibility that they might also enable new poetics and new poetic relationships.[26] Watts does not use social media. As a graduate of both Oxford and Cambridge universities, it can perhaps be assumed that Watts possesses enough *social capital* not to need it.

For Lisa Anderson of the online platform Black British Art, this is 'the era of black Twitter', one that enables art that is *for-us-by-us* ('FUBU'), rather than *by-them-for-us*.[27] The former, as Dave Randall points put, enhances community, while the latter reinforces hierarchy.[28] For those on the periphery of cultural institutions and media ownership, social media is an essential (if imperfect) cultural asset for generating not just audiences but solidarity as well. In the wake of Watts's attack on popular female poets, the #FEMALEPOETSILOVE hashtag exploded into a litany of tweets that identified and celebrated female performance poets. One of those tweeting was Katie Ailes, who points to the hashtag as evidence of 'the strong sense of community and mutual support underpinning this scene and insulating us from ill-informed attacks'.[29]

Social media helps poets access audiences and gain recognition. It also opens a space for those audiences as well as other actors (like promoters, bookers, and journalists) to find, commission, and enable new art. In this sense, the online 'field of cultural production' allows the *horizontal* networks to bypass more institutional routes of ascendancy.

*

The UK festival circuit is another space of DIY culture that is intimately connected with spoken word. Summer festivals, which have been growing in size and number since the late 1960s, have provided what Hakim Bey calls 'temporary autonomous zones': short-lived oases of subcultural activity.[30]

'You would create the festival you want to see,' says Jonny 'Fluffypunk' Seagrave, recalling the festivals in the eighties and nineties as more DIY and less 'corporate' than they are today.[31] His poem 'Summers Lament' jokes about the changes that have taken place:

> Do you remember the festivals, Miranda?
> Do you remember *real* Crusties?
> No, not the soft & fluffy tofu-sniffing trustafarians
> but the Real Deal: ragged, grey-skinned, glue-crazed
> nihilists, terminally pissed with
> 'Punk's Not Dead' tattoos
> syringes filled with Special Brew...
> they'd come up to you,
> see the cider-vomit dripping from your chin & go
> *Cor, Two's-up on that then, geezer...*

In her book, *Music Festivals and the Politics of Participation*, Roxy Robinson charts a history of rapid change in the scene. In the nineties, the large free party (or 'illegal rave') scene became criminalised, and much of their activities gave way to (or arguably gave birth to) 'super clubs' and more 'legitimate' gatherings.[32] The number of festivals listed on the eFestival website shows the extent of the change; with numbers jumping from just twelve in the year 2000 to one thousand by 2014.[33] For Robinson, the 'sweeping drive of commercialisation' continues in the new crop of boutique festivals. She also notes, however, that the scene is still composed of organisers who grew out of, or bear an allegiance to, the 'temporary autonomous zone'.

As festivals swelled to a more central role in British culture, so too did spoken word. By 2009, the annual poetry slam at Shambala festival drew audiences of over three thousand. The slam continues to hook in audiences, and often poets, whose only reason for attending (or performing at) a poetry event is that they stumbled across it in a field. The rapid increase of spoken word at festivals has been one of the main steps forward for spoken word in the last decade. During a 2008 collaboration with Hammer & Tongue, I wrote (with more than a touch of naive hyperbole) a funding application to support 'the first-ever festival road show of the new phenomenon in performance arts—slam poetry.' It is now almost impossible to find a festival without a spoken word tent or a slam. Spoken word communities have helped make the UK festival circuit one of the best of its kind in the world. Most major festivals, including Glastonbury, Latitude, Womad, and Boomtown have spoken word in their programmes.

For poet and organiser of the Phantom Laundry tent, Sally Jenkinson, the budget pressures of programming three days of entertainment makes festival poetry intensely collaborative and cooperative:

> You're pooling your resources in a way that doesn't happen in real life, you're like, 'OK, we're gonna put five people and all of our gear in this tiny car, cos we've got to get ten people there on two tanks of fuel' or 'I'm gonna get the coach from this place, but this person is driving, so they're gonna take all of my gear (even though I don't know them that well)'...Most of the people who have been performing with us have also been integral in holding the stage together. That's the sort of cooperative living that I yearned for growing up and didn't know how to find.[34]

For myself and many other poets, festivals are tribal homecomings; four-day stretches of camping, talking, dancing, and performing together. They cement friendships and throw poets from disparate parts of the country into a 'field' of spontaneity, creativity, and cross-pollination. The Tribal Voices collective, for example, holds a fireplace at Small World Festival where, year-on-year, poets share in the changing tides of each other's lives and work. There are many poets I only ever see at Tribal Voices, and the fire always feels like a homecoming.

Spaces outside the working week where we can sing, improvise, and tell stories or jokes are germinal to poetry. In a hyper-mediated world of digital entertainment, young people have less incentive and time to interact with environments and people beyond the home. As urban space becomes more controlled, surveilled, and privatised, a narrowing of sensory exploration leads to isolation and confinement and a form of 'cultural autism' emerges.[35]

For cultural anthropologist Kate Fox, festivals are a hiatus of British cultural norms. Reservedness and social stratifications are temporarily suspended, and people mix between age, class, and educational backgrounds.[36] While ticket prices and social cliques can turn festivals into spaces of privilege,[37] they do create new forms of *social capital* and interaction, where poetry can germinate and grow.

While this is true of the festival field, it is also the case for the entirely urban Edinburgh Fringe festival. Here, spoken word artists have found new audiences at the PBH Free Fringe, a self-acclaimed 'movement for the emancipation of performers' which has turned the financial superstructure of the world's largest cultural event on its head. The Free Fringe model gives poets access to venues without venue hire fees, and audiences pay by donation rather than by a brochure price. The vision of its founder, Peter Buckley Hill, is to end the excesses of 'pay-to-play', in which artists take huge financial risks (and often losses) in an 'arms race' of growing venue and publicity costs.[38]

Over the years, PBH Free Fringe venues (like the Banshee Labyrinth) have served as the engine room of spoken word, with poets from across the UK spending an entire August performing, promoting, drinking, and scheming. Through their footwork of flyering the Royal Mile, they have helped grow a global audience for the art form. Many, like Mark Grist, Rob Auton, and Sabrina Mahfouz have found international recognition for their work there.

Despite the successes of the PBH Free Fringe, the Edinburgh Fringe is a long way from being accessible to most artists. Growing costs and commercialisation mirror the path of the festival scene more broadly, and poets are often not in a position to risk losing money for the potential exposure.[39] As comic Abie Philbin Bowman once told me 'they used to say a good Edinburgh would make your TV career, now they say a good TV career will make a good Edinburgh'. [40]

*

Some poets have got around such problems by bypassing all me-diation of venue, promoter, and festival programming, delivering their poetry *im-mediately* as poetry buskers. In the modern era of amplification, the ballad singer has mostly morphed into the rap-per, but the ancient practice of street poetry lives on. I am not talking here of poets seated on pavements with typewriters (of which there has been a trend in recent years),[41] but the spoken (or shouted) performance of poetry on street corners. This is some-thing I have seen practised in many cities in Europe and Latin America by the street-homeless and travelling bohemians. I once stumbled across a poet in Berlin performing on the side of the street (with some success) to anyone who cared to stop and listen. His verse—loud, musical, and physically energetic—shows that poetry can work as a form of manual labour.

In the high streets of Devon, the poet Rich Butnotfamous takes spoken word busking into the next century. His unique brand of 'walkabout poetry busking' involves approaching pe-destrians with a menu of poems for them to sift through and se-lect.[42] Armed with a debit card reader and an iPad, Rich uses performance to open up long-term relationships of digital inter-action; collecting emails, and directing people to paid subscrip-tions to his Online Password Anthology. True to the missionary zeal of spoken word, Rich has set up a series of YouTube tutorials to teach other poets how to do it themselves.

Newcastle's Rowan McCabe started performing his poetry on the street and has since gone on to become 'the world's first

Door-to-Door-Poet'. Knocking on strangers' houses, McCabe tells residents that he is doing an 'art project'. 'To tell them that you are there to do poetry,' he told me, 'would be stupid'.[43] After chatting with them about something they care about, he leaves, only to return a day later with a poem to perform on their doorstep. Rowan's work has taken live poetry into the homes of Newcastle's roughest estates, proving that poetry can be valued, and practised, pretty much anywhere.

*

So far we have looked at a variety of grass-roots initiatives to create Bourdieu's 'universe of celebrants and believers' through events, books, reviews, festival shows, and busking. This mirrors the growth of spoken word in the US, where funding cutbacks and discrimination have inhibited certain voices in poetry, particularly from the black community. In response, American poets have developed 'alternative institutions' to transmit their work.[44] It is hard to overstate the importance of these attempts to galvanise. For sociologist Howard Becker, the relationships that constitute art are so important that the artist's success depends more on their 'celebrants' than on the intrinsic worth of the art itself.[45]

Poet and promoter Sam Berkson compares spoken word to the 'DIY professional scene' of Shakespearean theatre. 'It's not that Shakespeare was an isolated genius…Shakespeare was part of a scene…it's the scene that raises us up'.[46] In Tudor England, theatres were banned within the walls of the City of London and could only be found in the outlying suburbs (known as 'liberties'). Bawdy, subversive, and crowd-pleasing, Shakespeare's verse responded to the people's desire to be entertained. Without an elite education, the bard was sniffed at by his contemporaries, but he needed no special credentials or writers' guild approval; it was the audience that sustained and propelled him.[47]

Berkson goes on to recall the launch of Kate Tempest's first (self-published) book *Everything Speaks in its Own Way*. The event happened in 2012, just before she became one of the country's most renowned poets. With support from Chester P, Jam Baxter and Polarbear, the rap and spoken word community managed to take over the prestigious Old Vic theatre in London. 'It was like, *wow!*' Berkson continues, 'this is *ours*… we *did* this'.[48]

In his book *Surviving the Future*, David Fleming puts horizontal networks of cultural diffusion at the centre of his strategy to survive the predicted collapse of capitalism. In the long run, the *informal economy* is more resilient than the *formal economy*, because it is based on direct encounter, cooperation, and participation. Where the entertainment industry transmits cultural products produced elsewhere, to be passively consumed by the recipient (in the form of movies for example), the *informal economy* cultivates friendship, engagement, and even manners. The *trust* that it generates, claims Fleming, is itself a cultural asset and is 'both the producer and the product of *social capital*'.[49]

*

Spoken word's vertical linkages are, however, growing. With increased recognition comes increased interaction with institutions that hold more power of purchase. These include funding bodies and theatres, as well as publishers, agents, and broadcasters. Let's look first to the patrons.

Countless initiatives that started with no money (including the Saboteur Awards, the Door-to-Door Poet, and this book) were bought to fruition by Arts Council England (ACE) funding. On a larger scale, organisations like Apples and Snakes and Spread the Word have succeeded in becoming National Portfolio Organisations (NPO's), receiving regular 'core funding' from ACE to operate over many years. This finance has enabled them to go beyond live touring, to deliver school programmes, mentor schemes, and professional development through a network of regional staff.

While funding can provide a lifeline for skint poets, the expectations and guidelines that accompany it inevitably channel poetry in directions it may not want wish to go. As stand-up poet Byron Vincent jokes:

> I was homeless as a teenager. There was no funding
> for that. Maybe if I told the Arts Council that being

> homeless explored the tension between both the
> physical self and the real and theoretical constructs
> of a plutocratic hegemony, I wouldn't have had to
> shit behind a skip. I just want to get to a point in my
> life where, if I shit behind a skip, it's because I want
> to, not because I have to.[50]

Utter! Spoken Word questions spoken word's entry into the bureaucratic economy of arts administration:

> SW cannot be sustainable or independent
> while it relies for its survival on hitting the targets
> and building the careers of managers it does
> not appoint.[51]

Another way to see funding (and funded) institutions are as a means to demand public money from the state. This can shield poetry from the market and make it available to those who may not otherwise be privileged enough to take part in it.

For Lucy English, funding's real function is to put spoken word in a place where it can be funded by the commercial market. She points to the fact that grants are often predicated on 'match funding', 'in-kind support', and the income of predicted ticket sales.[52] In a funding landscape of growing scarcity and competitiveness, most poets enjoy these grants only sporadically. The UK's largest arts funder, ACE, has been forced to cut its 2018-22 budget by £156 million following a collapse in National Lottery sales.[53] To complicate matters, strict guidelines and complicated application procedures can bestow opportunities disproportionately to those with the time (and educational background) to write them. In practice then, the few grants that are available are usually supplemented by hundreds of hours of unpaid work by artists and promoters, as well as the ticket and book sales of punters. All this brings us back down to the *social capital* of spoken word.

*

So far, we have looked at the *horizontal* linkages that social media brings to spoken word, but its *vertical* transactions deserve attention too. Monopoly platforms like Facebook, Twitter, and Instagram, are increasingly pressuring their users to pay to have their content seen.[54] In doing so, they hold what Frank Baumgartner would call a 'meta power' that sets the conditions by which users interact, thus controlling them from a distance.[55]

The digisphere has drawn criticism from the spoken word community for creating a 'raced and gendered space' born of neoliberal markets.[56] Poets publishing online have no say over how social media is run (beyond giving it money). In Marxist terms, they do not own or control the *means of production*. Social media's motivation to dominate the attention of its users and generate advertising revenue is at odds with the democratic motives of the movement. While one seeks to dismantle financial barriers to participation, the other, in part at least, tries to erect them.

*

Poetry is also moving vertically, out of the pub basement, and into the black-curtained chamber. More and more theatres are hosting and helping to develop spoken word shows, and spoken word theatre offers a new path for connecting poets to their people. Yet dealing with theatres and larger arts institutions does raise concerns. Is the programming mandate of theatres interested in seeking out new talent? Do theatres have any interest in representing the diversity in the scene and fairly rewarding it? To borrow again from Utter! Spoken Word: 'Fair payment requires fair pricing; fair pricing means freedom from bureaucratic interference'.[57] Spoken word has a relatively new and precarious relationship with the theatre world. Poets are solo artists that usually have no agent or theatre company behind them. This makes it difficult to demand a just payment, or even secure a place in the brochure.[58]

Founder of the new Spoken Word Theatre Foundation, Sophia Walker, responded to the need for a 'we have your back' network of training, support, and opportunities for solo poets who tour shows. They now have a cross-continental network of partner organisations. In the words of Walker:

> There is this new genre bubbling up all over the world,
> but we have no links, no support, no infrastructure,
> no way to work together and no help to work individ-
> ually. Spoken word theatre needs to be taken seriously
> because it's one of the only financially sustainable
> ways of making a living in our corner of the arts world.
> So we decided to take it seriously ourselves, to be that
> artist-led organisation we so dearly wished existed.[59]

From its grass-roots inception, the Spoken Word Theatre Foundation has gone on to earn the 'consecration' of the British Council and the International Literature Showcase.

*

But who is consecrating whom, and to what extent is spoken word—as a whole—benefitting from such vertical relationships?

Since 2016, spoken word has become the vogue with marketing departments.[60] Most noticeably, a string of spoken word artists have been paid tens of thousands of pounds to write and perform a series of televised poems for Nationwide building society. This high watermark of media exposure has wrought divisions in the movements. Some see it as welcome exposure for underpaid and under-appreciated talent, and an opportunity to grow audiences for the art. Others see it as the death of poetry; the world of commerce plucking the low-hanging fruits of a sub-culture. Welcome to the mainstream media.

Spoken word poets are becoming regulars on the 'highbrow' BBC Radio 4, and gaining mainstream TV coverage.[61] Broadcasting opportunities are, however, infrequent. With the majority of literary agencies dealing with the world of publishing, most touring spoken word artists have not been picked up by agents. Some exceptions to this include Sabrina Mahfouz, Kate Tempest, Hollie McNish, and Vanessa Kisuule who, at the time of writing, are all represented by one literary agent, Johnson and Alcock.[62] In the words of live literature producer Sarah Sanders: 'it is impossible to make a singular career out of being a live literature agent based on the same model as that used for actors or comedy artists'.[63]

This may not always be so. The alternative comedy circuit of the eighties was changed beyond recognition when it became flooded with money. Large booking agencies like Avalon took ownership of entire touring networks, and comedy became less experimental and politically risqué.[64] Could the same thing happen to spoken word? Salena Godden, a poet whose career straddles two eras, has personal reservations about the growing tendency for agents to mediate between poets and audiences:

> Your dreams are a bucket of water. You carry it yourself. Do not give that bucket to someone else and expect them to not spill some…when you have an agent you may lose gigs, not money or corporate gigs, but grass-roots stuff… mates gigs and charity fundraisers. We need those home gigs, now and then, a hot, crowded room above a pub, just for fun, just for laughs, for a good cause, otherwise what's the point? [65]

*

Professionalisation is, however, necessary if poets are to earn a living and the 'artistic economy' of spoken word rarely deserves its own surname. Self-employed poets work with unpredictable income streams from short-lived projects, done through a multitude of clients. To exist in the (aptly named) 'gig economy', usually means being part of the 'precariat': a new class of workers, precariously tethered to short-term (or zero hour) contracts, temp jobs, and insecure work.[66]

Like all artists, poets make ends meet in any number of ways. I subsidise my writing by working as a street entertainer in the summer. Other examples of seasonal work include selling

Christmas trees (Steve Larkin) or tour guiding (Richard Tyrone Jones and James McKay). Some activities are related to the craft, like teaching, copy-editing and arts marketing, though most poets have a broad palette of (often unrelated) income streams. Some colourful examples include: 'tarot reading' (Jackie Juno), 'wedding celebrant and voice over' (Penny Ashton), 'life modelling' (Kat Lyons), 'hosting pub quizzes' (Josie Alford), 'engaging with the local railways' (Amy Wragg), and 'hanging round literary salons, doing sexual favours for novelists' (Jonny 'Fluffypunk' Seagrave).

By far the most significant income stream for spoken word artists is education. As long-time Apples and Snakes programmer Russell Thompson observes, the 'vast majority' of poets pay their rent with school workshops.[67] Yet with school cutbacks and the contraction of funding bodies, this income stream has become harder to find. As Joelle Taylor (a poet with thirty years of education experience) laments, 'three decades of Tory Rule have come to pass'. While I was working with the Spoken Word Education Programme in 2014, our fundraiser saw her success rate drop across all her projects, from nine-in-ten down to one-in-ten in the space of two years. Fees for visiting poets are dropping, and the extension of GCSE exam preparation from two to three years squeezes arts from the school timetable in a 'clampdown' on expression.[68]

While working as a spoken word educator in East London, I became acutely aware of the barriers preventing people from pursuing poetry professionally. A 2018 report by Create London shows that the proportion of young cultural workers from upper-middle class backgrounds more than doubled between 1981 and 2011 (from 15 per cent to 33 per cent). In the same period, the proportion from working class origins dropped by about a third (from 22 per cent to 13 per cent).[69]

Young poets, however, are perhaps less affected than older poets. While a plethora of high-profile initiatives exist to support 'young poets',[70] 'new poets' who are not 'young' are often left out of the picture. Then there are the established poets who need support to develop their work further. Add the demands of mortgages, children, and general fatigue to the mix, and a gigging poet can end up with a life span equivalent to that of a First World War fighter pilot. Though I have found no data on age in spoken word communities, I believe it is experiencing a crisis of eldership.

Writing for *The Guardian*, Joanna Walsh argues that age is 'a feminist issue' and disproportionately affects marginalised groups who are already suffering discouragement or delay in finding their voice as artists. These could be carers, the cared for, the disabled, or writers of colour. She continues:

> Older women are already told every day, in ways
> ranging from the subtle to the blatant, that they are
> irrelevant and should shut up. Multiply this by, say,
> race or gender, and the courage required to put work
> out is even greater.[71]

Spoken word, then, faces considerable challenges and must find ways to innovate and cooperate if it wants to avoid catering, call centres, and an endless stream of young(ish) middle-class white men (like me).

*

Where Marx proposed collective solutions to fend against insecurity, the profession of spoken word poetry is a long way from being unionised. Most of my fellow poets are not aware that they can join the entertainment union Equity. Even if they were, asking for union rates of pay and getting them are two different things.

Is there something about the solo art of spoken word that makes it innately unsuited to working collectively? Reflecting on her experiences of Scottish spoken word, Rachel McCrum warns of 'closed loop' communities of siloed professionals who refuse to share opportunities for fear of competition, or perhaps worse, professional cliques that are impenetrable from below. With few formal training opportunities and no conservatoires, theatre schools, or marketing departments, there is often a lack of a structured debate and 'explicit knowledge sharing' among practitioners.[72]

Organisation is not something traditionally associated with poets, who are renowned for being generally solitary and administratively confused. In the words of Jem Rolls, 'Poetry Society / irony bleeding irony?'[73] Even the word movement won't sit comfortably in the mouth of anyone who has ever tried to get a poet to turn up for something on time. If it is a movement, it is a groundswell, rather than a river running in a concerted direction.

The phenomenon of the self-employed solo artist, performing material they wrote about their own lives, is inherently individualistic, and poets often complain to me about the scuzzy task of self-promotion. I for one have been complicit in the image-building 'propaganda' of presenting myself as 'up and coming' and 'successful.' In his book, *Poetry's Afterlife: Verse in a Digital Age*, the poet Kevin Stein blames social media for encouraging artists to seek personal notoriety as vociferously as bankers pursue wealth.[74]

If poetry is individualist, few guarantees underwrite the security and health of these individuals. Musicians, by analogy, have the highest drug and alcohol use of any sector of the economy. Indeed, the UK's largest employer of musicians is The British Army; a source of regular pay that musicians can't find elsewhere.[75]

I have seen no data that links the practice of poetry and the use of drugs (perhaps because no-one will admit to doing it), though I do know from personal experience that being a jobbing poet can be lonely work that involves unsociable hours, lots of travel, and frequent contact with alcohol and late nights.

Being on stage can be life enhancing, but the exertion and excitement also has its comedowns. Gigging releases the stress hormone cortisol into the blood and results in higher resting heart rate that can stop performers from sleeping. In the long term these stresses can have serious health implications.[76]

Yet the *sociality* of spoken word also comes with benefits. Research from the late eighties and early nineties shows that poets have higher rates of mood disorders and suicide than other writers, like novelists.[77] In 2014, American researchers Nadia Alvarez and Jack Mearns extended this area of study to spoken word. A 'new form of poetry has taken rise' they write, 'in which performing and competing is incorporated in the medium.' The research shows that spoken word's emphasis on *community* builds trust and reduces 'rumination and passive coping'.[78] Its rituals of sharing also enable poets to draw insight, strength, and inspiration from other poets and audience members. Live performance is key, helping poets overcome their fears, and providing a coping mechanism that can help them regulate their mood.

The Chill Pill collective runs regular spoken word nights in London where members rotate slots to perform, MC, and promote. The 'family vibe' that comes from working together also provides a vital social function. One of its members, Raymond Antrobus, told me that banter and mutual 'piss-taking' helps to ground their egos. Beyond the events, they share professional opportunities and pool ideas for writing, performing, and organising.[79]

Explicit collectives like Chill Pill or Yorkshire's A Firm of Poets are vastly outnumbered by the countless *implicit* collectives who are putting on gigs across the country. Unlike Apples and Snakes in England, Scotland has no national support agency for spoken word. Poet Harry Josephine Giles, who co-founded one of Edinburgh's community poetry groups, Inky Fingers, says this is something it 'desperately needs'. 'Volunteer turnover has always been *high*' they continue, 'making sure that it was a collective endeavour from the start is what's enabled it to keep going against that background.'[80]

The People's Republic of Poetry is no utopia, but solidarity does exist and it provides a lifeline for countless skint poets trying to carve a space for poetry. With a lack of reliable vertical connections the spoken word movement is fuelled by its 'community vibe', and the love its participants have for the work.

*

Rapper KRS-One draws a distinction between your *work* (which involves fulfilling your own aspirations) and your *job* (which involves fulfilling the aspirations of others). With its sporadic relationship with the world of money, poetry is usually *work* (and *hard work* at that). In being *work*, it avoids what Marx described as *alienation*—where workers lack ownership and control over what they do. The work of spoken word is rarely done just to fulfil the aspirations of others. It doesn't turn people into 'wage slaves', or estrange them from their creativity or their destiny. As a small scale, artisanal craft, it gives us greater room to self-actualise and is relatively *disalienated work*. This quote from C.W. Mills captures it well:

> The worker is free to control his own working action…There is no split of work and play, or work and culture. The craftsman's way of livelihood determines and infuses his entire mode of living'[81]

An important characteristic of this creative freedom is that it is mostly practised outside of the expectations of academia. This can be both a closed door and an open one. For Gramsci, the 'organic intellectual' produces knowledge in ways that differ from socially closed educational institutions, who often reinforce established ways of doing things.[82] Though spoken word modules are increasingly common in universities, the art is rarely manufactured in the academy.[83] Instead, poets craft their work in conversation with the stage, as well as the poets and books that orbit those stages. Poet Jem Rolls calls this 'the coalface' of poetry.[84] I do not mean to argue here that formal training is wrong; instead that poets, through their apprenticeship to the scene, hone their craft in ways that formal qualifications do not recognise.

This could prove to be more valuable than it may appear. In the Spring of 2018, British university workers went on strike. Their picket lines (often accompanied by live poetry) protested against the privatisation of education, the rise in casual contracts, and the increase of tuition fees.[85] These measures further narrow opportunities for poets in further education. More widely, they amount to an assault on independent thought and critical enquiry, both of which we need for a healthy democracy.[86] In this context, the organic intellectual must seek new methods of sustaining the economy of ideas.

At the time of writing, initiatives are afoot to improvise new networks of human exchange from inside the scene. In January 2019, for example, I joined a team of poets at a retreat in rural Shropshire to prepare an inaugural four-day spoken word bootcamp (Hip Yak Poetry School) to be attended by fifty emerging poets from Southwest England. Training sessions cover the history of the movement, techniques for organising, and ways to tour, publish and educate others. The retreat (supported by ACE) offers bursaries and subsidised places for poets to convene, cross-fertilise, and find ways to survive financially. On the final day, the gathering will be joined by a number of spoken word organisations for a live-streamed debate on how to develop word-communities in the region.[87]

*

Throughout this chapter, I have analysed a variety of ways that spoken word has grown itself horizontally and (to a lesser extent) vertically. As a grass-roots practice, it has sustained lifelong careers for artists like Salena Godden who, in spite of the many barriers that affect female, working-class writers of colour, has gone on to become one of the country's most celebrated poets. The *social algorithm* that helped get her there, now more extensive and complex than it was in the mid-nineties, faces considerable new challenges in aiding new, and existing, talent.

In the face of these challenges, it is tempting to see salvation in the mainstream. But celebrity success, by definition, cannot sustain more than a small group of individuals. The majority of spoken word's achievements have grown from bottom-up, collective activities. Each night, organisation, and group of friends that compose it generate *social capital—auto-poetically*. Of all art forms, the intimacy of live poetry's personal disclosure make it particularly suited to this. It is founded on 'radical friendship' (see Chapter 8), a complex ecology of micro-interactions and empathetic exchanges shape its social form.

These communities are mobilising, not just for their own entertainment, but their own *cultural and intellectual transmission*. Outside the paywall of academia, the *organic intellectuals* of spoken word use the *informal economy* to develop their craft. They have built their own stages, publishing outlets, and touring networks. They have developed their own standards and tastes, with competitions, awards, and 'categories of perception' that are distinct to the genre. Though financially poor, they have found a way to *work*. In an age of economic and political turmoil, this form of cultural action can only be critical.

Notes

1   Bourdieu, *The Rules of Art* (1996), p.196.

2   I have borrowed the phrase 'event-based art practice' from Jacob, 'Groundless in the Museum' (2010).

3   DuBois, 'Oral Tradition' (2003), p.225.

4   Bourdieu, as above, p.111.

5   Mayakovsky, *How are Verses Made?* (1926), p.58.

6   Salena Godden Interview, Stage Invasion, Vimeo, (00:04:00)

7   Salena Godden email to Peter Bearder, 12 Apr. 2018.

8   Harvie, *Fair Play* (2013), p.156.

9   Dobson, *How to Save Our Town Centres* (2015), p.113.

10   National Rural Touring Forum, http://www.ruraltouring.org/about

11   Nymphs & Thugs, https://nymphsandthugs.net

12   Smith, 'SlamCulture 2011', 5 Apr. 2013, https://www.youtube.com/watch?v=MmH_ePoYCOM

13   Ailes, 'What Cult? A Critical Engagement with Watts' Essay', 6 Mar. 2018, http://sabotagereviews.com/2018/03/06/what-cult-a-critical-engagement-with-watts-essay/

14   Scottish Poetry Library, 2012, https://www.liverpool.ac.uk/media/livacuk/centrefornewandinternationalwriting/Longform,post,-,The,State,of,Poetry,and,Poetry,Criticism,in,the,UK,and,Ireland,FINAL.pdf

15   Trévien, 22 Nov. 2017, https://sabotagereviews.com/2017/11/22/the-challenges-of-reviewing-spoken-word

16   Watts, 'The Cult of the Noble Amateur' (2018).

17   Raymond Antrobus, email to Peter Bearder, 22 Jan. 2019.

18   Trévien, as above.

19   Jack, Oct. 2018, https://sabotagereviews.com/2018/10/14/joygernaut-andy-craven-griffiths-attenborough-arts-centre-leicester-11-october-2018

20   Quoted in Clive Birnie Interview, Stage Invasion, Vimeo, (00:25:00).

21   Clive Birnie, as above.

22   Clive Birnie, as above, (00:19:50)

23   I have borrowed this phrase from Johnson, *Killing Poetry* (2017), p.21.

24   Howe, *Crowdsourcing* (2009).

25   Godden, 20 Jan. 2014, https://www.standard.co.uk/comment/
        salena-godden-passion-and-hard-work-are-the-keys-to-writ-
        ing-9071749.html

26   Watts, as above.

27   Anderson, 'Uncomfortable Conversations in Black British Arts
        Practice Now', 22 Mar. 2018.

28   Randall, *Sound System* (2017), p.97.

29   Ailes, 6 Mar. 2018, http://sabotagereviews.com/2018/03/06/
        what-cult-a-critical-engagement-with-watts-essay/

30   Bey, *The Temporary Autonomous Zone* (1991).

31   Jonny Fluffypunk Interview, Stage Invasion, Vimeo.

32   Robinson, *Music Festivals and the Politics of Participation* (2015),
        p.36–40.

33   Robinson, as above, p.39.

34   Sally Jenkinson, email to Peter Bearder, 24 Jan. 2019.

35   Louv, *Last Child in the Woods* (2005).

36   Fox, *Watching the English*, (2004).

37   Laing & Mair, 'Music Festivals and Social Inclusion' (2015).

38   Peter Buckley Hill, email to Peter Bearder, 17 May 2018.

39   Varjack, 15 Aug. 2017, https://www.whatsonstage.com/edin-
        burgh-theatre/news/performing-fringe-costs-festival-paula-var-
        jack_44381.html

40   Bowman, unpublished interview with Peter Bearder, Beathearder
        Festival, 2013.

41   Patel, 1 Nov. 2013, https://www.theatlantic.com/national/
        archive/2013/11/a-verse-to-go-please-street-poets-and-the-lives-
        they-touch/281035/

42   Butnotfamous, https://www.richbutnotfamo.us/vision

43   Rowan McCabe Interview, Stage Invasion, Vimeo.

44   Johnson, as above, p.21.

45   For a look at Becker's thesis of Art Worlds in the context of other
        writing on the subject see: Hall, 'Interactionism and the Study of
        Social Organization' (1987).

46   Sam Berkson Interview, Stage Invasion, Vimeo. (00:30:00).

47   Greenblatt, *Will in the World* (2005).

48   Sam Berkson, as above.

49   Fleming, *Surviving the Future* (2006), p.41.

50   Byron Vincent & Dave McGinn, unpublished text of 'Live Before You Die', spoken word theatre show (2018).

51   *Utter! Manifesto,* (May 2018).

52   Lucy English email to Peter Bearder, 12 Oct. 2018.

53   Romer, 24 Jan. 2018, https://www.artsprofessional.co.uk/news/ lottery-shortfall-forces-ace-cut-2018-22-budget-ps156m.

54   Roberts, *Digital Publics* (2014).

55   Quoted in Hall, as above, p.6.

56   Johnson, *Killing Poetry*, p.133.

57   *Utter! Manifesto* (May 2018).

58   Sarah Sanders email to Peter Bearder, 17 Jun. 2018.

59   Trévien, 8 Dec.2017, http://sabotagereviews.com/2017/12/08/we-want-spoken-word-theatre-to-go-global-so-we-have-to-be-theforce-making-that-happen-in-conversation-with-sophia-walker.

60   See 'Why Brands are Using Spoken Word', Canvas8, 24 May 2016 https://www.canvas8.com/content/2016/05/24/rhymes.html.

61   Shows where spoken word artists have performed in recent years include BBC 1xtra's *Words First*, BBC 2 (Friday night prime-time) *Performance Live*, Channel 4's *Random Acts*, and *The Russell Howard-Hour* on Sky.

62   Johnson & Alcock, http://www.johnsonandalcock.co.uk

63   Sarah Sanders email to Peter Bearder, 17 Jun. 2018.

64   See 'Alternative Comedy' chapter in Double, *Stand Up* (1997).

65   Salena Godden, email to Peter Bearder 24 Apr. 2019.

66   McGuigan, *Cool Capitalism* (2009).

67   Russell Thompson Interview, Stage Invasion, Vimeo, (00:32:30).

68   Joelle Taylor Interview, Stage Invasion, Vimeo, (00:35:30).

69   Brook, O'Brien & Taylor, *Panic! Social Class, Taste and Inequalities in the Creative Industries*, 2018 http://createlondon.org/wp-content/ uploads/2018/04/Panic-Social-Class-Taste-and-Inequalities-in-the-Creative-Industries1.pdf p.17.

70   Some notable examples include *Barbican Young Poets*, the Poetry Society's *Young Poets Network*, Contact Theatre's *Young Identity* programme and the *Roundhouse Poetry Collective*.

71   Walsh, 'All the Awards for Young Writers Amount to Discrimination', 8 Sept. 2017, https://www.theguardian.com/books/books-blog/2017/sep/08/all-the-awards-for-young-writers-amount-to-discrimination

72   McCrum, 'The Ties that Bind Us' (2018).

73   Jem Rolls, 'I'd Rather Be Dead', unpublished poem.

74   Stein, *Poetry's Afterlife* (2010), p.93.

75   Randall, *Sound System* (2017), p.69.

76   See Thomson & Jaque, *Creativity and the Performing Artist* (2017).

77   Ludwig, 'Mental Illness and Creative Activity in Women Writers' (1994); Jamison, *Touched with Fire* (1993); Andreasen, 'Creativity and Mental Illness' (1987).

78   Alvarez & Mearns, 'The Benefits of Writing and Performing in the Spoken Word Community' (2014), p.267.

79   Raymond Antrobus, email to Peter Bearder, 22 Jan. 2019.

80   Harry Josephine Giles, email to Peter Bearder, 22 Jan. 2019.

81   Mills, *White Collar* (1957), p.220.

82   Gunster, 'Gramsci, Organic Intellectuals, and Cultural Studies' (2000).

83   I am aware of spoken word modules being taught in Bath Spa (Lucy English), University of Worcester (Jack McGowan), Brunel University (Benjamin Zephaniah) Canterbury Christ Church (Dan Simpson), Sheffield Hallum (Michael Markham) and London Met' (Niall O'Sullivan). Spoken word is also taught as part of a cabaret module at St Mary's University (Chris Redmond). Other universities with strong links to spoken word include Leicester, Goldsmith College and Warwick University.

84   Jem Rolls Interview, Stage Invasion, Vimeo.

85   Gardiner, 'Why I'm a Striking Lecturer', 12 Mar. 2018, https://www.theguardian.com/commentisfree/2018/mar/12/striking-lecturer-slow-death-public-education

86   Kadir, 'I'm Glad I Eschewed a Career in Academia', 31 Jul. 2017, https://www.timeshighereducation.com/blog/im-glad-i-eschewed-career-academia-there-are-plenty-of-alternatives-for-phds#survey-answer.

87   Hip Yak Poetry School also pledges 'to feed your soul as well as your brain' with an immersive guided walk through a forest. Here poets meet with other poets from history (in character and costume) who offer clues, riddles and provocations to help them get in touch with their motivations and aspirations.

Images

Chapter 1

Hammer & Tongue grafitti on the Cowley Road, Oxford. Artwork by Shtig. Photography: Hammer & Tongue.

Manchester's Thick Richard. Photography: Shay Rowan.

Hammer & Tongue poetry slam, Zodiac Club, Oxford, 2005.
Photography: Nick Cobbing.

Bang Said the Gun host Rob Auton presents the Golden Gun
competition. Photography: Wasi Daniju.

Carnival and competition: the Hatalyst cheerleader,
chosen from the audience at Bang Said the Gun, London.
Photography: Wasi Daniju.

Jury voting on the Republic aitys on the twentieth anniversary of
Kazakhstan's independence, 2011. Photography: Ministry of Culture
and Information of the Republic of Kazakhstan.
Photograph: Karimkhan Zanggar

Chapter 2

Literacy as a Percentage of Human History

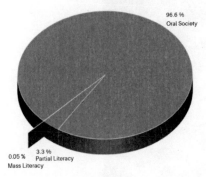

96.6 %
Oral Society

0.05 %
Mass Literacy

3.3 %
Partial Literacy

See chapter 2. Part 1.1

The European ballad singer tradition, street corner newscasters, satirists, poets and entertainers.

A griot praise poet with his chief. Senegal,
early 19th century. Names unknown.

Props, costumes and character poets. Is there still a place for cabaret quirk
in UK spoken word? Rachel Pantechnicon at Cheltenham Poetry Festival
2011. Photography: Cheltenham Poetry Festival.

#TeamTrending (Ben Fagan and Sarah Hirsch) at The Anti Slam.
Photography: Process Productions.

Poets vs MCs logo, Brighton. Artwork: Tom Hines.

Brighton's, Spliff Richard performs at the annual Poets vs MCs in Brighton 2018. Photography: Ashley Laurence.

Chapter 3

The Devastations occasioned by the RIOTERS of LONDON Firing the New Goal of NEWGATE and burning Mr. Akerman's Furniture, &c June 6 1780

Romantic poet William Blake attended this burning of Newgate Prison during the Gordon Riots of 1780, London.

A Chartist Meeting on Kennington Common, London, 1848.

THE VOICE OF THE PEOPLE.

'TIS the voice of the people I hear it on high,
It peals o'er the mountains—it soars to the sky;
Through wide fields of heather, it wings its swift
   flight;
Like thunders of heaven arrayed in their might.
It rushes still on, like the torrent's loud roar ;
And bears on its surges the wrongs of the poor.
It's shock like the earthquake shall fill with dismay,
The hearts of the tyrants and sweep them away.

W. H. C.

Chartist poem printed in a newspaper. © British Library Board
(MFM.MLD6* December 4, 1841).

A 1930s communist rally in Trafalgar square.
Photography: rarehistoricalphotos.com.

Allen Ginsberg at The International Poetry Incarnation, 11 June 1965.
Photography: "Ginsberg7" by John "Hoppy" Hopkins "© 1965 ESTATE
OF J V L HOPKINS"

Dada founder Hugo Ball at Cabaret Voltaire,
Zurich, 1916.

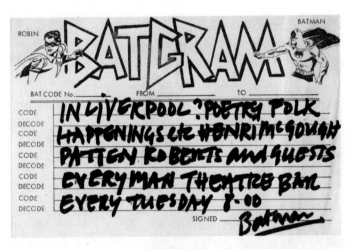

The Liverpool Poets: Adrian Henri, leaflet for Batnight, c.1966. © Adrian Henri estate, by permission of Catherine Marcangeli.

Black Arts Movement: Gil Scott-Heron.
Photography: Brian Kavanagh.

Queen of dub poetry, Jean 'Binta' Breeze.
Photograhy: Robert Huggins.

Punk poetry: Joolz Denby touring with New Model Army.
Photography: courtesy of Joolz Denby.

Alternative Cabaret: John Hegley's 1980s band The Popticians.
Image: courtesy of Bill Muir.

Chapter 4

Salena Godden's first homemade pamphlet published in 1995 in collaboration with Tim Wells' poetry zine *Rising* (now in its 70th edition).

Phantom Laundry Poetry Tent, Shambala Festival, 2018.
Photography: Tilly May.

Breakout sessions at the Hip Yak Poetry School, May 2019. Led by
Chris Redmond & Matt Harvey. Photoraphy: Tasher Kuler.

Breakout sessions at the Hip Yak Poetry School, May 2019.
Led by Kate Fox. Photoraphy: Tasher Kuler.

Poetry Collectives: Yorkshire's A Firm of Poets. Left to right:
Matt Abbott, Ralph Dartford, Genevieve Walsh, John Darwin
and Matthew Hedley Stoppard.

Spoken word theatre: John Berkavitch's show *Wrong*.
Photography: Belinda Lawley.

A selection of British spoken word artists.
Artwork by Scott Tyrrell, poet.

'Poet Tree' by poet Cat Brogan, prepared for the Politics and
Creativity conference at Portsmouth University, October 2018.

The Door to Door Poet, Newcastle's Rowan McCabe.
Photography: Opie Productions.

Chapter 5

Jasmine Gardosi. Photography: Thom Bartley.

Kat François.
Photography: Sloetry.co.uk.

Hannah Silva performs poetry on a loop machine.
Photography: Magdalena Fabianczyk.

Chapter 6

Rob Gee making a cheeky aside.
Photography: Nick Rawl.

Emotional contagion: audience members at An Evening with
The Last Poets, Rough Trade East, London, 18 May 2018.
Photography: Suzi Corker.

Chapter 7

Rachel Rose Reid performs her show Silence, 2018.
Photography: Raymond Van Mil.

Ecstatic poetry: Salena Godden performs at Nasty Women,
Stour Space, Hackney Wick. Photography: Suzi Corker.

Kate Tempest on the Holts Stage, Glastonbury Festival, 2017.
Photography: John Kerridge.

THE ILLUSTRATED LONDON NEWS

MR. CHARLES DICKENS'S LAST READING.

The hypnotist Charles Dickens with his custom made performance table.

Chapter 8

Protesters enter Hambacher coal mine, Germany.
Photography: Ende Gelände.

The BP or not BP? 'Ramira and Juliet' stage invasion at
Cadogan Hall on 18 April 2016. Photography: Hugh Warwick.

Shakespearean flashmob in the British Museum, 18 November
2012, by BP or Not BP? (formerly Reclaim Shakespeare Company).
Photography: Kristian Buus.

Protest and 'The Gift of Pain': David Lee Morgan.
Photography: Jon D. Barker.

Sam Berkson performs at Occupy London, 2011.
Photography: Peter Macdiarmid, via Getty Images.

Chapter 5:
The Path of the Poem
Through the Body

'*The Word, a vital force, a corporeal vapour,*
a spiritual and carnal liquidity'
—Paul Zumthor

'*Language overflows the voice and seeps into the body*
causing it to twist and contort.'
—Anthony Howell

'*Your face is a poem.*'
—Spanish saying

*

I often find myself here: an empty car park, a foyer, a corridor. Today it is the alley behind a curry house. I pace, gesticulating and muttering at the floor. I go through the poems, the intros, the pauses. I lightly bounce on bended knees with my arms jiggling loose by my side. Shaking my hands releases unwanted energy. Beatboxing loosens my face muscles and sharpens my pronunciation. I stick my tongue out as far as it will go and keep it there in a stretch. The air tastes of saag aloo. A passer-by is staring at me. We turn our heads away. I take eight deep breaths to oxygenate my mind. I'm nervous, adrenalised, and channelling. I'm here. I'm now. I'm on…

*

In live poetry, the body is the material, the media through which the poetry is published. In entering it, poetry becomes a product of that body; from its muscles, gut, and cardiovascular rhythms, through to its larynx, eyes, and facial expressions. This chapter is about poetry as it stands before us—a resonating body of flesh. It will look at what is outside of the poem's text: the *choreography*, not the *script*, the *music*, not the *score*, and the *topography of the flesh* rather than the *typography of the page*. This is not a comprehensive dissection of sound and movement in live poetry, which has been done more fully elsewhere (see Julia Novak 2011). Instead, it will present poetry as a *musical-muscular blueprint* and sketch its journey through the body. In *writing through the body,* spoken word in-corporates the flesh (and its inseparable musicality) as an intrinsic part of its design. On the way out, the poem can transform and 'purge' emotional imprints to heal the performer.

Since literary criticism bifurcated from performance studies in the early twentieth century, 'poetry' has been analysed as text, and the physical discipline of literature has been consigned to 'drama' and 'theatre'.[1] The result has been a split from the oral tradition which has left many 'readings' figuratively and literally anaesthetised from the neck down (from *an-aesthesia*: 'not aesthetic').

This is not to say that the body has been absent from our understanding of poetry. Textbooks abound with exercises on evoking 'sense data' into our verse.[2] Yet more attention has been given to 'writing *from* the body' than writing *into* it. Dylan Thomas captures this idea when he says that verse 'comes to life out of the red heart through the brain'.[3] Thomas (one of the most famous poet-performers of all time) knew that this is only part of the passage. Through performance, it returns to the heart, and the rest of the body, dictating its pace and workload.

When performance poetry surged in visibility in the post-war period (most visibly through the Beat poets), it was Charles Olson's essay *Projective Verse* that served as the ideological blueprint. What poetry had suffered from, claimed Olson, 'is manuscript, press, the removal of verse from its producer'. For Olson, poetry should be written for the ear, with the breath as a guiding principle. By invoking the body in the writing process, poetry can become a 'projectile' and 'percussive' discharge of energy.[4]

Yet Olson's concern with 'the kinetic of the poem' was more to do with the performance of poetry on the *page*. What happens when the poem comes, not as a desire to write, but a compulsion to say, or perhaps sing?

*

Kat François is a poet who works extensively with the body and I will return to her several times in this chapter. In my interview with her she told me that poems begin their lives as 'an itch', a *blueprint*, that seeks fruition through the body:

> I find that on the stage, the piece finds itself. And a rhythm might be tapping away in my head, it's *telling* me…Maybe at first, I haven't really got the confidence to really sing it and really claim that rhythm. But then after a while, it's just tapping, tapping, tapping and I *must not but* listen to it.[5]

Many of us will be familiar with the feeling that a poem is passing through us. At an early, purely musical stage, it can be said to be pre-linguistic; a hurtling inarticulacy flung from the muse. One night, as I lay in my bed, I was struck by the compulsion to write a poem that caused me to get up and sit scrawling at my desk. There were fragments of metaphors and images, but its life in me at that time was principally that of a rhythm, a melody, and a tension in my gut. Below are a couple of passages from the poem:

> You maligned silence swelling inside of me
> Warm, moist creature
> Sssssitting in my viscera.
> Sssssssssiting in my bathroom
> Ssssssssssiting in my head

As I started to write it, I was compelled to randomly repeat words as if caught in a stutter or muscle spasm. The body was writing itself into the poem. It felt necessary to capture these sound effects, which wanted not just to be written, but enacted and sung.

You who loiters in the garden of madness
maligned matrix
inescapable algorithm
monotonous chant
gesticulation
reartic, tic, tic,

Does the p
Does the paast
Does the past not keep,
Does the past not keep constr
Are you the blueprint of a lurching edifice?

A few nights later, while working on the poem (by muttering into a booklet at the back of a pub), the poem moved through me with such a shuddering intensity that I awoke with swollen glands in my throat. I was sure this came from the poem working its way out of me.

*

Jasmine Gardosi inscribes the blueprint of 'Unidentified Crying Object' into her performance to make the breath itself a metaphor, with strained breathing (speaking on the in-breath) used to simulate toxic attitudes in the classroom. In and out breaths are accompanied by a slow point of her finger; outward in accusation, inward in self-questioning. Lines performed on the in breath are italicised.

[…]
No one knows you're gay.
Not even you

but still, these speech bubbles will expand as clouds
that become a part of the atmosphere.

bunch of queers
homo

poofter
bumboy

What they speak,
you absorb.

Your brother's car will be fuelled by it.
The science corridor will swirl in it.
This isn't your kind of oxygen.
Maybe you belong to an alien race
that would explain why you're that
unidentified crying object in the school toilet [6]

'Unidentified Crying Object' stretches the articulatory parameters of Olson's *breath*. As the poem crescendos in near hyperventilation of strained breathing (Gardosi often had to lie down during rehearsals), we are made to feel the strain of the poem, from her insides.

For Walter Ong, the spoken word has unique expressive capabilities because it deals in sound. Of all sensory fields, sound has the unique ability to communicate the insides of something. While sight and touch deal with surfaces of things, the ear can stretch into the innards, without having to open them up. Sight alone, for example, cannot tell us if the box is empty. We can knock on its side with our hands, but its 'voice' is given by sound.[7] Similarly, we can read the emotional state of the poet (or the character they are performing) through the quiver of the breath, the tightness of the throat, and the tangle of the gut. The heart of the performer, and (as we will see in the next chapter) that of the listener, is carried on the flow of the poet's breath.

*

Having established the idea of what our insides can bring to spoken word, let's now shift focus to the place of movement.

Kat François trained as a dancer before moving over to music, then theatre and poetry to express herself 'more fully'. As a performer, she always *owns* the stage, moving around it to deliver memorised poems and dramatic monologues. When she won the 2005 World Poetry Slam Championship in Rotterdam, she entered the final round barefoot to help her feel unbound and grounded. Decisions like these are part of her craft: 'For me, poetry *sits* in my body, it's a physical, emotional thing. It's not *just words*'.[8]

In spoken word theatre, (see Chapter 2, Part 1.3) poetry has become the object of stage positioning, costumes, dramaturgy, and directors. Vanessa Kisuule's one-woman show, *Sexy*, combines comedy, spoken word, dance 'and various states of undress', to unpack the concept of 'sexy' as construct, institution, fashion, and feeling.[9] Working with a movement director, Kisuule charts the growth of her body, and her relationship to it as she grew up. At one point, wearing only a bra and knickers, she introduces her different body parts to the audience. The body becomes both the *subject* and the *object* of the show, and the idea of biographical poetry (or 'life writing') is expanded into the flesh.

When writing through the body, movements and gestures become part of the poem's articulation. As Kisuule exclaims in the opening lines of one of her pieces:

> Just pick one.
> Come on, just [CLAP] *pick* one!
>
> There's no way you can like pole dancing
> *and* respect yourself.

The clap (a coded sound for 'now!') is timed to metric precision and lends surprise to help launch the poem. In this sense, the clap is both linguistic and poetic.

By evoking the physical correlates of speech, spoken word transfers, to quote Teresa Brennan, 'from one register/alphabet to another'.[10] Spoken word poetry is not a purely 'verbal art', but rather what Julia Novak calls a 'bi-medial' art form (text and body together).[11] Stage directions are written into the script of *Sexy*.

Kisuule reflects on her practice:

> I believe in the physical poetry of the body, in
> dance as a form of poetry and poetry as a form of
> dance. I think both art forms do similar things,
> they elevate the stories and feelings that cannot be
> articulated through every day speech.[12]

This position mirrors Jacques Lecoq's philosophy of physical theatre, which is founded on the idea of the 'poetic body'. Here, the
actor is first of all a poet. Their language is movement, and their
body is the instrument.[13]

In spoken word, performers (consciously or otherwise) test
choreographed and memorised poem-dances on audiences.
These poem-dances deliver characters and feelings that are literally *beyond words*. The poem ripens into the body, spilling down-
ward (or perhaps upwards) through our flesh. Its rhythm and
phrasing lengthen into us and ripple through our limbs. The
body begins to interject with pauses, sighs, and shuddering *crescendos*. Punch-lines arrive in the form of pointed fingers, gazes,
or facial expressions. All of this becomes part of the poem's lineation, the full realisation of the poem's *musical-muscular blueprint*.
Kristine Stiles calls this the 'rhetoric of the body'.[14] It is all at
once scenic, music, and kinetic.

*

So far we have looked at a few ways that the voice, lungs, and
other parts of the body can augment the poem's capacity to communicate. But performance is contentious in poetry and it is these
controversies that I will turn to now.

The main concern with live performance is that it can detract
from the written content of the poem (see Chapter 2, Part 2.1). As
Paul Vermeersch complains:

> The idea, I suppose, is that the flailing, stylized vocals
> will be interesting enough on their own that no one will
> notice how bad the actual writing is… the 'performer'

> must jazz it up with all kinds of forced rhythms and
> hand signals to make it 'entertaining' enough for an
> audience.[15]

While Vermeersch raises a vital point about the need to cultivate both the writing and performance of this 'bi-medial' art form, the data I collected from the Hammer & Tongue 2018 Slam Final shows the 'over-performance' complaint is often unfounded. The use of gestures gives one indication. 27.8 per cent of poems made heavy use of gestures, 40.8 per cent made notable use, while a full 31.3 per cent had almost no gestures, or restricted their gesticulation to the face (for more on this see Chapter 2, Part 2.5 and the Appendix).

We have all seen poets use performance in ways that mask bad writing, let down good writing, or just send us to sleep. This passage from Taylor Mali's performance 'I Could Be a Poet' captures what can happen when one half of this 'bi-medial' art form takes over.

> I'm not afraid to
>
> SHOUT! WITH INTENSITY! AND LONG,
> DRAMATIC...
>
> PAUSES
>
> FRAUGHT WITH ANGST!
> [...]
> And then the end
> Spoken softly, hauntingly tender,
> Though not devoid of irony,
> Ending abruptly as if there is
> more... [16]

Purposefully un-artful delivery can also be a rhetorical decision. Charles Bernstein calls this the 'anti-expressivist' performance style.[17] We can see this in action at the award ceremony of the prestigious T.S. Eliot Prize (an award founded by the Poetry

Book Society). Here, performances (or 'recitals') are typically read from the page with an air of intensity and a stately pace of delivery. While it is impossible not to generalise, there is clearly an 'anti-expressive' performance style and a desire to ensure complete immersion in (and minimal distraction from) the written word.

While this is an entirely valid approach, a rigid ideology of stripping back all embellishment to let the words speak for themselves, also risks being an over-performance of the page. 'Why are you not thinking about your *audience*?' complains Joelle Taylor about some poets she has watched. 'Those people just spent ten quid to come and see you, you *arrogant bastard.*' Reflecting on the changes in the scene, Joelle believes the worlds of 'page' and 'stage' are now meeting in the middle, with performers becoming better writers, and writers learning to 'own their own hands'.[18]

We can also see an 'anti-expressivist' style in the spoken word of Rob Auton and Zia Ahmed. Both use a relatively narrow range of pitch and volume, and the default frequency and pace of voice are low and slow. Hannah Silva's research into 'spoken word voice' shows how this bucks the trend of faster and higher pitched spoken word performances.[19] Yet Auton and Ahmed's 'anti-expressivist' style diverges from that of the T.S. Eliot Award Ceremony. Both are professional performers (as well as writers), who exploit 'anti-expressive' style to convey an almost comic sense of mundanity. This becomes even more effective when the dry persona is broken, and they say something absurd.

Exploring and playing with the uniqueness of one's own voice is part of the spoken word poetic. Kat François, for example, was influenced when growing up by singers like Ella Fitzgerald, Nina Simone, and Tracy Chapman. 'These were black women with depth and a resonance to their voice,' says Kat, 'I'm learning to play with that and accept that and sit in that and embrace that.'[20]

While the 'art worlds' of poetry are certainly blurring, the historical divide between the poetry gig and the 'formal poetry reading' has made the body a site of intense controversy.[21] There is, of course, no right or wrong physicality, only appropriate. Writing for the body (whether for understatement or overstatement) does at least honour the fact that the body exists.

*

Unlike the relatively anonymous transaction of the page, the existence of said bodies comes with baggage. In his analysis of social class, Paul Fussell shows how class imprints itself on our nervous system from early childhood. The result is that we wear our background as gait, stance, and even gesture. The 'lower orders', he argues are more exuberant with their gestures, while the 'upper classes' have a more controlled and restricted body language, with arms kept close to the body.[22] Perhaps this is why T.S. Eliot (the bowler-hatted employee of the Lloyds Bank Colonial and Foreign Department) had a famously rigid and deadpan 'performance' style. For French novelist and poet Jacques Roubaud, the austere and well-behaved delivery of some poets comes from a desire to perform their 'high culture'.[23]

This does not, however, amount to a clear correlation between performance style and class. These styles can change throughout a poet's, and a poem's, life. What's more, simplistic groupings of 'class' are difficult to define. The winner of the 2018 Hammer & Tongue Final, Usaama Minhas, was noticeable for the hip hop idiom of his hand movements. Yet this doesn't show class so much as the influence of a global cultural phenomenon. This is to say nothing of how his body may perform conventions of gender, age, race, or any other way one might decide to look at it.

Still, body language, like all forms of communication, is inscribed by the settings and styles of our social groups. Erving Goffman's landmark book *The Presentation of Self in Everyday Life* sees an almost constant state of 'stagecraft' in how we manage our expressive behaviour to the point where 'he and his body merely provide the peg on which something of collaborative manufacture will be hung for a time'.[24] Unsurprisingly, this extends into the performance of poetry, which Julia Novak's research concludes is partly 'culturally conditioned'.[25]

While there are many reasons to hold reservations about performance in poetry, it would be surprising if cultural chauvinism is entirely absent from the controversies. If we insist that poetry should also be judged on appearance, it will be judged on appearance. Given that forces are writing into our bodies before we even open our mouths, these appearances come with their own politics.

*

For Haun Saussy, language is a 'mechanical reminiscence' that etches itself on our nervous system. From this perspective (that of *media theory*) our brains, muscles, and nerves make the material base, or *medium*, of poetry. Saussy's interest here is how the world has inscribed itself—as a stream of patterns—onto our motor system and muscle memory. Language is 'a set of vibrations,' and knowledge itself is 'the sum of learned gestures, including verbal gestures such as poems and proverbs'.[26] He points to the fact that we acquire language first in its oral, bodily form, as rhythms, emphases, melodies, and gestures. *Atishoo! Atishoo!* We all fall down!

As with the rest of our bodies, the way we organise pitch, rhythm, and timbre (or colouration) of the spoken word, is culturally conditioned. This is everywhere apparent in the verbal music of head teachers, sports commentators, or indeed any other performative role we may step into. A fun way to explore this is to recite 'The Lord's Prayer' in the call of a market trader, present the weather in the voice of someone giving a speech at a protest, or deliver the News at Ten in the voice of a homeless person asking for money. Each of these vocal performances has their own rhythm, volume, and melodic contour. They also come with their own pace, emphases, and range of volume and pitch. The strength of their music only becomes apparent when it is taken away or altered. At that moment our attention shifts from 'meaning' to the musical 'surface of the language.'[27]

For Cornelia Gräbner, spoken word artists appropriate these 'socially coded rhythms' and re-express them through the body in performance.[28] In this way, the body becomes an instrument for the rhythms that feed the writing. This could be the rhythms of chain gangs and hip hop, or the tense and accelerated distractions of urban superstructures.[29]

The music of the spoken word then, is something we inherit from the world around us. In live performance this can be harnessed, toyed with, and inverted in the service of poetry.

*

One poem by Hannah Silva gives us a flavour of how far we can go with this music. What follows is my own transcription of a novel and moving performance she gave at the Warwick Arts Centre, Coventry.

Silva uses an electronic device to layer vocals in a sequence that repeats in a loop. The poem begins with a rhythm of scatted vowels:

O ee uh e o oh i o   e o i o o a i o oh

The pitch of the vowels bounces hypnotically between D# and F#, a jump of a tone-and-a-half in pitch. This minor interval gives a menacing, uneasy feel to the phrase. The fact that the notes are vowels also gives them a tender and exclamatory feel. She then overlays some monotone vowels on top of the sequence to give emphasis to certain syllables of the phrase,

e   oh   e   i   a   oh

Then comes a layer of consonants that adds a subtle vocal percussion to the loop:

ty p s tf th   w prsth tic lmswah g b k t wha

The jilted, fractured collage of sounds gives a sense of dismemberment. With a vocal backing track now laid down, a degree of sense is recovered with a series of (non-looped) phrases:

prosthetics prosthetics   prosthetics   prosthetics
Backintowar b backinto backinto b b backintowar backintowar

The tone of her voice becomes strained and forced:

Amput *A* tion isthe*first*
isthefirst *STEP*   in reha bilitassshun

Riffing on the phrase, she repeats it continually, breaking-up, stretching, and clipping syllables in a passage of verbal freestyle (or as Silva likes to call it 'live writing').[30]

'*It's a positive thing*' she declares in a new voice. The tone is formal and reassuring, perhaps that of a medical professional. The line is repeated. This time, it is disturbed by the introduction of a pause, and a falling minor-interval that objectifies the 'thing' with sneering discrimination:

> it's a positive
>
> > > *thing*

'A little girl cuts the eye out and arm off her doll', she continues in a neurotic tone of voice, before shifting to the voice of a little girl:

> *It looks like a monster now,* she says
>
> just like her father.
>
> Back into war, back into war, back in to…

Silva's face, body, and voice start to contort:

> *am*put *amputatation is the first step*
> *in rehab rehabilita biliatation is the first step*
> *is the first step in reha rehabili tation*
> *It's a positive thing, it's a posi it's a posi it's a positive thing*
>
> A little girl cuts the…
> It's a positive it's a positive
>
> A little girl cuts the…
> It's a positive it's a positive thing

As we approach the *crescendo*, more voices are layered in a menacing monotone voice:

Forty percent of those with prosthetic limbs will go back into war
Forty percent of those with prosthetic limbs will go back into war
Forty percent of those with prosthetic limbs will go back into war
Forty percent of those with prosthetic limbs will go back into war
Forty percent of those with prosthetic limbs will go back into war...

The thickening texture of voices feels like a growing body of people, morbidly marching forwards. The utterance is superimposed over the opening vowels and consonants (looped at the beginning of the piece), which make sense—retrospectively—as the constituent parts of the *re-membered* conclusion. It becomes apparent that the entire rhythm of the piece (laid down in that opening vowel scat) was composed to the natural emphasis of the phrase as it is spoken. Stressed syllables are highlighted here in bold:

Forty per**cent** of th**ose** with pros**thetic lim**bs will go **back** into **war**
Forty per**cent** of th**ose** with pros**thetic lim**bs will go **back** into **war**

As the march builds in numbers, the voice of the medical professional returns to speak over them:

It's a positive thing   it's a positive thing

It's a positive thing

It's a positive thing it's a positive thing

It's a positive thing   IT'S A POSITIVE THING!

These phrases are also layered into the mix (in various tones of voice) that escalate into a montage of conflicting sentiments, from the reassuring and defiantly declarative, to the manic and desperate. The assertions build into an argumentative cacophony against the testimony of the marching 'forty per cent'; a world of amputated bodies, lives, and families. Silva hits her machine, the voices fall silent, and after a short, winded silence, the audience applaud and the video ends.

*

It is remarkable that 'Prosthetics' can convey so much with just eight lines of text. The way that these lines spill into the voice and body speaks volumes about the *musical-muscular blueprints* of words and what this means for poetry. Thanks to the internet, you can watch and listen for yourself, and I encourage you to find the piece on YouTube and elsewhere.[31]

First, let's look at the melody and the timbre of the voice. The piece puts the same sentences (like 'it's a positive thing') in the mouths of several different characters (the family member, the nurse, the amputee) who are brought to life onstage. With help from the loop machine, contrasts in volume and tone create a collage made of a single phrase. Changes to pitch-range and pitch-contour infuse the voices with conflicting emotions, from pain and anger to reassurance and morbidity.

The rhythms of the poem also carry meaning. The vowels layered in the opening passage sever the phrase of meaning, foregrounding the percussion of language instead. These vowels provide the rhythmic signature of the piece. When the fully articulated phrase ('Forty per cent of those…') is later sewn back into the vowels, music is healed with meaning to create a moving body of sound and sense. We can also find evidence of Gräbner's 'socially coded rhythms' in the finale's layered cacophony ('Forty per cent of those…' and 'it's a positive thing'), which appear to mimic the reiterative streams of verbal snippets, trending and conflicting through social media feeds.

Painting with sound in this way embodies a fundamental principle of creative writing—*show don't tell*. Yet the way it does this is very different to the standard advice of poetry textbooks. Instead of using 'concrete language' or 'sense data' to make the subject feel tangible, the amputation is *shown* through its manner of speaking. This manner comes not from the typographic layout of text, but a poetic body of music and movement. The dismemberment of 'Prosthetics' is *performed* (from Old French *par-fournir*: provide through). This provision is all in the music of the body.

In using her voice as a musical instrument, Silva dives into the *materiality* of language. Here Roland Barthes celebrates this as:

> pulsional incidents, the language lined with flesh, a
> text where we can hear the grain of the throat, the
> patina of consonants, the voluptuousness of vowels,
> a whole carnal stereophony: the articulation of the
> body, of the tongue, not that of meaning, of lan-
> guage… it granulates, it crackles, it caresses, it grates,
> it cuts, it comes: that is bliss.[32]

The fragmented words and phrases of 'Prosthetics' (sped-up, slowed-down, and rewound) mimic the prosthetics of sound editing software. Words are tangled through the vocal processor of the human body to create *ideophones* (sound effects). Indeed, Silva used computer software to reverse recordings of her voice during the rehearsal: 'you reverse the physiological experience of speaking' she explains. 'You swallow words. Consume your own speech.'[33] These effects are not extraneous embellishments to the words, but part of the architecture of the poem's meaning; a bionic soundscape of pain and dislocation.

> noitatupma is the first step, the first step in… reha reha
> rehabilitation tion noit noit

In his investigation of the expressive capacity of sound patterns, Reuven Tsur shows how 'divergent sound patterns' can become poetic devices by breaking the conventions of language and disrupting 'the smooth functioning of cognitive processes.'[34] By this analysis, Silva's word-mangling is a heightened, renewed, and surprising use of language. It is, therefore, highly poetic. A single sound can, in the words of Steve McCaffery, touch on 'a hundred ideas at the same time without naming them'. Tearing words and phrases apart holds a trapdoor open to hidden meanings and the 'drives of the unconscious'.[35]

*

It is to the passage of these unconscious drives that I will turn to now. To do so, I will borrow from the practice of *biodynamic* ('life-movement') psychotherapy, as well as *body based* and *movement* psychotherapy. In all of these fields, therapists work in conversation with the body to locate tension and trauma stored below the surface. By working with posture, massage, and even dance, therapists are able to help emotional imprints ripen and surface from their patients. As we will now see, this corresponds directly with *writing through the body*, which enables stored trauma to emerge from the poet.

As a physically expressive activity, live poetry takes its place within the cyclical progression of emotions through our nervous system. Therapist Gerda Boyesen describes this as stimulus – charge – expression – equilibrium.[36] This cycle is particularly relevant to spoken word artists, who are known for performing material about their own lives. What we could perhaps call *biodynamic poetry*, has implications that go beyond the well-known therapeutic benefits of expressive writing to a more holistic and embodied view.[37] *Biodynamic poetry* recognises verse as physically *expressed* as well as *ingested*. The body is in the composition, and the composition is in the body.

In her study of theatre, Anna Sigg argues that the stage is a platform for commemorating and transforming trauma in the service of healing. The performance is a 'somatic intervention', where the performer 'interpenetrates the audience' with defiant resistance.[38]

Salena Godden's poem 'Voodoo' is a perfect example. At a 2015 performance at Tongue Fu (accompanied by the in-house 'improv' jazz band), Godden recounts the racial bullying she experienced at school.[39] 'In this era of my life I was bullied horribly' she told me in an interview 'rough times, both at school and at home, life was shit.'[40]

The performance begins with her trapped in the woods. Her bullies are taunting her for wearing a beaded necklace her mother gave her. 'What's that shit you've got round your neck anyway, some sort of voodoo African black-magic *nigger* shit is it?' The scene escalates into confrontation '*BLACKY, BLACKY, BLACKY, FIGHT, FIGHT, FIGHT!*' Surrounded, alone, and desperate to avoid a fight, Godden holds up her necklace 'like a crucifix'. She starts shuddering her head, rasping (as if possessed) and screams 'I *curse* you. I *CURSE* YOU! MAY YOUR CROPS FAIL!... MAY YOUR WATER BE POISONED... MAY ALL YOUR CHILDREN BE DEFORMED!' Her tormentors are terrified by the outburst. Godden has become what they fear. Vulnerability and isolation morph into a howling parody that is hurled at her bullies and, in the context of performance, her audience and her past.

In the words of Sigg: 'The body on stage literally and metaphorically "screams back" to trauma by emitting a countermelody of agency and resistance.'[41] Who's laughing now? Everyone in the room. In turning this trauma into live art and comedy, its significance is transformed, and Godden is applauded.[42]

Kat François offers another example of how trauma can be transformed through performance. In December 2018, I saw François perform at Raise the Bar in the Arnolfini Theatre, Bristol. Half speaking, half singing, she tore through her poem 'Poetry Whore', the back of her hands pumping outwards from her chest: '...I perform for need, I perform for greed / I perform for love, for lust and just so I can breathe...'. On finishing the poem, she thanked the audience for 'letting me get that off my chest.' 'I've had a difficult week' she continued, 'I think I needed to purge that from my body'. As she finished the sentence, she gestured with her fingertips, as if pulling something up and out from her diaphragm. 'It's a liberating experience,' she told me after the gig. 'I guess some people would use counselling, or they may use drugs or drink...poetry is a way to put everything together and then get it out'; stimulus – charge – expression – equilibrium.[43]

Poems like these are (to quote the title of Joelle Taylor's book) the *Songs My Enemy Taught Me*. We store them in our body as 'mechanical reminiscences'. As we lie in bed staring at the ceiling, these blueprint songs return to animate us. Like a faceless army marching through a valley, they are carried only on the current of an inescapable rhythm and the metric thud of beating skin. They may impel us to leap from our beds and scrawl it down. They may also impel us to sing it on a stage. Writing through the body enacts the emotional truth of the poem and slings it back at the world with all of the music and theatre it deserves.

*

I will end by returning to the strange noises in the alleyways, the people muttering, pacing, and shaking their limbs. The warm-up removes muscular blockages so the poet can enter a state of intent, flow, and presence. A responsiveness is created between the poet's inner world and the moment and place at hand. The poem is prepared for its (final?) journey.

On stage, the poem inhabits the flesh, and the flesh inhabits the poem. In this sense, the piece is integrated and authentic, that's to say, the author is present in the fullest sense. Spoken word, then, dissolves the mind/body distinction implied in text-centric terms like 'reading' or 'recital'. Poets do not *have* bodies, they *are* bodies.

To return to Charles Olson's 'Projective Verse', the poem is 'energy transferred from where the poet got it'.[44] As such, it operates in accord with an important biological principle that life is *the flow of energy through matter*: chlorophyll, flesh, larynx, and lip. From inspiration to transcription and into performance, the text and the body inter-animate. In its passage, it speaks the poetry of words, music, and movement combined. Spoken word, so often described as 'visceral' and 'alive', treats words as 'anatomical processes'.[45] The Spoken Word Renaissance, then, is a *somatic renegotiation of literature,* a *re-membering* that heals the 'body of text' with its *musical-muscular* extremities. As we will see in the next chapter, the path of the poem through the poet's body is only the beginning of a much larger journey.

Notes

1   For an overview of this see: Novak, *Live Poetry* (2011), p.16–17.

2   Dobyns, *Next Word, Better Word* (2011), p.35; Lee,
    Writing from the Body (1994).

3   Thomas, *Dylan Thomas Early Prose Writings* (1971), p.165.

4   Olson, 'Projective Verse' (1950), http://writing.upenn.edu/~taran-
    sky/Projective_Verse.pdf

5   Kat François, email to Peter Bearder, 16 Jan. 2019.

6   'Jasmine Gardosi - Unidentified Crying Objects', 11 Oct. 2017, https://
    www.youtube.com/watch?time_continue=55&v=og4l4bG43zQ.

7   Ong, *Orality and Literacy* (1982), p.71.

8   François, as above.

9   'Vanessa Kisuule, Sexy', http://thewardrobetheatre.com/livethea-
    tre/sexy.

10 Brennan, *The Transmission of Affect* (2004), p.149.

11 Novak, as above, p.49.

12 Vanessa Kisuule, email to Peter Bearder, 25 Jul. 2019.

13 Fusetti & Willson, 'The Pedagogy of the Poetic Body' (2015).

14 Stiles, 'Performance' (2003), p.88.

15 Vermeersch, 'Why I Hate "Spoken Word" Poetry', 23 Jan. 2014,
    https://wordup411ng.com/why-i-hate-spoken-word-poetry.

16 Mali, 'I Could Be a Poet', https://www.stpatricktheatre.org/up-
    loads/4/9/2/7/4927337/taylor_mali_poetry.pdf.

17 Bernstein, *Close Listening* (1998), p.10.

18 Joelle Taylor Interview, Stage Invasion, Vimeo, (00:05:00).

19 See 'British Spoken Word Voice' chapter in Silva, 'Live Writing' (2018).

20 François, as above.

21 Stern, 'The Formal Poetry Reading' (1991).

22 Fussell, *Class* (1983).

23 Roubaud, 'Prelude: Poetry and Orality' (2009).

24 Goffman, *The Presentation of Self in Everyday Life* (1956), p.234.

25 Novak, *Live Poetry*, p.145.

26   Saussy, *An Ethnography of Rhythm* (2016) p.37, p.117.

27   Lopez quoted in Silva, 'Composing Speech' (2010), p.41.

28   Gräbner, 'Hurricanes don't Roar in Pentameters' (2011).

29   Gräbner's observation echoes early academic writing on the oral
      tradition. In 1960, Albert B. Lord observed how oral cultures ap-
      prentice themselves in the songs of their people from birth: 'From
      meter and music he absorbs in his earliest years the rhythms of epic,
      even as he absorbs the rhythms of speech itself and in a larger sense
      of the life about him. He learns empirically the length of phrase,
      the partial cadences, the full stops…Basic patterns of meter, word
      boundary, melody have become his possession, and in him the
      tradition begins to reproduce itself.' See: Lord, *The Singer of Tales*
      (1960), p.33.

30   Silva, 'Live Writing' (2018).

31   This analysis is taken from 'Apples and Snakes - Wordsmiths & Co.
      Featuring Hannah Silva', 11 Jul. 2014, https://www.youtube.com/
      watch?v=yCy9YS_UYeE&t=352s. On Soundcloud, you can find
      a previous version which is rhythmically more complicated because
      it removes a vowel on each iteration of the line. Silva stopped
      performing it like that because it was so challenging to deliver.
      See: https://soundcloud.com/hannah-silva/prosthetics. There is
      a new version of 'Prosthetics' on her record *Talk in a bit*. Here the
      rhythm is: 123 45 123 45 1234 (2 sets of 5 then 1 set of 4 - or 5+9).
      This most recent rendition omits the pause between each iteration
      of the sentence. You can hear it at: https://humankindrecords.
      bandcamp.com/album/talk-in-a-bit.

32   Quoted in Silva, 'Live Writing' (2018), p191.

33   Silva, 'Composing Speech' (2010), p.43–44.

34   Tsur, 'Sound Affects of Poetry' (1997), p.115.

35   McCaffery, 'Cacophony, Abstraction, and Potentiality' (2009),
      p.124.

36   Macnicol, 'Biodynamic Massage - an Introduction', http://www.
      yobeely.f2s.com/articles/massintro.html.

37   The majority of literature on poetry therapy, often building on the
      work of James Pennebaker, relates to the page. New research on
      spoken word finds that its ethos of sociality (see Chapter 2, Part
      3) extends these benefits through human connection, ceremony,
      and ritual (see Alvarez & Mearns, 2014). At the time of writing, I
      have found no research that explores the path of autobiographical
      writing through the nervous system in the form of live poetry.

38   Sigg, 'Therapeutic Theatre' (2015), i.

39   'Salena Godden - Voodoo - Live at Tongue Fu', 25 Jun.
      2015, https://www.youtube.com/watch?v=dl9oQ0rnGhU.

40   Salena Godden, email to Peter Bearder, 18 Sept. 2018.

41   Sigg, as above, i.

42   'Voodoo' is an excerpt from the 'Girls Just Wanna Have Fun' chap-
      ter of Godden's memoir *Springfield Road*. Godden made the passage
      into 'its own kinda beast and a story telling performance'. 'Voodoo'
      was also included on the LIVEwire album (see Chapter 4). The
      track can be found at https://nymphsandthugs.bandcamp.com/
      album/livewire.

43   Kat François, as above.

44   Olson, as above.

45   The idea of words as 'anatomical processes' is taken from Brennan,
      as above, p.70.

Chapter 6:
The Contract of 'Emotional Participation' and the Rhythms of Audience and Affect

'It is the flint and steel meeting that brings forth the fire.'
—William Cobbett, radical
Victorian journalist and orator

It's around midnight in a barn at Cock & Bull Festival, Wiltshire, 2018. The stage is mounted on the back of a lorry in front of an audience of around five hundred who are watching MC Dizraeli and DJ Downlow tear into a headline set. The dance floor is fluid and charged. We are immersed in its field of energy, held together by waves of sound and feeling, our nervous systems cooperating in movement. The music stops and Dizraeli launches into a high-octane poem. He is inside the piece as an actor is inside a character. We are all swept along, transported by the images and the story, as well as the music and sheer physicality of the performance.

Imperceptibly my pupils dilate, my pulse quickens, and my blood pressure rises. The microparticles in the air synchronise my hormones with those around me. The sweat on my hands and feet increase, and my skin becomes more sensitive. I feel like I am witnessing a small, yet significant moment in history, one consecrated by the shared attention of everyone in the room. Small muscles at the base of my hair follicles contract as if I am experiencing cold, shock, or fright. The trauma held in the poet's body speaks to the trauma stored in mine, gripping me by the solar plexus and the throat. My breathing changes, and something warm and wet rises from inside me and into my eyes. An imprint from the past I had forgotten was there appears to leave me, making sense somehow as it goes. In its passage, it takes stress hormones from my blood, creates disease fighting molecular compounds, and strengthens my immune system.

*

This chapter is about the conversation between bodies in live poetry. Through the lens of *affect theory* and *rhythmanalysis,* it will look at the ways that poet and audience inter-animate (overtly and covertly) at spoken word events. It will present spoken word as a specialist performance discipline that lives inside a contract of attunement between audience and performer, forged in a matrix of affective, trans-personal rhythms that elicit (and even heal) emotional imprints stored in our bodies.

I have always been fascinated by the humanity that accumulates in the radius of the voice. In the part-improvised, part-conversational theatrics of live poetry, the speaker is with us in the room, addressing us directly about the intimate details of their life. Stand-up poet John Hegley describes his work as 'emotional participation'.[1] This phrase (a play on 'audience participation') captures the way emotions circulate between us. What, then, are the chemistry and mechanics of this participation? What fields of energy that are we subjecting each other to? How do we ingest live poetry? How do we make *sense* of it all?

Part 1: A Short Introduction to *Affect* and *Rhythm*

First, some important theoretical grounding on *affect theory,* and how it relates to live performance. Affect theory is concerned with how feelings pass through and between us.[2] While it is often used as a synonym for emotions, I will use it here to describe the raw feelings and sensations that are distinct from emotions. Though two audience members may be in the same space, experiencing the same poem (and the same *sensations*), the resulting *emotions* may be totally different. Emotions are about our individual orientations and relationships towards things. Because these orientations are influenced by our history and upbringing, emotions are social and cultural practices.[3] In short, '*affect* is biological, *emotions* are biographical'.[4]

Another way to see affect is as a 'passage from one experiential state of the body to another.'[5] As emotion-inducing signals enter our nervous system, we synchronise, align, and react to them. These coded biological signals function in the same way as a language, and our bodies learn them intuitively.[6]

In her landmark book, *The Transmission of Affect*, Teresa Brennan investigates how the pheromones we emit through our sweat can arouse affect in those around us. These messenger micro-particles are subconsciously registered by specialist chemo-receptors in the mucous membranes of neighbouring noses.[7] Applying Brennan's 'fleshly codes' to live poetry, poet and academic Jack McGowan presents the poem as a chemical journey that circulates between performers and audience members.[8] Unlike sight and sound, smell is a sense of *proximity*. In the intimate settings of live poetry, it is part of the economy of human transactions.

Affect theory shows us how, in live performance, 'the explicatory power of language is usurped by experience'. In this *pre-conscious, preverbal* realm of raw feeling, there is a gap between our *senses* and our *thoughts*.[9] This gap is a multidimensional space of flux and sensation that transcends any single cause. Like the communicative breath of a collective consciousness, poems pass through us, *affecting* the chemistry of our brains and bodies. These 'endogenous drives' can spread through crowds like a contagion and cause us to lose our individuality.[10] Live poetry, then, can be a form of *mob behaviour*.

When we become 'the crowd', we become part of its rhythms of affect, movement, and noise. In this chapter, I will marry affect theory with that of *rhythmanalysis*; a way of seeing the world that was developed by the philosopher Henri Lefebvre. Lefebvre would look down from his apartment in Southern France to see pulsations of interlocking rhythms: traffic, lights, pedestrians or, more broadly, the passing of days, nights, and seasons. *Rhythmanalysis* seeks to understand the world as an unfolding process of flow, repetition, and variation.[11] Indeed, 'the regulation of rhythm' has been noted by physicists and neurologists to be 'a fundamental organizing principle of all living systems'.[12] We can see this in the oscillations of eyelids, heartbeats, and breathing. We can also find it in daily broadcast schedules, or the cycle of political elections.

In live poetry these rhythms could include the undulating pace, volume, or intensity of speech. They might also be the patterns of eye contact, laughter, and interaction. For Brennan, rhythm has 'a unifying, regulating role in affective exchanges'.[13] Understanding these rhythms is a vital part of the craft of spoken word, its flows of affect, and its 'emotional participation'.

Part 2: Convening the Conversation, the Role of the MC

'...ladles and gentle spoons, without further ado...'

The MC is the Master of Ceremonies, the host or compère of the night. More than perhaps anyone else in the room, they are tasked with managing the affective rhythms of the crowd. As they finish their sentence, they scan the room, reading the energy, enthusiasm, and attention of the audience. What joke can be thrown in here? What do they need? Where could they be taken? Verbally they are on autopilot, subconsciously they 'take it all in', formulating new interactions in a simultaneous process akin to circular breathing.

I once attended a workshop at Occupy London which compared the facilitation of crowds to the wet finger moving lightly over the rim of the wine glass. The facilitator's job is to allow energy to move around the room in the way it needs to. In this way, without too much friction, the room begins to sing. In facilitating the circulation of *affect*, the MC can permission a crowd to a climax. 'Please show your love...' is a ritual invitation to elevate a performer to a stage on a wave of energy. 'Let's hear it one more time...', is a permission for us to express our emotion again, together.

In a poetry slam, their role is so central that the 'MC spiel' has become a common term in existing scholarship.[14] Its role is to mediate between artists and the place, moments, and people surrounding them. The MC sets the tone, the expectations, and calibrates the audience for participation. There are often ritualised warm-up games, such as 'building the applause' (which is swept through the room from a gentle patter to stamping and whooping) or rehearsed participations, such as 'finger-clicking' (a way to show appreciation without drowning out the poem).

Such an orchestrated MC role suits spoken word poetry, an art that still occurs mostly in informal settings with low stages or no stages at all. Like comedy and cabaret with which it shares a history (see Chapter 3, Part 11), this personal, informal arrangement recognises the audience's potential to talk back. The MC defines the rules of engagement (phones off, no talking during poems etc.) They also prime them for the conversation, 'warming them up' with jokes, banter, or a performance of their own. This serves to align the audience to the show and to each other. The result is a collective flow state; a shared sense of rhythm, feeling, and collective power. In channelling the attentional resources of the room, the MC creates (to borrow from Dierdre Osborne) 'a contract of public contact'.[15]

Note to the Host

The following passage was inspired by a dream of my friend Julian Cottee that was later read out at his wedding.

We're about to consciously craft a memory. Like a potter crafts her clay or a painter her painting, we're going to become amateur craftsmen of memory. But you have so many more tools than a painter. Your scene can be 4D…

Halfway through her speech, the speaker invited the audience to hug, shake hands with, and speak to those around them. A 'memory blanket'—made intricate by its many-headed loom— was woven for the newly-weds 'to wrap around themselves on cold evenings'. From that moment, its threads sprawled out through time and space:

…maybe we will share our memory with others, and we will imagine with a warm-hearted smile that other people are doing the same, in various parts of the world, and the memory tapestry will keep growing with ever more voices and detail.

The MCs and promoters of spoken word, as with celebrants at weddings, are weaving people and moments into memories. In the words of famous NYC slam master, Bob Holman, 'the Show is yours to shape and form and play as if it were a poem or a piece of music.'[16] Poet Jeff McDaniels expands on the idea: 'The MC is editor. The atmosphere is the typography. And whoever is on stage is the page you're on'.[17]

I once found myself on one such page, looking out over a field from a park bench. I remember the dog walkers approaching each other from opposite sides of the field. I remember their two labradors circling the field in a sprint, looping into the opposing side of the field and back round to their owners and each other. I remember the dog walkers chatting silently in the distance, exchanging numbers, hugging, and finally walking on in a geometric knot of romantic symmetry. That was the introduction. I remember nothing of the poem.

Perhaps the poem (cleverly written and performed though it may have been) was incidental to this act of witness, or to the fact that this particular group of people had coalesced at that place and moment in history for a ritual of word sharing. Perhaps the poem is a mere aesthetic embellishment, an excuse to participate, or a seal of approval that certifies the testimony and gives it currency in the living canon of 'the conversation'.

The 'editor's' job is of the highest importance. They gather and publish, not just people and performances, but moments, places, and memories. They are artisan crafters of textile memories.

Part 3: The Synaesthetic Ingestion of Poetry

The spoken word artist is now onstage, and the activity of receiving them has begun. We will now turn our attention to the 'audience' (a name that unfairly emphasises one sense over others), to see how it absorbs an awareness of the performance synaesthetically (from *syn-aesthesia*: literally 'together-sense'). The poem comes to us from a co-mingling of sensory information and much of this is below our conscious attention.

It is beyond the scope of this section to fully account for how poets and audiences communicate and interact through body language and sound. The study of kinesics and psychoacoustics are huge disciplines. Instead, what we will now do is zoom out to a soft-focused, inclusive reading of the spoken word artist.

When a poet performs in a language we cannot speak, we see how, in the words of T.S. Eliot, 'genuine poetry can communicate before it is understood'. We detect their blockages, their 'vibe'. We read, if you like, their aura. Even if we are being spoken to in our own language, we often inadvertently stop listening to the words and just gaze at the speaker.

The micro-physiological shifts of the poet's face and body convey what Brennan calls the 'information channels of the flesh.'[18] To borrow from Deborah Kapchan, we use our *whole body* to read the 'reverberations of the rhythms and intensities of performance'.[19] Since ninety-eight per cent of our thoughts take place in our subconscious, much of the communication is both unscripted and indescribable.[20] Nonetheless, it is central to what poetry is—an *affective* exchange.

We do not just read this information, we are also altered by it. 'Motor mimicry' (or the 'chameleon effect') is a subconscious, automatic behaviour, where we involuntarily adopt the action of the person we are observing.[21] A similar process takes place when we read silently. As we look at the text on the page, our lips, tongue, and larynx make tiny movements 'as if we are preparing to read aloud'. Silent reading, then, is 'a physical act'.[22] Off the page, this mimicry moves beyond words to enable us 'to "read" others' thoughts, feelings and emotions'.[23]

We can register and mimic facial expressions within 300–400 milliseconds (just under half a second).[24] The same responsiveness extends to mannerism and posture.[25] This strange capacity to be possessed by those around us is made possible by the existence of 'mirror neurons' in our brain.[26] These neurons are key to our ability empathise, sympathise, and function as *social animals*.[27] They are, therefore, key to our understanding of the 'emotional exchange' of poetry.

Joelle Taylor describes highly performative poetry as 'speaking to the rhythm of your heartbeat and making it go faster'.[28] Physiologically speaking she is absolutely right.[29] Through *automatic mimicry* our bodies synchronise heartbeats, as well as the behaviour of our pupils (as we will see later), and even our hormones. All of this is part of emotional contagion.[30]

Poems that remind us of past trauma involuntarily trigger *autonomic responses* in the body's stored memory bank. When aroused, the aptly named *sympathetic nervous system* is engaged, triggering a 'fight or flight' reaction that raises our heart rate and blood pressure.[31] Tiny muscles at the base of our hair follicles contract in a process known as piloerection (goosebumps) and our sweat pores open up. Though these reactions can be caused by a variety of things (exercise for example), they can also indicate emotional response in the body.

The poet might also engender a more relaxed state in the audience by engaging the *parasympathetic nervous system*—the body's 'rest and digest' mode. Storyteller Rachel Rose Reid describes how she works with the tension in the room:

> If I breathe slowly, you will breathe slowly. If I'm
> really stressed about my performance and barely
> breathing, you will also barely breathe… If I speed
> up, your breathing will speed up.

She explains further how rhythm is used to contour tension and create moments of poignancy:

> If this silence, where a character is meant to speak
> and they *don't* speak, if everyone is meant to *feel* that…
> If this silence now *really* matters… I can't have loads
> of random pauses in the ten minutes beforehand.[32]

I once attended a workshop by John Berkavitch where he asked us to get into pairs and deliver phrases (consisting only of varied and articulated breathing) into each other's ears. The listeners then drew lines on a page (from left to right) to try and capture the shape of how the utterance *felt*. The exercise threw up a series of dramatic skylines. Sounds and feelings inflate, spike, and fall away inside us. For Berkavitch (an experienced practitioner of spoken word theatre), surprises, silences, and energetic cliff edges can create 'vertical drops' that can knock the wind out of audiences.

We can see this in the closing passage of Dizraeli's poem 'My Brother Can't Help Himself' (2018), which builds in speed and volume:

> [...]
> my brother can't think.
> my brother can't think.
> don't ask questions of him
> my brother can't thinkParty time!
> My brother does just the one sniff
> Then another then another one
> Then another then another then another one
> My brother's munted
> Just for fun
> My brother's quite mardy
> My brother's quite gone
> My brother's quite ill
> my brother's quite ill
> My brother might
>
> .
>
> him
>
> self
>
> My brother can't help himself [33]

The breathing and tension in the audience build alongside that of the performer, and the vertical drop comes at the punchline ('.'), where Dizraeli pauses and decreases in volume. During that pause, he holds his breath and we in turn do the same. [34] This could be caused by suspense, motor mimicry, or both. Having all held our breath, we exhale. Dizraeli grips our solar plexus, stealing our breath and synchronising the rhythm of blood and oxygen in our bodies. The deep breathing this creates also simulates the experience of crying.

Ana Pais picks up on the frequently expressed idea of tension as a tangible *thing* that performers can hold in their body. Tension can hold us, just as we can hold others with tension. [35] As poet

Mark Gwynne Jones puts it, 'I'll communicate it with my *toes* if I can get you *with me!*'[36] Tension meets attention, which, as Pais points out, both come from the Latin *tendere*: 'to stretch'. It is as if the poem is held on an invisible elastic web, whose threads are held in the bodies of everyone in the room.

What we can see from these examples are some of the ways live poetry 'makes us feel'. Since many of these experiences happen subconsciously, it is in *the blur* that poetry is fully apprehended. A holistic, soft-focused reading of the poem offers a more expansive 'subject matter' than the text alone allows. It accounts for the *energetic geography* of the poem and the poet. It recognises live poetry as a multidimensional process between bodies; as much *physiological* as *verbal*.

Part 4: Reading the 'Vibe' of the Audience

Affective information passes in both directions, stage to crowd and vice versa. The poet is the *audience's audience*, reading their performance just as keenly. Seasoned spoken word artists, like Lemn Sissay, Mark Gwynne Jones, and Francesca Beard, have studied audiences for decades, developing a nuanced working knowledge of the 'vibe in the room'.

When poet Matt Harvey first started performing in the nineties, he would suffer chronic anxiety to the point of needing visualisation exercises and herbal medicines (Rescue Remedy to be precise). He learned to harness this tension, holding it in his body as a way of being present and alive to the moment. In time, he started to play with it, joke on it, and exaggerate it as a 'reverse double bluff':

> I can feel in my body when I'm not making the connection...and it's to do with the quality of *authenticity* in that moment. Even when I'm in the middle of telling big lies, it's something to do with the quality of *being there* which is a very physical thing. [37]

Harvey's dissection of this communicative tension resonates with recent thinking in theatre studies. Nicholas Ridout, for example, talks of those shuddering moments in live performance 'in which both a compulsion and a resistance to representing oneself for others generates a momentary organic dis-ease.' This shudder, he continues, 'may in fact be communicative, that it vibrates between performer and spectator.'[38] As with theatre, live poetry is a 'vibratory transmission', a reciprocal exchange of energy.

Harvey's 'connection' with his audience is what Julian Henriques would call a 'whole-body vibrotactile experience'. Henriques studied the circulation of affect in Jamaican dancehalls, concluding that feelings act like sound vibrations that pass through our bodies. As instruments of 'the vibe', humans can amplify and re-propagate affect, changing its volume, frequency, and timbre. A group of people, and indeed society as a whole 'literally pulsates with cycles of exertion and rest'.[39] We are creatures of oscillation: from the weekly cycles of work and play, through to surges of collective excitement. On the dance floor, skanking bodies are carried by the rhythms of heart and lung, and the electrical pulses of the central nervous system. Like music, spoken word stimulates and attunes these 'whole-body' frequencies into a collective whole: 'the one-who-is-many and the many-who-are-one'.[40]

For those moments when poets feel 'out of sync' with their audience, they have at their disposal the *paratext*. The *paratext* (the 'beyond-text') is the words that surround, frame, and enable literature. On the page, this might include the author's name, the preface, illustrations, or title. In spoken word, the *paratext* comes in the form of intros (before poems), outros (after them) and asides (within poems). In theatre, these are known as prologue, direct address, and epilogue respectively. On the page, the *paratext* is fixed, but on the stage it can adapt, mediating between the poem and the moment, people, and place at hand.[41]

Lemn Sissay is one poet who has been studied for his epic asides. Hannah Silva counts one 'poem' as nine hundred words long (only 258 of which are written on the page).[42] In the asides of live verse, the concept of the 'poem' becomes fuzzy and porous. The box of text haemorrhages speech bubbles: 'I think that's my favourite line in the poem' (Mark Gwynne Jones), 'I'm sorry you are not having such a good time, I think I'm having a slightly better time' (Matt Harvey). To hack another quote from T.S. Eliot, 'poetry is what happens between the lines'.

Lucy English compares these asides to that which can happen on the page between the writer and the reader. She identifies Vladimir Nabokov as a novelist who 'leans forward' to address the reader directly, punctuating their immersion with the narrator's presence. 'A bad accident is about to happen quite soon', he interjects in the novel *Lolita*. The reader is reminded that behind the narrative is a chronicler who is leading the 'puppet show'.[43] 'I shall not exist if you do not imagine me', comes the voice and the reader is drawn in, no longer an observer, but a participant.

On stage, this interplay serves other functions. Matt Harvey has some 'ad-libbed-then-crafted-and-kept-in' asides that are later written up and used, in his words, 'to refocus any part of the set where I get flustered and faff about.'[44] Another stand-up poet, Rob Gee, has crafted his entire poetic around the *paratext* (especially in his earlier work of the noughties and nineties). His frequent and extensive asides could break out at any moment, like live info-boxes or footnotes: 'It gets proper awkward doing this one in schools'. The script of his first stage show *The Genghis Khan Guide to Etiquette*, is made up entirely of shorthand prompts for the asides and intros that accompany the memorised poems. The script is colour-coded to show parts that should only be performed in certain places. The following aside is from the poem 'Every Good Man Should Read Cosmo' (which he still performs today) and took place at the Edinburgh Comedy Rooms in August 2002:

> That line, 'Not tonight darling, I've got a Prozac', comes from an article that was in the New Scientist recently saying that Prozac and clomipramine, two of the more recent SSRI anti-depressants, have been known rarely to cause involuntary orgasm when yawning. [audience laugh] Which I think is *fucking magnificent*, especially if you've got depression, it's the drug of choice. 'Take that ... go to a lecture, go

see your grandma.' [mimics an orgasm] [audience laugh] It gives a whole new meaning to the phrase bored stiff. [audience laugh] [45]

Gee's asides offer trapdoors to comic and theatrical interludes. The frequent shifting between modes of address creates a sense of anticipation and surprise which keeps listeners on their toes. Below are some show notes for his asides, which read like a meta-narrative on the poem. Activate these performances with your imagination:

Epiphany:

Commissioned/BBC/no less/got to/studio/producer/do you mind if I/quick look at it/hmm/okay/not quite/spirit/what we had in mind/never heard from them since/so I fucked that one up but I got a cracking poem out of it.

And my favourite:

Guy Ketamine (Charlie/Football intro):

Mate theory/it's you/Guy/sketchy nightclub/white powder/in goal, don't need to be over everything like a rash/Ketamine/isolated pockets of mirth/major horse tranquiliser/body paralysis, visual hallucinations and if you're lucky, near death experiences/16-0/half-time/sitting by goal post/mates yelling/why can't pick up post on other side of pitch/never doing that again - football/Cocaine/meth/easy to spot/sunken eyes/inability to shut up/all you need to know about coke/nought to dickhead

Rachel Rose Reid explains how she carries people's attention through stories that might last twenty minutes:

We might be entirely in that room in 1823…and then I'll be like, 'you know what that's like, don't you?'… If I'm in that realm for ages, and you've squidged off a bit because of the lighting…If I remind you that I'm *here* with you and that the story *needs* you – you'll come back to this present moment. And then, you'll go more *deeply* with me. There's a kind of trust that we build up.[46]

In keeping with the discipline of hypnotism, Reid adjusts the rhythms of her script to the *biorhythms* of the audience. The show becomes a somatic cadence, a pattern of tension and release, a cycle of charge and expression.

Clever though these tactics may be, they may also be spontaneous and involuntary. For the rapper Carpetface, managing the crowd's energy happens below the level of conscious attention, in the peripheral awareness of his embodied cognition:

Like jazz drumming, you feel it you don't think it, you've learned the math, now you become the math so you can forget the math…This 'hidden mathematics' enables a performer to mentally and physically multitask effortlessly while onstage and be several chess moves ahead of a crowd.[47]

As with Carpetface's work, much spoken word consists of memorised performances that minimise the distance between the reading of the *poem* and the reading of the *room*.

Spoken word artists learn the language of the 'vibe' as the tightrope walker learns the language of the wind, or the surfer learns the language of the waves. As a conversational practice, it parts ways with other forms of performing arts, where the actor or dancer might be tied to a scripted routine. The text of the poem may be fixed, but the full act of verbal artistry is not. Like stand-up comedians, live poets orchestrate the rhythms and tensions of the room into their art. They are, if you like, fulfilling their side of 'the contract'.

Part 5: The Conversation of Eyes

Yet no contract is as binding as that created by the eyes. Having seen how audiences 'read' performers and vice versa, let's zoom in to examine the parts of the body that, perhaps more than any other, regulate human interaction.

From infancy, the joint attention of eye contact is central to the maternal bond, helping us gain the trust, reassurance and dire ction we need to grow.[48] In the 'emotional participation' of poetry, eyes are key to the direction and distribution of attention and affect.

I often pause before a particular line (usually the last in the poem) to look around the room and get the gaze of as many people as possible. I find this builds suspense and creates complicity with those I look at. Below are the closing lines of my poem 'Manifesto for a Revolutionary Poetic'. I have inserted spaces between lines here to show where I pause to look around the room.

> [...]
> We come with sharp pointed implements behind our
> teeth,
> amplified devices in our chests
> and love in our clenched fists.
> We are the iambic heartbeat of the human race.
>
> We are communities of words
>
> and actions.
>
>
> We are poetry.

The pauses come at the end of an energetic finale which italicises both the silences and the eyes. The more eyes I reach before delivering the line, the more people I am 'saying it' to.

Pupilometry, the study of pupil size, shows that our pupils expand in response to evocative words, sounds, and images.[49] Pupil behaviour is not just a way of adapting to light, it can also be a symptom (and sign) of emotional connection and arousal. As with other forms of mimicry, our pupils mirror each other in a process known as 'pupillary contagion'.[50] Yet unlike other types of synchronisation (such as that of heart rate) our pupils are visible to each other and, consciously or unconsciously, they speak to us. In one experiment, men were shown pairs of photos of young women's faces. The images were identical apart from one small difference: in one of the photos, the woman had larger pupils than the other. Unaware that they had been manipulated, the men found the women with larger pupils to be warmer, friendlier, and softer than those with smaller pupils.

Yet the eyes' ability to arrest us also comes with its problems. When I first encountered spoken word (see Chapter 1), I was closed in on by the eyes of Thick Richard. Shuffling with discomfort, I averted my gaze and even asked my friends 'why is he looking at me?' The proximity of the encounter is what got me, its fierce eloquence, and those *eyes*, which I still remember, even though I no longer recall what the poem was about. Thick Richard was using his eyes rhetorically (and thus artistically) as part of the poem's tool kit of incision.

Eyes are political, committing acts of agency and power,[51] and in spoken word, these power dynamics are uneven and continually shifting. On arriving to the stage, the performer may have already practiced (consciously or otherwise) how to use their eyes in a particular piece. In 'A Manifesto for a Revolutionary Poetic', for example, the eyes are part of the design, scripted in at a later stage, but scripted (in part) no less. These inscriptions are not written down but inscribed into my embodied cognition as *musical-muscular blueprints* (see Chapter 5).

In accruing 'stage time' performers are more accustomed to dealing with eye contact and using it to their advantage. As the object of attention, they are invested with power, not just over how and where to speak, but how and where to *look*. In the 'conversation without words', say Whalley and Miller, 'to break eye contact is to signal that the conversation is over'.[52] It is the performer who decides where the conversation moves next. But alongside this power and reward is vulnerability and risk. Our collective power to 'witness' makes things sacrosanct (as with marriage), but it also makes things accountable (as with crime).[53]

For spectators, inviting the eyes of the poet is also a small gamble. The gaze can create a sense of connection and arousal, or threat and accusation. The poet, rich in attention and privileged by the silence of those listening (or noise should they wish to invoke it), might direct everyone's attention onto the spectator. If that spectator is not entirely comfortable or engaged, they may feel implicated or unwelcomely involved in the politics of the eyes.

When the collective psyche tunnels into us, it sees not just our fire, but our frailty and our fraud. Like all other school kids, we had nightmares of arriving at assembly naked. Prejudices and stereotypes dance in the air between us. The eyes bring the fear of rejection, the thrill of the chase, and the rush of endorphins when a face in the dark silently cries *Yes!* We are dealing with more than words here, we are looking *into* each other. Eyes infiltrate us. Holding them can be harder than holding hands. In some studies, *glossophobia* (fear of public speaking) is the number one reported fear among humans, above dying (number seven) and, ironically, loneliness (number nine).[54] I would guess that much of this is the fault of the eyes.

The non-verbal behaviour of the eyes helps string together all the affective and rhythmic exchanges in this chapter. Intersecting their lines of communication, something else orbits the mic, and it is usually the loudest and most frequent expression in the room.

Note to the Poet / Self

The auditorium is a classroom. Though you may have something to tell others, you are (and always will be) a student. Study hard. Charisma, spectacle, and honesty are not substitutes for homework. Use the privilege of the mic to grow understanding, and challenge people (especially yourself). Ask yourself, how can I increase the complexity of feeling and consciousness? You are standing before one of the most ingenious things in the known universe—human attention. A group of nervous systems moving together through a landscape of thoughts, images, and emotions is a magical and creative force. Have you deliberated over every line? A thirty-minute set in front of fifty people amounts to twenty-five hours of psychic entrainment. Grasp this opportunity with all thirty-two of your teeth.

To perform is to surf a wave which can drown you in disapproving silence, and elevate you in euphoria. Make libations to the gods of the sea. They are your teacher, your passage, and your sustenance. They are also, potentially, your downfall. You can learn to navigate these waves, but you can never really control them. Watch your breath, your ego, and your tongue. The creatures of the sea love to see you taken by the swell, so elicit the storm and cry out to the void. The law of echolocation applies here. Cry loudly, with conviction, and the call will hear its response. They want to see you jump. They love it when you teeter, regain balance, and surge back into the roar. No one wants to see you drown.

Show leadership and take responsibility for this voyage. Draft a set list, then *redraft*, taking care to orchestrate the energetic contours of your performance. Plan and rehearse your introductions, outros, and asides. Vary the length and style of your poems to prevent monotony. Leave time for banter. Take risks. Take prisoners. Don't apologise. Leave your ego at the door. You are the latest manifestation of a tradition that is bigger and older than you. Expect the worst, but remember, everyone wants you to enjoy yourself, so do your job.

Read, write, read, read,* edit, perform, edit,** rehearse, perform, edit, perform, perform and edit,*** then meditate, and for god's sake, *go to bed.*

*Stare at clouds
**Stare at cobwebs
***Lay in the bath listening to Chopin / Abba / Metallica

Part 6: Laughter: A form of Audience Participation

Laughter passes between us, shaking our bodies beyond our control. Sniggers, giggles, and full-on convulsions are acts of audience participation that heckle, chorus, and do the call-and-response. More a polylogue than a dialogue, laughter circulates between bodies as a form of affect. Though rarely looked at in poetry scholarship, laughter is the most noticeable and volatile rhythm in poetry performance.

Stand-up comedians know, almost intuitively, that getting the laugh is a *team effort*. They will often check in with lighting technician before a crowd arrives. Too much light and the audience may feel exposed: *Will people think my laugh is weird if I laugh at that?* Too little light and the audience won't feel part of the body of laughter. As a contagion, laughter often passes more easily when carriers are supple and receptive.

While scholarship on laughter has traditionally focused on *humour* and the things that *cause* laughter, a new area of study is looking at it as a physical interaction and a form of *affect*. Laughter is an undulation of waves, bursts, and swelling intensities that subsumes bodies into its affective environment. Palpably atmospheric, it *incorporates* our bodies into the environment it creates.[55]

For Phil Emmerson, laughter has its own physical 'trajectories' and exists in space as a rhythmic communication. In the cadence and pulsation of social discourse, laughter acts as a 'refrain'.[56] Just as a poetic refrain gives structure to a poem (by anchoring it with a particular rhythm or sentiment), laughter punctuates social interaction, giving it structure, re-articulation, and a sense of return. As with daily conversation, it can both open and close a conversation, letting people in and signalling a point of departure.

The reciprocal 'energy exchange' of laughter can make or break a performance.[57] As Ridout shows us, this is a quality it shares with applause. Performance, he argues:

> generates an eddying of physical and emotional activity, a kind of turbulence out of which confusion emerges a

rhythmic logic which is the applause's own. This rhythm
then transmits itself to the performer, in such a way
that she is carried to apparent heights of performance
which now seem, it appears, to be the logical cause of the
mechanical applause.[58]

And yet, to a degree, the poet can facilitate these rhythmic out-
bursts. Comic asides (like Rob Gee's semi-scripted refrains) simultaneously break the tension of silent listening and gauge the
presence of the crowd. Many stand-up poets I know have a number of 'bankers', sure-fire jokes they can throw into the beginning
of a set to test where the audience is at. 'If you're alive say AYE!',
says Steve Larkin as he arrives on stage. The audience responds
accordingly. 'If you're dead say NAY!'. The crowd *nays* with almost the same volume, then laugh. 'Right, I can see that some of
you need waking from the dead…'.

Like everything, laughter lives inside the oscillating charge-
and-release of tension. In developing his craft of stand-up poetry,
Matt Harvey drew inspiration from the comic Hannah Gadsby
who describes her work as the *setting-up* and *breaking-down* of tension (the set-up / punch-line dyad).[59] We see this in Harvey's 'really intense piece about home furnishings', 'Curtains':

> 'I need some material.'
> He said, 'What's it for?'
> 'It's for curtains
> [...]
> I want them to represent me.' I felt myself blushing as
> I said this, but he said: 'Don't be embarrassed. This is
> a haberdasher's. We get all sorts in here.
> [...]
> 'I'm a velvet person.'
> 'Velvet, Sir. Any particular velvet?'
> 'Crushed velvet. Crushed, but not ultimately defeated.
> [...]
> 'I want a pattern that says: Here is someone who's taken
> a good look. Who's looked at life, held it up to the light
> and said, "I see." Who's looked into the dark corners of

> their own soul, held the gaze of what looked back
> at them, and said, "That's me."' And the assistant
> said: 'I'll just see if I have that in stock, Sir.' [60]

Harvey's poetry is frequently 'punctuated' by more tense or solemn passages out of a commitment to 'owning all the parts' of himself. 'Paradoxically,' he told me, 'the levity brings it earthward each time it aspires to gravity'.[61]

We can see the same modulation of tension in the self-deprecating jokes that poets use to open their sets. Through their introduction, the MC builds the suspense of expectation. The poet comes on stage and breaks it, we all resonate together, and the power balance is restored:

> If you are expecting the same calibre of poetry as you
> got from the last acts, lower your expectations now.
> (Mark Gwynne Jones)

Stand-up poets are *literally* writing other people's nervous systems into the architecture of their performances. With pinpoint precision, they can make large collections of diaphragms spasm simultaneously. In doing so, they orchestrate the breath and motor systems of the audience.

But the poet can never really know how a line will land. Laughter is a 'muscular phenomenon', that has an agency of its own.[62] It spreads like a contagion that unites bodies in movement. It also shifts the significance of a moment, redefining relationships between people in the room.[63] A knowing smirk, a freak-sounding guffaw, or a laugh that just keeps going, can stop the show and change the significance of what, and where, we are. A refusal to work with these rhythms can close off potential affective territories of the poem. Engaging with it is part of the craft of spoken word—where a poem is a social event.

As part of the 'contract of public contact', the laugh is both commissioned and commissioning. It is often the laughter that carries the performance, and the stand-up poet gets the laugh as the elected get mandates to lead. Laughter consents (from Latin *con-sentire*: 'feel together'). These small rhythmic acts of empathy and agreement carry poetry in their flow.

Part 7: Audience Participation

So far we have analysed the less apparent forms of participation. We have looked at the mediation of the MC before and after the poet, and the micro-dynamics of 'the vibe' once that poet is on stage. We have then seen how the conversation of eye contact and laughter intersects the spoken word. I will now turn my analysis to the most *overt* acts of involvement, commonly known as 'audience participation'. Though obvious and explicit, they are no less fascinating. In fact, as I will argue here, they are complex rituals of affective transfer, founded on rhythm and trust.

In the tumult of political demos, bodies of people are held together by sound. This could be anything from the call and response of chants (or antiphonal poetry as it is known to anthropologists) through to samba rhythms, whistles, and horns. Poets performing at protests are well aware that activists need little encouragement to interact. By definition, activists *get involved*. Poetry that elicits their energy honours the fact that a demo, occupation, or protest camp is a ritual of participation.

At a 2017 climate protest camp in Germany (Ende Gelände) we prepared for a mass action to close down Europe's largest coal mine by practicing formations to break through police lines. In the following feedback sessions, we came to the consensus that chanting together made it easier to break on through to the other side. Like the '*haul away!*' of sea shanties or the '*heave!*' of tug of war, chanting creates cohesion and force. Slave owners of the Americas used this for their profit, paying a higher price for lead singers who could set the pace of work songs.[64]

The idea that the audience should sit in silence and not contribute to the sonic experience of poetry is arguably a symptom of a modern, text-centred society.[65] Foley cites indigenous Kaqchikel Mayan poetry, where supporting performers interject with refrains: 'uh-huh' and 'oh!'. He also points to the *naamunaa-muna* ('encourager'), whose chants of 'mmm', 'indeed' or 'true' are integral parts of West African epics. Such occurrences are frequent in West African poetic traditions and the 'call and response' is an inheritance that informs African American verbal artistry today.[66] Citing the influence of the black church on his poetry, American poet Sekou Sundiata called this the 'living text' of bible, music, and congregation.[67]

Audience participation can be infinitely varied, and need not even be vocal. I remember a gig in Oxford where John Hegley got the entire audience to dance around the pub in a line behind him like guillemots as he sung a song on his ukulele (about guillemots). Other colourful examples include passing a bottle of rum around the audience (the Gypsy Unit band), and (my favourite) a fourteen thousand strong 'to me!...to you!' from the Chuckle Brothers at Camp Bestival in 2015.

British spoken word poet Jasmine Gardosi also moves beyond the standard 'call and response' interaction with her poem 'Raise Your Hand', which I saw performed at Bristol's Milk Poetry in October 2017.

The opening line gets everyone involved and launches the poem with a laugh:

> Raise your hand if you sometimes feel uncomfortable talking about sex.
> I'm glad we got that out the way.

Gardosi plays with tension and pushes the boundaries of 'comfortable', provoking awkwardness alongside the titters of recognition. Some of the invitations are tactfully subtle, recognising the resistance people have to make personal revelations to those around them:

> If, one Christmas, you were basting the turkey
> when you realised
> 'this is the nakedest thing I've handled all year...'
> Blink.
> [...]
> If you only learnt what sexual consent was in your late teens
> then grip your knees
>
> and if you've ever felt pressured
> then don't do anything for me.
> [...]

If you're still working out how to be happy on your own
touch someone on the shoulder.
Even if that someone is yourself.
[...]
If you're single and you fucking despise Valentine's Day
cross your arms.
If you have a partner and you fucking despise Valentine's
Day
cross your arms.

Then hug yourself.
Hate and love can look the same sometimes.

The poem weaves the stories of audience members into the meaning of the verse. As I listened to the poem, I was confronted by a decision at the end of each line. Even the decision not to act carried meaning, presenting me with my blocks and anxieties over appearing vulnerable. It was 'touching' to see how the men in the audience (including myself) came onboard with the gestures as others around them did the same. The message of the room moved through the auditorium in a ritual of collective gesture and built trust as it went:

If there are things you wished you talked about
more
look at your hand.

If you can find a way to start the conversation
raise it.[68]

Designing interactions is one of the more audacious ways that page meets stage in live literature. These can be loud and rhythmic exchanges that create an 'incandescence of an alternating current' (to pirate a phrase from E.P. Thompson).[69] They can also be subtle, silent, and ritualistically physical.

In his comparison between hip hop theatre and the oral poetics of South Africa, Daniel Banks considers these exchanges as nothing short of *transcendence:* 'the performer's body is one with the body of her culture and, in this way, connects to the bodies of her audiences'.[70]

Note to the Audience

What are you doing sat there? Are you rebirthing the oral tradition or planning your next Facebook status (or both)? Is the poet stood before you better than YouTube? If not, what are you going to *do* about it?

Art evolves when there are fanatics who are vocal in comparing artists and expressing strong opinions. Be discerning. Don't tolerate cliché. Review gigs online. Read books from and about poets. Write dissertations and even your own books if you can. Speak to other audience members about what's going on. Ask if you can give feedback to the poets. Shout, clap, boo, walk out of the room in protest if you really have to. Don't wait for someone else to do it, this is a DIY movement. OK, if it's an open mic or an intimate reading then be respectful, but if people are paying (and being paid) don't allow your evening to be turned into a group therapy session. If we return to passive, genteel, and accepting audiences, then we are back to stage one. Heckling doesn't have to be abusive, it can be done cleverly and in good faith. Heckling it is a form of critical dialogue. When the poet uses the stage to deliver a series of political opinions—heckle. When the poet uses the stage to deliver bad stand-up comedy—heckle. If there is no art, no attention to performance, or just self-indulgent ego—heckle. Don't do what you are told.* Do your job.

Don't do what I tell you.

Part 8: Debating Interaction

In her study of affect in theatre, Ana Pais argues that the *func-tion* of the audience is to circulate and amplify affect. What's more, she says, it's an ethical and political decision as to whether this agency is designed into the show.[71] Radical theatre maker Augusto Boal invited his spectators to become 'spect-actors'. In his 'forum theatres', performer-facilitators open a discussion mid-show and even summon the crowd to get on stage and change the plot.

As an *agonistic*, conversational event, spoken word shares some of this ethic. In the early days of slam, founder Marc Smith actively encouraged heckling.[72] Smith felt that poetry was not challenging audiences, and audiences were not challenging poetry. In Smith's slams, score-carded knock-out bouts enabled the audience to programme the remaining poetry of the night. Audience passivity was engineered out of the performance ritual.

Bristol rapper and spoken word artist Clayton Blizzard sometimes confronts passive audiences by walking off stage and delivering lines (off mic) three inches from people's faces. He quotes former manager of Liverpool FC, Bill Shankly, to justify his manoeuvres: 'If he's not interfering with play, what's he doing on the pitch!?'[73]

Yet for Jacques Rancière, being a spectator 'is not the passivity that has to be turned into activity. It is our normal situation'.[74] He warns against romanticising performances that 'liberate' spectators. In their silence, spectators are *already* actors. There is nothing passive about consuming, processing, and interpreting a performance with mind and body:

> Is there something more interactive, more communal,
> that goes on between [theatre goers]... than between
> individuals who watch the same show on TV at the same
> time? I think this 'something' is nothing more than the
> presupposition that theatre is communitarian in and
> of itself.[75]

For Mikhail Bakhtin there is much to do in the simple act of consuming language, which is 'entangled' and 'saturated' with associations, assumptions, and value judgements. Speech bubbles grow inside us, 'pregnant with responses and objections'. As readers or listeners, we all have our own relationships to what is being said.[76] In the words of Yoko Tawada:

> we hear selectively, we correct, add to, and adulterate
> what we are hearing...we contribute to this process
> by bringing in our own knowledge, preconceptions,
> imagination, and repressed thoughts. Thus every active
> listening is already a dialogue, even before we open our
> mouths to reply.[77]

In literary studies, 'reader response theory' describes the process by which the reader animates the word's images, characters, and empty spaces inside their head. In doing this, they complete the production of literary works.

In *live* literature, this responsiveness takes on a new dimension. Sound theorist Deborah Kapchan calls performance a 'social field of listening'. This field of *activity* not only auto-translates (as in the sense of reader response theory), but *witnesses*, recognising the 'pain (and praise) of others'. In short, listening acts *do things* in the world.[78] Like a lone person looking skyward in a crowd of people, human attention can infect those around us. A single 'deep listener', though silent, can transform a space and act as a conduit for the transformation and transmission of affect. 'Affective listening' involves tact and engagement,[79] as one psychotherapist describes it:

> The quiet focussed attention of the witness helps
> to create a secure containing environment in
> which the person ... can experience a sense
> of feeling held and seen. The function of the
> witness is to hold the person's experience in his
> own mind.[80]

The act of *transformational listening* bridges the gap between Rancière's idea of live audiences being no more involved (or 'liberated') than TV viewers, and radical theatre that seeks to make the audience part of the show. Spoken word's 'contract of public contact' lies somewhere between these two extremes. This respectful intimacy, as we will now see, has ramifications for the health of those in the room.

Part 9: Live Poetry as Therapy?

I will end this chapter by analysing how spoken word's codes of connection can bring healing. In the last chapter, we saw how emotional imprints pass through the bodies of performers in a way that can be therapeutic for them. The poem, to return to Charles Olson, is 'energy transferred from where the poet got it'.[81] This transfer of affect enters the bodies of the audience and comes back to the poet full circle.

I, personally, find the stage to be energetically cleansing. As the sweat of performance cleans the pores of my skin, the poem, which comes from my insides, goes *into* the audience and circulates back to me as positive affect. Though exhausting, it can also be intensely energising.

Should we put this down to adrenaline alone? Psychotherapists, who have a practical and theoretical understanding of affect, know how a deep listening can enable a client to process the emotions stored in their bodies. Allan Schore, for example, argues that attuning to others' emotions and rhythms can create complimentary inner-states that we reflect back to them. This, he says, 'results in the coupling between the output of one partner's loop and the input of the other's to form a larger feedback configuration'.[82] Both participants are changed by the interaction. He goes on to liken the process to the notion of sympathetic resonance in physics, where objects pick up on an external vibration and begin to 'sing' back like tuning forks.

Hegley's idea of 'emotional participation' ripens through the 'social field of listening'. This 'field' doesn't merely receive and interpret the poem but mirrors it back to the performer in a bounce-back of new affective information. This, in turn, further alters the physiology of the poet. In terms of affect, the performed poem is completed not just in the witnessing, but in the *re-witnessing*.

Teresa Brennan's theory of affect (introduced at the beginning of this chapter), argues that this circulation can be 'life-enhancing'. The 'living attention' of love is a biological drive, she says, that energises and unblocks us on an emotional/physical level. This, in turn, frees up energy that might otherwise be spent on repressing trauma stored in our bodies (see Chapter 5).[83]

Though some poetry events can resemble group therapy sessions, poetry is not psychotherapy. The poet is not involved in an unscripted conversation and is not being questioned by the listener. Neither is the audience trained to listen without judging or distorting what they are hearing with their own feelings. It should also not be automatically concluded that performers are using the stage as therapy. One study of spoken word communities suggests that poets often resolve their trauma before performance out of 'the sense of responsibility' not to burden audiences with their 'emotional baggage'.[84]

Nevertheless, it is well known that live art boosts not just our mood but our mental and physical well-being. Benefits to our immune system include a reduction in stress hormones and inflammatory processes, as well as an increase in antibodies and improved coronary health.[85] Indeed, the 'controlled and safe environment' of spoken word performance is now beginning to receive attention for its health benefits.[86] This includes the prevention of social isolation and mood disorders,[87] the reduction in anxiety,[88] the increase of emotional literacy,[89] the growth of confidence and personal development[90] and the affirmation and acknowledgement of those who have suffered trauma and abuse.[91]

Support networks are central to our health[92] and (as we saw in Chapter 2) *sociality* is central to spoken word. Poetry activists strive to create 'a safe space' of respect where personal stories can be given and emotions participated in. In this sense, live poetry is (in part at least) a group form of *folk therapy*.

Summary

All of these considerations have implications for how we view the discipline of poetry. Many poets I have interviewed consider performance as part of the writing process. Performances allow them not just to run the poem through their own bodies, but to run it through a collection of bodies. This is what deep ecologist Arne Naess called 'the social self'—our wider selves, where our extended cognition occurs.[93] Spoken word spaces, then, offer opportunities for *live drafting*. As such, a spoken word artist is perhaps less likely to attend a 'writers group', with its sober analysis of texts in quiet rooms, and more likely to scratch poems in the alchemical play of the live setting.

In the viscous soup of gas and water vapour that surrounds us, it is more than just words that make our hair stand to attention. Spoken word engages with the chemical-electrical environment of chaos, surprise, and flux. It tests the power of poetry by putting it into an agonistic relationship with the audience: a 'social field' made of frequency, pheromone, and the subtle interplay of power and consent.

Through their apprenticeship to the stage, spoken word artists can learn to attune themselves to the rhythms of live performance. This is not one rhythm, but an interlocking matrix, a state of *polyrhythmia* as complex as the rhythm and metre of the poetry itself. Part of the craft of spoken word is, I believe, to develop a literacy for these affective frequencies, responding to them and incorporating them into the show.

All of this blurs the boundary of 'the poem' as it is understood on the page. Spoken word experiments with the stagecraft often associated with theatre and live music (adapted to a more conversational setting), and that of stand-up comedy (but with a broader spectrum of emotions). This inheritance, which has really always belonged to poetry, gives us an ancient and elaborate toolkit to impress literature into the human nervous system.

The practice also involves profound acts of trust. By aligning ourselves, we enter into a contract of roles and responsibilities. Affect is not only created but circulated, amplified, and altered in the *forcefield of human attention*. The bodies of the poet and the audience are held in this field. Some cultures may prefer to describe it as *prana*, *chi*, *mana* or *spirits*. Within it, the poem meets the conscious and subconscious participation of everyone in the room. Poetry funnels into us as streams of coded somatic data that, in turn, elicit emotions. In spoken word then, empathy is like combustion ('the flint and steel meeting'), it is fed by breath and spreads through contact with others. It is, in short, an airborne contagion.

Notes

1   John Hegley Interview, Stage Invasion, Vimeo.

2   See Brennan, *The Transmission of Affect* (2004); Nathanson,
        Knowing Feeling (1994).

3   Ahmed, *Feel Your Way* (2014).

4   Nathanson, as above.

5   Brian Massumi quoted in: Shouse,'Feeling, Emotion, Affect' (2005).

6   Brennan, as above.

7   Brennan, as above.

8   McGowan, 'Slam the Book' (2016.)

9   Whalley & Miller, *Between Us* (2017), p.79.

10   Brennan, as above.

11   Lefebvre, *Rhythmanalysis* (2004), p.15.

12   Iberall, A.S. & McCulloch, W.S. paraphrased in Schore,
        Affect Dysregulation and Disorders of the Self (2003), p.143.

13   Brennan, as above, p.70.

14   Schmid, 'Performance, Poetics and Place' (2003), p.20; Wheeler,
        Voicing American Poetry (2008), p.145.

15   Osborne, '"Set in Stone"' (2011), p.212.

16   Holman, 'DisClaimer' (2000), p.19.

17   McDaniel, 'Slam and the Academy' (2000), p.36.

18   Brennan, as above, p.138.

19   Kapchan, 'Listening Acts' (2017), p.236.

20   Estimates vary on this figure. I have also heard the figure pitched
        to around 88%. The percentage I have used is taken from: 'George
        Lakoff on Embodied Cognition and Language', 22 October 2013,
        https://www.youtube.com/watch?v=XWYaoAoijdQ&t=2254s>

21   Scheve, 'Collective Emotions in Rituals' (2012).

22   Wheeler, as above, p.25.

23   Hatfield et al., 'New Perspectives on Emotional Contagion' (2014),

24   Scheve, as above.

25   Prochazkova & Kret, 'Connecting Minds and Sharing Emotions
        Through Mimicry' (2017), p.100.

26   Umiltà, 'The "Mirror Mechanism" and Motor Behaviour' (2016).

27   With the existence of mirror neurons, it is tempting to say that
        empathy lives in the brain. Yet the prevailing consensus in neuro-
        science is that all cognition is, to a degree, embodied and that the

brain is necessary, but not sufficient, for thought and experience, see: Falletti, 'Introduction' (2016); and Yakubovskaya, 'Emotions, Empathy and Drama', 10 Oct. 2014, https://sites.tufts.edu/emotiononthebrain/2014/10/10/82/

28   Joelle Taylor Interview, Stage Invasion, Vimeo, (00:08:40).

29   Thomson & Jaque, *Creativity and the Performing Artist* (2017), p.10

30   Prochazkova & Kret, as above.

31   University of Twente, BMS Lab, 2017, https://imotions.com/gsr-guide-ebook

32   Rachel Rose Reid Interview, Stage Invasion, Vimeo, (00:58:00)

33   This text provided by Dizraeli, the poem can also be watched at: Dizraeli, 'My Brother Can't Help Himself', https://www.facebook.com/Dizraeli/videos/10154853842292611.

34   Dizraeli, email to Peter Bearder, 6 Sept. 2018.

35   Pais, 'Re-Affecting the Stage' (2016).

36   Mark Gwynne Jones Interview, Stage Invasion, Vimeo, (00:04:00).

37   Matt Harvey Interview, Stage Invasion, Vimeo, (00:12:00).

38   Ridout, 'Welcome to the Vibratorium' (2008), p.221.

39   Henriques, 'The Vibrations of Affect and their Propagation on a Night Out on Kingston's Dancehall Scene' (2010), p.69.

40   Henriques, as above, p.67.

41   For a fuller discussion on paratext in performance poetics see: Novak, *Live Poetry* (2011), p.75.

42   This figure is given by Silva, 'Live Writing' (2018), see the Chapter, 'Lemn Sissay: Defamiliarising the Poetry Performance'. See also, Gräbner, 'Is Performance Poetry Dead?' (2007).

43   Appel, 'Nabokov's Puppet Show, Part II' (1967). Lucy English's observation came from personal correspondence.

44   Matt Harvey, email to Peter Bearder, 22 Aug. 2018.

45   Rob Gee, email to Peter Bearder, 1 Aug. 2018.

46   Rachel Rose Reid Interview, Stage Invasion, Vimeo, (00:54:00).

47   Carpetface, email to Peter Bearder, 22 Nov. 2018.

48   Prochazkova & Kret, as above, p.105.

49   Gruber, 'Suasive Speech' (2016).

50   Harrison et al., 'Processing of Observed Pupil Size Modulates Perception of Sadness and Predicts Empathy' (2007).

51   For a classic thesis on the patriarchal power of the 'male gaze' see: Mulvey, 'Visual Pleasure and Narrative Cinema' (1975).

52   Whalley & Miller, *Between Us* (2017), p.7.

53   This is to paraphrase Whalley & Miller, as above, p.13–14.

54   Cited in Taransaud, *I, Monster* (2016), p.3

55   Emmerson, 'Thinking Laughter Beyond Humour' (2017).

56   Emmerson, as above.

57   Gay McAuley quoted in Ridout, 'Welcome to the Vibratorium' (2008), p.221.

58   Ridout, as above, p.223.

59   Matt Harvey Interview, Stage Invasion, Vimeo, (00:13:00)

60   Harvey, 'Curtains' (2005).

61   Matt Harvey, email to Peter Bearder, 22 Aug. 2018.

62   Hannah Macpherson quoted in Emmerson, 'Thinking Laughter Beyond Humour', (2017).

63   This is to paraphrase Emmerson, as above.

64   Hoyles & Hoyles, *Moving Voices* (2002), p.32.

65   Ong, *Orality and Literacy* (1982).

66   See: Dowdy, 'Live Hip Hop, Collective Agency, and "Acting in Concert"' (2007); Foley, *How to Read an Oral Poem* (2002), p.154.

67   'Sekou Sundiata on music, poetry, East Harlem and activism', 1 May 2012, https://www.youtube.com/watch?v=M0FIzRj7prY

68   Gardosi, 'Raise Your Hand', unpublished poem.

69   Thompson, *The Making of the English Working Class* (1963), p.833.

70   South African poet Pitika Ntuli, paraphrased in Banks *'From Homer to Hip Hop'* (2010), p.240.

71   Pais, 'Re-Affecting the Stage' (2016).

72   Smith & Eleveld, *The Spoken Word Revolution* (2003), p.116.

73   Clayton Blizzard, email to Peter Bearder, 8 Oct. 2018.

74   Rancière, 'The Emancipated Spectator' (2007).

75   Rancière, as above, p.287.

76   Bakhtin, 'Discourse in the Novel' (1982), p.281.

77   Tawada, 'The Art of Being Nonsynchronous' (2009), p.189.

78   These are the premises of Kapchan, 'Listening Acts' (2017).

79   Kapchan, as above, p.278.

80   Wyman-McGinty, 'The Body in Analysis' (1998), p.239.

81   Olson, 'Projective Verse' (1950).

82   Schore, *Affect Dysregulation and Disorders of the Self* (2003), p.141.

83   Brennan, *The Transmission of Affect* (2004), p.34.

84   Alvarez & Mearns, 'The Benefits of Writing and Performing in the Spoken Word Community', (2014).

85   Bronte, 'Health Benefits of Going to Musicals, Theatre Touted' (2014).

86   English, 'The Growing Popularity of Performance Poetry Is a Boost for Mental Wellbeing', 2 June 2016, https://www.theguardian.com/culture-professionals-network/2016/jun/02/performance-poetry-boost-for-mental-wellbeing

87.   Alvarez & Mearns, as above.

88   English, as above.

89   Bearder, 'Communities of Words' (2015); Sam-La Rose, 'The Rise of Spoken Word Educators in UK', 3 October 2013, https://www.theguardian.com/teacher-network/teacher-blog/2013/oct/03/spoken-word-educators-poetry-schools

90   Dyson, 'Crafting "The Humble Prose of Living"' (2005); Reyes, 'Finding the Poetic High' (2006).

91   Lee, 'Spoken Word as a Way of Dismantling Barriers and Creating Space for Healing' (2018).

92   Bronte, as above.

93   Naess, *The Ecology of Wisdom* (2016).

Chapter 7:
Reviving the Ecstatic:
Live Poetry, Transcendence &
Altered States of Consciousness

Poets are often compared to shamans, oracles, seers, and sages. Clarissa Pinkola Estés places the poet among an 'ancient community of holy people, troubadours, bards, griots, cantors... bums, hags, and crazy people.'[1] But the image of the poet as a tribal word-magician, who casts spells, alters consciousness, and spiritually elevates their listeners, is not one that most spoken word artists cultivate for themselves. Most jobbing poets I know are fairly down to earth people and would probably reject such language as 'a bit wanky'. Yet we are indeed massive wankers. It is not fanciful or inaccurate to compare spoken word poets to bards and shamans, since they use many of the same techniques and achieve many of the same results. Moreover, science is beginning to find evidence that these techniques work, and to suggest some of the mechanisms involved. This chapter will embrace the language of 'ecstatic poetry', 'altered-states', and even 'transcendence', but it will bypass the usual conceptions of ecstatic poetry as found in printed anthologies. Our interest here is in the ecstasy of poetry in *performance*. I will start by examining ecstasy as *peak experience*, and move on to the dissociated states of hypnotism, to show how some spoken word artists have a working understanding of trance induction.

*

The word ecstatic derives from the Ancient Greek *ekstasis* ('standing outside oneself'). An ecstatic experience can be used to describe a wide spectrum of states, from raptured contemplation and absorption (akin to a child looking at a spider's web), right through to a state of trance in which people lose their sense of self and become rigid, unresponsive, and impervious to pain or tiredness (as with the 'spirit possession' of some African vodou practices).[2] Ecstasy is *peak consciousness.* Whether it's a mystical state of spiritual enlargement, or simply one of joyful exuberance, the ecstatic transports us out of our inner monologue and into the wider patterning of life. It can be achieved in rituals both religious and secular, through meditation, dancing, spinning in circles, extended isolation, repetitive chanting, flickering lights, and even via the sense of smell. It most certainly can be caused by poetry.

Indeed, it is impossible to separate the ecstatic from the music and metre of poetry. Some authors believe that the ritualised and elevated speech of oral poetry (like singing, chanting, or the imitating of animal noises) has been at the centre of spirituality since pre-historic times. Alongside shaking, swaying, and beating of simple wooden drums, rhythmic and expressive release enables us to transcend ourselves and find healing in ecstatic states.[3]

Edward Ahearn looks to the texts of Coleridge and Rimbaud in an attempt to find 'a model of ecstatic poetry'. He defines it as 'a transforming experience provoked, mastered, enacted by words'.[4] In contrast to this, writers like James Landau find an ecstasy on the dance floors of electronic dance music which is closer to the orgiastic passion of carnival.[5] For the sake of this chapter, I will take a little from both these ends of the spectrum; treating the ecstatic as something that can be induced by words, but which also incorporates the subliminal knowledge of the body.

The poets usually associated with 'mystic' or 'ecstatic' poetry tend to be drawn from the canon of literature, such as Blake, Rumi, Coleridge, or Rilke. This emphasis on the *textual* inheritance of dead poets has created a conspicuous blind spot for the role of *performed* verse in creating altered states of consciousness. W.G. Kraemer, for example, acknowledges that poetry can induce a trance in the audience (as well as the reader), but argues for the *'hypnotext'* as a *'literary genre'.*[6]

Studies that join forces with anthropology have expanded the picture. Research on *ethnopoetry* has cast new light on the vocal artistry of shamanism and tribal cultures, looking outside the written word to embrace different settings and musical contexts. *Ethnopoetics* put the human (*ethno*) back into poetry in the fullest sense of the word.[7] Yet between these two poles there is a gulf. A search through the library may leave you with the impression that ecstatic verbal artistry was practiced in the past by now-dead poets, or in distant, non-industrial societies. This, as we will see, is not the case.

*

The spoken word 'gig' will be considered here in opposition to the 'readings' and 'recitals' of the 'Formal Poetry Reading' which Frederick Stern describes as '*not* "ecstatic"'.[8] I believe poetry's text-fixation has shifted our understanding of the ecstatic away from the social and the somatic, toward a more contemplative, reflective, and solitary communion with the page. One of the most famous 'ecstatic poets'—Rainer Maria Rilke—crafted an entire philosophy around solitude. 'Only the individual who is solitary,' he argued, can be brought under 'the deep laws' of spiritual knowing and inner reflection.[9]

Such attitudes may be the result of the Global North's long tradition of suppressing what anthropologist Émile Durkheim famously called *collective effervescence*.[10] In her book *Dancing in the Streets: A History of Collective Joy*, Barbara Ehrenreich traces the Christian church's crackdown on ecstatic exuberance. In the thirteenth century, seats were installed in churches in order to prevent dancing and, for the following five centuries, the church stifled intuitive and affective approaches to spiritual experiences. These included trance states, the belief that one is temporarily 'possessed' by spirits, and 'speaking in tongues' (where people are inhabited by a voice other than their own). Worshippers who did these things were persecuted for heresy, superstition, or madness.[11]

Uncontrolled physical exuberance was unacceptable to the church because of its association with sex and rioting. Having evicted disorderliness, the church channeled the people's continued desire for 'collective effervescence' away from festivity and abandon and into ritual and ceremony.[12] The Catholic Mass, for example, is a '*controlled* ecstatic event' where the priest leads the worshippers into a 'trance-like state' through prayers, chants, and call-and-response.[13] Anthropologist Felicitas Goodman agrees. For Goodman, the church is to blame for the shift from physical participation to 'thinking about religion instead.'[14]

As the modern era approached, 'Enlightenment' values of scientism and rationality combined with Protestant puritanism to purge certain forms transcendental rapture. A sensible religious experience of 'high art' and solemnity prevailed. The industrial era was dawning and under the observance of the 'Protestant work ethic' disciplined workers and restrained audiences were the order of the day.[15]

The effect of this disembodiment was that physical pleasure itself was stripped of its sense of sacredness. In the uniformly religious societies of old, 'exalted' and 'rapturous' experiences were very often considered direct encounters with a higher power. This changed as the population became increasingly non-religious.[16]

Traces of this world view, however, live on in the words we still use to describe poetry. Poetry that brings us the distant or imagined, summons and invokes (from Latin *invocare*: 'to call in'). The emotional transcendence of poetry is indeed *sublime* (literally 'to lift up'). All these terms were once imbued with a divine enthusiasm (from *en-theos*: to have 'god in'). In the wake of secularisation, such spirited activities came to be seen as purely hedonistic. Today, 'ecstatic' has two commonly understood meanings: (i) mystic self-transcendence, and (ii) exuberant joy. Much of the world of poetry has sided with the former at the expense of the latter.

The gulf between these traditions became glowingly apparent in May 2018 when the black American preacher, Bishop Michael Curry, took to the pulpit of St George's Chapel, London for the wedding of Prince Harry and Meghan Markle. His part-improvised and stirringly theatrical sermon was lauded in the press as a 'complete contrast to the solemn and stationary ecclesiastical address that preceded his'.[17] A perfect ten as they say in slam. The service was also treated to the singing and (god forbid) dancing of the Kingdom Choir gospel group.

Scholar of oral poetry Paul Zumthor credits the black

churches of the American South as being 'so saturated with the presence of African music that they evoke voodoo; collective ecstasies'.[18] He also cites the arrival of opera in late sixteenth century Europe as helping to reestablish a 'modern equivalent of archaic rituals of trance and possession'.[19] Later, popular cultural movements like rock and roll ignited congregations of music fans who abandoned themselves to rhythm.[20]

The ecstatic, then, didn't die but transmuted and re-infiltrated culture. As we will now see, the musical and theatrical poetics of spoken word draw on both pop culture and the black prophetic tradition. They are heavily implicated in the ecstatic tradition.

*

Spoken word artist James McKay may have been excommunicated in days gone by. Here he recalls his first 'real gig' in 2000:

> I had a *literal* out of body experience. I had the
> experience where you stop experiencing your voice
> as yours, and you seem to be another voice speaking
> through you. And I *swear*, I was at the top back of the
> room, looking down at myself... (like I was when I
> had my nipple pierced).

McKay, who was so adrenalised that he was 'shaking and smiling for about a week afterwards', compares his experience to the trance states of Pentecostal church meetings:

> the idea of 'speaking in tongues' is the experience of
> speaking, but you're not speaking; the Poem is speak-
> ing itself, or the Voice is speaking and it's not you.[21]

Mystical ideas like these are not as rare as you might think. In November 2016, the poet El Crisis performed alongside the Jamaican dub poet and philosopher Mutabaruka at an event in Brixton, London. During his set he used the ecstatic participation of call-and-response, and invited the audience to sing the chorus lines of poem. 'It's a griot ting' he explained, referencing the praise-poets of the West African oral tradition:

> The ancestors are all here, they're with us ya' know.
> When we're calling out…them is reflecting the vibration
> to us ya' know. So we have to remember the ancestors
> speak *to* us, the ancestors speak *through* us and we have
> to recognise some of us are ancestors as well, ya' know.
> [poet laughs] So we have to appreciate this kind of vibra-
> tion what we're bringin' right now. TO THE *FULLEST*.
> YO WHAT UP? [audience cheers][22]

El Crisis, who we will return to later in this chapter, has a compellingly musical delivery. His vocal style is sermonic, not just because he speaks of esoteric themes but because it 'trespasses into song' and 'gets involved in the energy of the world'.[23] To further explore this I will now turn to the work of Kate Tempest who performed to an audience of twenty thousand at Glastonbury 2017 in what must be the biggest event of ecstatic live poetry in modern British history.[24]

During Tempest's set, poems appear alongside songs that she raps with the accompaniment of a backing band. The audience dance, sway, and nod, apprehending the music with their bodies and the bodies of those around them. On the dance floor—that sacred space of connection and abandon—whooping and cheering are never far from the surface:

> They've taken everything from us
> Telling us nothing is ours
> but here we are dancing in the rumbling dark
> [audience cheer]
> So come a little closer give me something to grasp
> give me your *beautiful, crumbling* heart.[25]

Tempest's voice climbs in pitch and intensity as she progresses through poems that frequently border on shouting. She paces, gesticulates, and bobs on the front of her feet, jumping into her lines as if held back only by the mic. Some passages are delivered with closed eyes and trembling open palms. She dispatches poems like 'Brand New Ancients' and 'People's Faces' with all the devastating tenderness of a marital argument, her voice quivering with difficult truths. By whipping herself into exaltation, Tempest is inhabited and transported by her words.

Audience members respond accordingly, swaying with their eyes closed and palms held above their heads. Others can be seen crying and holding each other while focussed intently on the words. YouTube comments below the Glastonbury footage show that this peak experience is also felt by viewers beyond the festival: 'Goosebumps', 'Incredible', 'I'm shivering', 'makes me cry like a baby every time I watch it' and 'she's an amazing therapist'. If this is therapy, it is one grounded in the ecstatic experience of the body. As rapper Marv Radio puts it, 'performance that makes people move, feel, sing and shout takes them out of their individual problems and into an interconnected bliss state.' [26]

Tempest's fifty-minute set contrasts between music/acapella, loud/quiet, and fast/slow to work the bodies of the crowd and orchestrate their energy. Expert on *flow states* Mihaly Csikszentmihalyi credits performers with creating 'optimal experience' which channels 'psychic energy' and brings 'order to consciousness'.[27] This *flow* is a valued skill in rap and spoken word and it relates directly to shamanic traditions which use an intense rhythmic stimulation (or 'sonic driving') to propel listeners into new realms. The rhythm of chanting, singing, or drumming engages the mammalian brain to help listeners bypass conscious thought to feel receptive and connected to 'the flow'. [28]

Tempest's faster pieces have an attrition of syllables that reach 330 beats-per-minute (BPM). This is well within the 160–400 BPM that Timothy Thomason identifies as the speed needed to induce trance states.[29] The rapping creates a voice-as-drum effect that lasts in excess of the 'several minutes' required to bring a listener to trance. Yet Tempest's sonic driving parts ways with Thomason's trance drumming which, he says, should have 'no accents and no breaks.' Nevertheless, her double-time vocal pyrotechnics create a sensory bombardment that drowns out external stimuli. Our attention ricochets between racing syncopated rhymes and emphasised syllables. Rap's ability to create what

David Banks calls 'a momentary rhythmic Utopia' is what makes it so entrancing.[30]

In their scientific study of ecstasy, Becker and Penman note that there is relatively little test-based research into trance states. Unlike other altered states (like meditation) trancing subjects are often moving which makes them hard to monitor.[31] Their research shows 'transcendence' doesn't only happen in places of worship. 'Pentecostal ecstatics' who are 'possessed' during church services, show strong physical responses when listening to religious music they love (namely the excitation of the sympathetic nervous system we looked at in the last chapter). The same responses can be found in non-religious 'deep listeners' (like music students), who develop intense emotional connections to music they are familiar with.[32]

Hannah Silva relates Tempest's poetry to the Caribbean and African American sermonic traditions. In the YouTube comments below Tempest's videos, Silva finds 'a kind of "amen corner" with remarks like; "amen"; "Damn! Preach!"; "preach the truth you blessed"; "such spirit".' [33] This *co-signing*, or 'talking back' of the congregation is a hallmark of ecstatic oral practice.

Tempest's Glastonbury performance makes blessings like 'we are still godly, call us by our name', and invocations such as 'PLEASE CONNECT, PLEASE CONNECT... PLEASE REMEMBER, PLEASE REMEMBER, PLEASE WAKE UP AND LOVE MORE!' [34]

A passage like this may not get you marked up in a creative writing assignment, but it is entirely valid in ecstatic poetry. Delivered to a swelling finale of instruments, rolling drums, and white lights that blare into the screaming crowd, it has the feel of a religious benediction.

Though Tempest's invocation isn't accompanied by ritual or traditional religious language, it can be described as a *charm*, which is defined by the *Princeton Encyclopedia of Poetics* as 'a verbal formula used for magical effects'.[35] The magic we are witnessing is not the supernatural magic of fantasy, but *mundane* (or everyday) magic. Aleister Crowley famously describes such practices as 'the science and art of causing change to occur in conformity with Will'. The following part-improvised outburst becomes the defining moment of Tempest's closing poem 'People's Faces'. She performs it from the front of the stage while emphatically plunging her head to waist height. It is met by a huge outburst from the crowd.

> I'm listening to every little whisper in the
> distance singing hymns.
> And I can, I can feel things, changing.
> I *CAN*, I FUCKING *CAN!* [36]

Passionate this may be, but is this really 'causing change to occur in conformity with Will'? Tempest's declaration of change is *performative*, not in the sense of it relating to performance, but as an act of speech that not only declares, but enacts. A phrase like 'I love you' is *performative* in that it elicits and performs the love it describes. Similarly, the utterance 'I Knight thee' instantly makes a noun out of its verb. [37] Spoken before thousands of festival goers, the 'change' in 'People's Faces' creates the change it describes. The passage *charms* the audience into action, evoking a palpable euphoria that combats dis-*illusionment*, and conjures a sense of hope, togetherness, and resolve. This, as we will see in the following chapter, has everything to do with change.

Satire and political exhortations have roots in ancient occult practices. [38] Tempest's 'verbal missiles' (to quote Bronisław Malinowski) are akin to the Babylonian incantations which accompanied the ritual burning of images of one's enemies. [39] Charms, blessings, invocations, and other 'magical' speech acts are founded on a belief in the ability of sound to evoke and transmit power, and the tradition is alive and well in spoken word.

Spoken word can, then, be a form of peak experience where physical exuberance can be cultivated to bring a crowd to states of physical, emotional, and even spiritual abandonment. In this state of rapture, audiences can be charmed and enemies burned. Let's now turn the volume down a little to explore the more dissociative states of spoken word.

*

Spoken word doesn't get volunteers to cluck like chickens and forget their own names, but it could be described as a type of 'stage hypnosis'. In essence, hypnosis is a method of bypassing logical, critical thought and 'wrapping the mind around an idea'.[40] The music of the voice, as well as the *relational* processes of spoken word have a big part to play in this.

Writing for the *International Journal of Clinical and Experimental Hypnosis*, experts in hypnotic poetry Snyder and Shor outline the key elements of trance-inducing poetry. Two of these relate to the *content* of what is said: (i) vague imagery, and (ii) obscurities that tire the listener's mind. Both of these make the reader (or listener) less inclined to grasp onto thoughts that could prevent them 'going deeper'.

From the perspective of spoken word it is significant that the remaining components of 'hypnotic poetry' have more to do with the way the words *sound* and, by extension, the *manner* in which they are spoken. These are:

- A regularity of a soothing rhythm
- Refrains and frequent repetition
- The avoidance of abrupt changes that might create alertness
- Ornamental rhythmic embellishments to fix attention [41]

Any of this sound familiar? We are back to the *flow* of the rapper and spoken word poet. The idea here is not to drone on monotonously, but to elaborate the poetry with rhyme and rhythm. The hypnotic poem plays on the sonic properties of language, threading passages together with a 'heavy play on little groups of vowels and consonants'. A 'regular cycle of rising and falling pitch' may also be used to help the listener go deeper.[42] This two-pitch pendulum of 'reciting tones' acts like the swinging of the hypnotist's pocket watch. It can be found chanted around the world, from the devotional chants of Russian Orthodox priests, to the mantras of Buddhist monks.

We can also see it in the work of spoken word poet El Crisis. His poem 'So Many Wonders' shows (with sound) how the poet's 'soul flies'. There is, he says, 'a natural mystic in the air in tune with the words I say' that is 'blowing my mind'. It is sung and chanted at high speed with the flow of dub rhythms and the backing of a djembe drum.

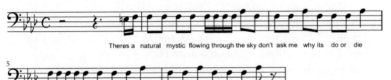

Theres a natural mystic flowing through the sky don't ask me why its do or die

Listen to the voices take you high   thoughts run by through my third eye

'So Many Wonders' fits the model of hypnotic poetry. The soothing rhythm and melody prevents 'abrupt changes' and lulls the ear with its repetition. At the same time, 'ornamental rhythmic embellishments' tug back at our attention. Of course, the poem has to be heard to be truly felt. Its value is not in detailed images but in the compelling stream of syllables that carries the poem's message. The speed of the poem's flow forces the listener to stop trying to dive down for sense and just swim in the sound.

To this model of hypnotic poetry, we can also add *texture, tone,* and *pace* of the poet's voice. A reassuringly confident and soothing voice can instil a sense of abandon the listener. A hypnotist, for example, might say in a soft voice 'you may wish to become *relaxed*', elongating the final word of the phrase. Here the manner of delivery is itself a *hypnotic suggestion*, stewarding the listener into a state of absorption.

Like a joke that loses the listener's interest after the interruption of a postal delivery, the spell is broken if the speaker loses the *flow*.[43] Before performances, many poets use facial warm-ups to avoid tripping over their own tongues. The slurred or forgotten word can cause the crystal ball to fall and smash, casting the listener out of the poem and back in front of someone who has memorised a text (badly).

Marrying poetry with hypnosis has a long history. Written records find hypnosis in the incantations of Chinese healers over four thousand years ago. In pre-Roman Europe, Druids combined their oral practice with music to induce a palliative 'magical sleep'. [44] Such examples only scratch the surface of this history which is likely to have been practiced since prehistoric times. In the repeated words of Kate Tempest at Glastonbury, 'we are the brand new ancients'.

Being ancient isn't new. Beat poet Allen Ginsberg chanted Buddhist mantras to aid concentration and meditation in his listeners. [45] In the nineteenth century, one of history's most famous performers of live literature Charles Dickens made extensive use of his training in hypnotism to captivate his audiences. People would pack into tiny windowless rooms in mid-summer to see his now legendary performances. One scholar believes it was probable that he hypnotised himself before his shows. [46]

Though most spoken word poets don't describe their warm-up routines as self-hypnosis, many have extensive techniques to seduce themselves into apparently limitless confidence, presence, and self-control. Breathing exercises can help performers relax and concentrate (see Chapter 5) and affirmative mantras can focus the performer's attention away from anxiety, doubt, and other intrusive thoughts. London-based poet Jah-Mir uses meditation to prepare for his improvised spoken word. 'I fill the energy and sit with it,' he told me. 'Sometimes small sentences or ideas will come to me. I try not to follow them but hold them like seeds'. [47] More kinetic warm-ups like shake-downs and stretches create rhythms and postures that could be described as *somatic mantras*, releasing tension and setting intention.

From self-hypnosis, the poet can then lull the listener into a state of susceptibility. In the last chapter we looked at how live poetry controls the audience's experience through the regulation of rhythm. This is also true of hypnotism, a discipline that makes extensive use of repetition. Hypnotic suggestions like 'your eyes are feeling heavy' or 'you're going deeper' are synonymous with poetic refrains, like Tempest's 'we are the brand new ancients' that imprints its message on the listener through reiteration.

Poetry is what Goodman would call 'controlled dreaming'. As the Amazonian shaman guides the ayahuasca-induced trancer through their visions, [48] the poet leads the listener into the imaginarium. Poet and storyteller Rachel Rose Reid describes how her audiences come to wrap their minds around her stories:

> If I say to you, 'in my hand there is a rose', you see it,
> as much as if you say 'there was a city', around the
> outside of the city there was a wall. Like, *we all know
> this is my hand!* It's not possible for a city to fit on my
> hand. Yet we *do* create this world where we start get-
> ting tingles down our legs because we feel this magic
> being created that's a *complicity* between us.[49]

Tempest helps to create this complicity in her poem 'End Times'
by addressing her audience about it directly. Mid-poem she
opens her eyes, pauses, and her voice softens:

> Look, when I'm tellin' rhymes I shut my eyes
> cos' it helps me see stuff. These words they're
> like the leaves in the bottom of the gypsy's tea
> cup. If you look at them right you might see your
> future in 'em.[50]

Both spoken word and hypnosis can be intensely inter-personal,
requiring a willingness from the listener to be effective. To return
to our experts Snyder and Shor:

> The audience should be quietly relaxed, com-
> fortable, in sympathetic rapport with the reader
> who is preferably an authority-figure, and there
> should be minimum outside distracting noises [51]

The poet, then, is not just a speaker of words, but a Master of
Ceremony (MC). Like hypnotists,[52] their practice is one of observation and intuitive response to those being addressed. In spiritual terms, both hypnotist and listener could be described as
filaments. Through them, the 'electricity' of a shared or 'greater'
consciousness passes. As Judith Becker puts it:

> Deep listening is a kind of secular trancing,
> divorced from religious practice but often carrying
> religious sentiments such as feelings of transcend-
> ence or a sense of communion with a power
> beyond oneself.[53]

259

The research on Pentecostal ecstatics mentioned above concludes 'the skill of ecstasy' resides not in the MC, but in the one who is ecstatic. As the listener's relationship with art grows, so too do the emotional associations attached to it.[54] This could come from their familiarity with a place or community, or perhaps a melody or rhythm. Music itself is understood to provoke 'quasi-hypnotic states' for reasons that are as much social as physical. This has implications for the *sociality* of oral poetry, which is essentially a form of music.

Hannah Silva's analysis of Spoken Word Voice cites research on African-descended oral practices which show that recognisable patterns of intonation can create conditioned reactions in listeners. In the words of Henry Mitchell, 'it automatically makes some folks "happy" just to hear the tonal aspect of their religious mother tongue sounded in the pulpit'.[55]

It is entirely plausible that the dub rhythms and sermon-like incantations of El Crisis are euphonies that entice his listeners to be carried into absorption. Since such processes are below the level of our knowing attention, they are able to bypass our critical faculties, triggering a *waking hypnosis* that speaks to the subconscious knowledge of the body.

To sum up, hypnosis is intimately connected to spoken word. As a *flow*-based musical poetic, melody and rhythm combine with the tone and texture of the voice to induce semi-trance like states in its listeners. Performers can alter their own consciousness with warm-up techniques to help steward the audience into 'controlled dreaming'. These verbal rituals are intensely inter-personal. With a little rapport, poetry seduces us with visualisation and hypnotic suggestion, helping us to surrender our critical faculties.

*

Poets need to, in the words of a Luke Wright poem, 'embrace the wank'. Spoken word can spellbind, entrance, and hypnotise audiences into altered states. Consciously or otherwise, poets are aware of this and manipulate it in their writing and performance. At its most compelling, spoken word is a revival of the 'archaic techniques of controlled ecstasy.'[56] These techniques have shuddered in the air of the shaman's drum and danced in the sparks of the fire for as long as there have been tongues to fan the flames. My decision to use magico-religious language in this chapter is an attempt to convey due reverence for what we are experiencing. In live performance, we have all felt moments when some ineffable, trans-personal chemistry shimmers through us. We have all been stolen by a poem and absorbed into a totality that goes beyond our singular intellects. This is, if you like, a mystical experience.

I will stop short of equating poets with 'shamans', 'healers' and 'sorcerers'. The intention of spoken word is very different. Poets don't lead rituals to heal people, harness 'supernatural powers', or summon spirits or ancestors. (Most) poets do not alter their consciousness with sleep deprivation, fasting, or mind-altering substances (though there is no reason why we shouldn't and we might have a lot more fun if we did).

We should also not dismiss what has survived through the centuries on the printed page. The work of ecstatic poets such as Blake, Whitman, and Rumi are treasured possessions that we can all learn from. But these poets, and indeed all poets, should *sing* from time to time. Ecstatic poetry that lives only in printed word can limit the participation of the body, and it is here that ecstasy so often lives.

Spoken word, then, invites us to reconceive the ecstatic by marrying contemplative rapture with physical exuberance. As a tangibly *sensual* experience it permissions some of 'the repressed "shadows" of industrial civilisation'—the 'visceral event'—the body.[57] Teresa Brennan helps us marry our idea of the 'spiritual' with the everyday processes of human attention:

> Nothing is more material than mysticism.
> Through sustaining living attention by concentration the mystic enters into a timeless state
> that eventually yields an experience that is
> evidently sensual and spiritual.[58]

Ecstasy is being *beside ourselves* with laughter or reduced to tears by a spell caster with a microphone. Ecstasy is the divine stream of incomprehensible verbal rhythms flying from the mouth of the jungle MC. It is the call, the response, the cheer, and the stamping of feet. Ecstasy absolves us of responsibility for our cheers and tears, sweeping us along in 'the one-who-is-many and the many-who-are-one'.[59] As we will see in the next chapter, this is not only spiritual but highly political.

Notes

1   Estés, *Women Who Run With the Wolves* (1997), p.19.

2   I use the word *vodou* here rather than *voodoo* as it is the proper term
      believers use to call their religion. The word *voodoo* is a foreign term
      that denotes a colonial and often racist worldview unrelated to that
      of *vodou* believers.

3   See: Révész, *Introduction to the Psychology of Music* (2015); Sachs,
      The Rise of Music in the Ancient World, East and West (1944).

4   Ahearn, 'Toward a Model of Ecstatic Poetry' (1982), p.42.

5   Landau, 'The Flesh of Raving' (2004).

6   Kraemer, 'The Hypnotic Literary Genre' (2009).

7   For an overview of this see Uzendoski & Calapucha-Tapuy, *The Ecology of
      the Spoken Word* (2012), p.2, p.4; See also: Bauman, *Verbal Art as Perfor-
      mance* (1977); Tedlock, *The Spoken Word and the Work of Interpretation* (1983).

8   Stern, 'The Formal Poetry Reading' (1991).

9   Rilke, 'Rome, December 23rd 1903' (1993).

10   This phrase originates in the classic work: Durkheim,
      The Elementary Forms of Religious Life (1920).

11   Fowler, 'The Anatomy of Joy' (2016).

12   Ehrenreich, *Dancing in the Streets* (2015).

13   Lucy English, email to Peter Bearder, 2 Dec. 2018.

14   Goodman, *Ecstasy, Ritual and Alternative Reality* (1988), p.35.

15   Ehrenreich, as above.

16   Bruce, 'The Sociology of Late Secularization' (2016).

17   Evans, 'Michael Curry's Royal Wedding Sermon Will Go down in
      History', 20 May 2018, https://www.theguardian.com/comment-
      isfree/2018/may/20/bishop-michael-curry-sermon-history-har-
      ry-meghan-wedding

18   Zumthor, *Oral Poetry* (1990), p.151.

19   Zumthor, as above, p.143.

20   Ehrenreich, as above.

21   James McKay and Keith Jarrett Interview, Stage Invasion, Vimeo,
      (00:49:45).

22   'Nat Nye - El Crisis – Performance', 14 Jan. 2017, https://www.youtube.
      com/watch?v=WavHElgpk20&t=1428s

23   'trespass': Thomas, 'Neon Griot' (1998), p.310; 'gets involved':

Zumthor, as above, p.66.

24   Area organiser of Glastonbury Festival's West Holts stage, John Kerridge, estimates the figure to be 20,000. John Kerridge, email to Peter Bearder, 28 Mar. 2019.

25   Tempest, 'People's Faces', 25 Jun. 2017, https://www.youtube.com/watch?v=CmHgQT9zP_c.

26   Marv Radio, email interview with Peter Bearder, 28 Nov. 2018.

27   Csikszentmihalyi, *Flow* (1990).

28   Thomason, Northern Arizona University, http://www.cuyamungueinstitute.com/articles-and-news/the-role-of-altered-states-of-consciousness-in-native-american-healing/

29   Thomason, as above.

30   Banks, 'From Homer to Hip Hop' (2010), p.244.

31   Penman & Becker, 'Religious Ecstatics "Deep Listeners," and Musical Emotion' (2009), p.50.

32   Penman & Becker, as above.

33   Silva, 'Live Writing' (2018), p.124.

34   Tempest, 'Live at Glastonbury, 28 Jun. 2017, (00:45:30), https://www.youtube.com/watch?v=mLzJUalxZYM

35   Welsh, 'Charm' (1993), p.183.

36   Tempest 'People's Faces', as above.

37   For a full exploration of performative utterances see: Austin, *How to do Things with Words* (1962).

38   Welsh, as above.

39   'verbal missiles' quoted in: Welsh, as above; for 'babylonian incantations' see Evans, 'Incantation' (1993), p.581.

40   Livingstone, 'Waking Hypnosis', http://www.hypnosis101.com/hypnosis-tips/waking-hypnosis.

41   Snyder & Shor, 'Trance-Inductive Poetry' (1983).

42   Snyder & Shor, as above, p.4.

43   This analogy taken from: Kraemer, 'The Hypnotic Literary Genre' (2009), p.10.

44   Hearne, 'A Comparison between the Concept of Western Hypnosis and African Trance' (2012), p.12.

45   Wheeler, *Voicing American Poetry* (2008), p.132.

46   Kraemer, as above, p.22.

47   Jah-Mir, email interview with Peter Bearder, 12 Feb. 2019.

48   Goodman, *Ecstasy, Ritual and Alternative Reality* (1988), p.47.

49   Rachel Rose Reid Interview, Stage Invasion, Vimeo, (01:00:00).

50   Tempest, 'End Times', 7 Dec. 2009, https://www.youtube.com/
        watch?v=jYMtmQ_H570&t=152s.

51   Snyder & Shor, as above, p.6.

52   Rossi, 'Mind/Body Communication and the New Language of
        Human Facilitation' (1987).

53   Quoted in: Hagedorn, '"From This One Song Alone, I Consider
        Him to be a Holy Man"' (2006), p.2.

54   Penman & Becker, as above, p.64.

55   Silva, as above, p.129.

56   This phrase is borrowed from: Karafistan, '"The Spirits Wouldn't
        Let Me Be Anything Else"' (2003), p.162.

57   Berman, *The Reenchantment of the World* (1981), p.279.

58   Brennan, *The Transmission of Affect* (2004), p159.

59   Henriques, 'The Vibrations of Affect' (2010), p.67.

Chapter 8:
Poetry, Protest & Political Renewal

'Culture unites us, it's what makes us human. It is a sacred space
for resistance, the basis of resistance. Culture feeds hope.
That's why they attack it, and that's why we must defend it.'
—Berenice Celeita, Colombian human rights defender

'It is not enough to be like Wordsworth... poetic sensibility
to the death of the planet is not what we are striving for here.
What we are striving for is to halt, overturn and back out
of the impending death of the planet.'
—Terence McKenna

It is 2017, and I am with five thousand protestors from across Europe. We
are marching towards Europe's largest coal mine, Hambach Mine, Germany,
to occupy it and shut it down. In groups of between five hundred and a thousand, we progress out of the town, down country roads and over fields. People
are erupting in song, 'There's a hole in my planet, oh scheiße! oh scheiße!...'.
Drum rhythms, chants, and call-and-responses spread outwards.

The force of this cadence helps us break through lines of police armed
with batons and pepper spray. We descend into a lunar deathscape the size
of neighbouring Cologne (a city with a population of one million). Some of
us will make it onto the world's largest diggers, and the most destructive
machines humanity has created, the infamous Bagger 293s. Standing at 96
metres tall and 230 metres across, each one is the height of a small skyscraper
and consumes energy equivalent to a small town.

But we are not there yet. After thirty minutes of walking through the
mine, we arrive at a reformed line of cops. Our target—the Bagger—lies
no more than a hundred metres away. The police break into the crowd with
horses and assault protesters with pepper spray. Surrounded, the circle comes
together around the samba band, and we are kettled.

Kettles are a tactic used by police to detain protesters in an enclosed space.

Their purpose is to discourage and dehumanise protestors by denying them access to food, water, and toilet facilities for hours at a time. We have lost our freedom to move, and we are fast losing light and heat. People are using insulation blankets as makeshift urinals. Many feel shaken by the police incursions, and some are dealing with the sting of pepper spray. Everyone is tense and wondering what will happen next. This is not fun. This is not where we want to be. This is not winning. We have to do something drastic to turn this around. Given the circumstances, there is only one sensible thing we can do—a cabaret.

Introduction

We can't speak of poetic movements without speaking of their politics, and we can't speak of political movements without speaking of their poets. In one sense, spoken word *is* protest, from the Latin *protestari* (to give testimony). Spoken word artists are on picket lines, sit-ins, demos, and occupations. They are speaking on the radio and at conferences, and in pubs and basements. They are also eliciting stories in schools, workshops, and community centres. Broadly speaking, their work is to engineer what I once heard MC Angel describe as 'moments of collective empathy'. Their means is that ancient and democratic tool of human action, the voice. As a social rhythm of events, spoken word gives us an expressive economy of profound political implication.

This chapter shows how spoken word is cultural equipment for progressive change. I will first examine how it contributes to the *carnivalesque* elements of activism, and how it can itself be a form of *non-violent civil disobedience.* Later, I will look beyond the poet to see how poetry cultivates 'radical friendship', the micro-bonds of empathy and trust at the heart of every social movement.[1] Finally, I will show how all this ties together to help propel movements for change in the cause of *political renewal.*

Part 1: What do we Want? When do we Want It?

Why Poetry?

Nothing is more political than the voice. In *Why Voice Matters*, Nick Couldry defines 'voice' as a political concept, namely 'the ability of people to give an account of themselves', both as a 'process' and something that has 'value'. The importance of voice is not just that people have one but that their testimonies have the power to make things change.[2]

In Germany, voice and vote are the same word. The act of bearing witness and telling one's story is at the heart of democracy, which is essentially a conversation and a contestation. For Jacques Rancière this process of representation is 'a way of framing, among sensory data, a specific sphere of experience'.[3] Poetry excels at this. It instantiates, it testifies, it is a 'conduit for social remembrance'.[4] Through our voice, we represent ourselves and our communities. By giving them shit, we hold those in power to account. By having our say, we get involved. These are the building blocks of democracy: Representation, Accountability and Participation. That, as they say, is a RAP.

Yet it is often claimed that poetry is above such matters. Quoting Auden's famous maxim ('poetry makes nothing happen'), James Fenton argues that poetry is about the 'individual conscience' and any idea that it can be useful to society is 'Stalinism's legacy'.[5] Explicitly conservative positions like this mingle with the implicitly conservative idea that poetry is a 'still, small voice' that belongs to solitude, meditation, and reflection. While it is undeniable that poetry can be at right angles to the 'clamorous' world of flashing screens and pop-up windows,[6] it can also be outspoken and visibly involved in the conversation of digital media and current affairs. Critic Dave Coates welcomes 'work that forcefully states a philosophical case for love and solidarity' in the context of 'a poetry culture in which "apolitical" lyric niceties tend to reap the greatest rewards'.[7] Maintaining the regime of 'apolitical niceties' is the mantra that poetry should strive to be '*affective* rather than *effective*', yet this should not blind us to the fact that it can be both. As I hope to demonstrate here, poetry loses much of its power if confined only to the private sphere of processing emotion.

Why Now?

Poetry in protest is not new. Most of the poets looked at in Chapter 3 and countless more that I am unable to chronicle here, have put themselves in political flashpoints at some time or another. Today, this tradition faces considerable challenges. With authoritarian governments casting a growing shadow over the continent there is a significant need to protect and enrich protest. Under expanded and misused 'anti-terror' legislation, peaceful protestors are increasingly becoming the victims of espionage, police brutality, and imprisonment.[8] In some parts of London (including near Parliament) you can be arrested, fined, and banned from the area for the crime of carrying a megaphone.[9] At the time of writing, three of my friends (the Fracking Three) are facing prison terms for climbing on top of stationary lorries that were headed for a fracking rig. Fifteen more (the #Stansted15) are facing possible life sentences under 'terrorism' charges for a peaceful protest to stop the deportation of asylum seekers.

All of this impacts free speech more generally. Under the same 'terror' legislation, careless words of dissent can be interpreted as the 'encouragement' or 'glorification' of terror. The UK's Investigatory Powers Act 2016 (the 'Snoopers' Charter') demolished processes of prior approval that once stood in the way of the government spying on our telecom and internet use.[10] What's more, Brexit looks set to further reduce our human and civil rights protection.[11] A 2018 report by the UK civil liberties group Big Brother Watch warns that 'the state is building the most totalitarian style surveillance regime of any democracy in history.'[12] It is not without reason that Wikileaks founder Julian Assange calls this generation 'the last free generation'.[13]

And yet there is so much to speak out about, from the growth of fascism or migration caused by war and economic devastation, to the evisceration of public assets, spiralling inequality, and ecological collapse. It would be senseless for any artist not to consider the role of their work in the face of these approaching tsunamis.

Why 'Protest'?

Much of the writing on political spoken word has been centred on *identity politics* (including matters of ethnicity, gender, class, and sexuality). Most of it has been written in the US where (much like the UK) spoken word has served as a tool for cross-cultural communication in a multiracial, and often very fractured, society. A majority of the commentary, however, focuses on political spoken word as it appears in poetry events[14] or educational settings.[15] This chapter will look at spoken word as it appears *outside* the spoken word night, mixing with speeches, chanting, and dancing, as well as in 'direct actions' like sit-ins, occupations, and picket lines.[16]

Part 2: Arrest that Poet!

It's March 2011, and Oxford-based poet Danny Chivers walks through the doors of the high-end London grocers Fortnum & Mason with hundreds of other protesters. The chain store's parent company, Wittington Investments, have dodged around £10 million in tax at a time of savage cuts to essential public services. He recalls:

> Banners are waving, people are chanting 'pay your taxes', slogans are strung around the stairwells. Staff watch in bemusement as protesters sit on the floor next to the £20,000 Fortnum's hampers and get their own home-made picnics out of their bags, or throw a beach-ball to each other over the display of chocolate bunnies, pausing to put back any that get knocked over.

'People of Britain!' Megaphone in hand, Chivers launches into a poem. The poem is delivered in the style of a public service broadcast that implores people to: 'try to keep an eye—OK, to spy—if you think your wealthy neighbours are tax-dodging on the sly.' He continues:

> Have you spotted the boss of Marks and Sparks
> sneaking out after dark to meet his accountant on
> a bench in the park?
>
> Have you figured out the whereabouts of Richard
> Branson's hidden ransoms, Murdoch's dirty
> stocks or Lord Ashcroft's cash loft?
>
> Has your future been nicked by some comfortable craven
> Relaxed on his back in a sunny tax haven
> On a luxury, tax-free plush sun lounger?
> Don't take this lying down: shop a corporate scrounger.

The poem implores the listeners to take action, recalling the message of 'a friend who was sat on the floor of a Vodafone store, tax demand in her hand, banners blocking the door':

> [...]
> We just can't ignore all this stuff anymore
> Let's cash in our passion, not hold it offshore
> Drag them out of their loopholes, lay their assets bare
> And calmly demand that they pay their fair share
> Till the case for the cuts melts away in the air.[17]

Shortly after Chivers's performance, 145 peaceful protesters were mass-arrested in a staggering act of police repression.[18] Since the arrestees were too numerous to fit in the courtroom, fourteen of the more visible participants were singled out, and ten were charged with 'aggravated trespass'. Chivers was one of them. The judge pointed to CCTV footage of him reciting a poem 'in a ranting and polemic style', and he was fined £2,300. In Chivers's words: 'I've done some badly paid gigs in my time, but that one's going to be pretty hard to beat.'[19]

One way to view this 'sub*versive* incident' (sorry) is as an artistic embellishment to the protest, but I would instead see it as *part* of the protest, on a continuum of verbal creativity that includes press releases, banners, leaflets, songs, and chants. Much of activism and campaigning revolves around 'getting your message out'. In 'direct actions' such as the above, the emphasis is more on *deeds* than *words*, yet the occupation was a 'symbolic action' as it is known in activism; a way of speaking that we turn to when the conversation of conventional politics fails us. Symbolic actions occupy the discussion, centring it on voices that have been left out (in this case a generation who have had their future stolen by bank bailouts and tax evasion). Like a protestor speaking to camera while their head is fastened to the gate with a bicycle D-lock, Chivers's poem is simultaneously an action, a testimony, a factual broadcast, and a campaign statement.

The potency of this dissent comes from its audacity. Through disobedience, it challenges what Rancière called the 'distribution of the sensible'. By 'sensible' Rancière refers to what the authorities decree as 'reasonable' political expression, carried out in an 'appropriate' place.[20] Performing a poem in a 'ranting and polemic style' is fine if you do it among yourselves. Do it on the shop floor of a tax-evading multinational corporation and you are breaking the law.

*

In a world of rapacious privatisations, closures, and evictions, there is now a spatial imperative to all protest. In the words of Allon White, 'the history of political struggles has been the history of the attempts to control significant sites of assembly and spaces of discourse.'[21] Nowhere is this truer than in the protest camps of the Occupy movement, which sprang up in fifteen-hundred cities across seventy countries in 2011. Ordinary people set the agenda of the national discussion, alerting millions to a popular critique of capitalism and inserting terms like 'the one per cent' and 'the ninety-nine percent' into the language of politics.

Poets like Cat Brogan and I lived in Occupy London camps outside St Paul's Cathedral, the London Stock Exchange and the offices of Bloomberg financial news service. The camps were awash with spoken word performances and in the opening weeks, performances were happening daily. This is not a comprehensive list, but I remember seeing performances from David Lee Morgan, Deanna Rodger, Sam Berkson, Stephanie Dogfoot, Loudspeaka, Dennis the Menace, Dizraeli, Danny 'the ranting and polemical' Chivers, Attila the Stockbroker and Thick Richard (and yes, half of us had silly names). At its best, Occupy was an Athenian agora of ideas, testimonies, and newly forged friendships. Armed only with polythene tents and a propensity to be outspoken in places of embarrassment to political and business elites, the camps were evicted (and often brutally) by police. Political philosopher David Graeber later concluded that their greatest crime was to be an 'outbreak of democracy'.[22]

Spoken word artists (or 'professional gobshites' as James McKay prefers) are often on the mic or the megaphone at protests.[23] Their poems intersect with call-and-response chanting (antiphonal poetry), as well as speeches and announcements. Amid extremes of tension and revelry, 'crowd control' can be construed as 'incitement' and poets are frequently singled out as 'ring leaders' by police. I personally know many who have been targeted by police surveillance and the cameras of Forward Intelligence Teams. While at Occupy London, an activist legal observer alerted me to my repeated appearance (megaphone in hand) on video footage that was being presented in court. In countries with more precarious human rights, it is easy to see how politically-inflected poetry can be deemed 'illegal'. 'Resist my people, resist them,' wrote Palestinian poet Dareen Tatour in a poem she posted on Facebook. She was sentenced to five months in jail for 'incitement to terrorism'.[24]

In short, spoken word adapts well to the accelerated spontaneity and action of protest. Sometimes it even qualifies as *nonviolent civil disobedience*, a *direct action* that looks beyond voting and letter writing to make head-on, and often physical, interventions in the course of human affairs. Like all forms of 'improper' political expression, it can become arrestable. Though this is rarely the intention of poets, it does evidence an ability (and a willingness) to use live poetry to confront and mobilise power.

Part 3: Spoken Word as Riotous Joy

The Coal Mine Cabaret that we landed in at the beginning of this chapter has begun. Data on this artistic practice is scarce, but we suspect it may be a world first. We start with some audience participation (call-and-response, silly noises etc.), then some poetry. 'Up next' is Bee Powers with a high-octane poem-protest-chant hurled at volume to a line of amused (and slightly confused) German protesters whose arms are linked to block police:

> We came here to undo the tragic mistakes
> Of the twin institutions of capital and state
> They pinned down the routes that the radicals take
> Jackboots on the rooftops with canisters of mace.
> Capsicum in faces, vans full of police dogs
> I am the Lorax, listen when the trees talk
> Roots crack through the tarmac where my feet walk [...]

For all the criticisms of 'ranting poetry',[25] we should credit this poem for capturing the spirit and textures of the event ('capsicum' and 'mace' refers to the chemical weaponry used by police). Though it's unlikely to go down well at a literary festival, the poem's defiant indignation is as legitimate an emotion as any for 'collective empathy'. As the poem ends, it merges with an internationally recognised protest chant:

> my mother said I could change the system from
> the inside I took it literally to mean the innards
> of a coal mine chillin on a digger in the middle
> of a blizzard
> A! - ANTI! ANTICAPITALISTA! [26]

Powers then returns to help protesters hold out against the police. I later found out he was dragged into a police van minutes after performing the poem. Rock 'n' roll? [27]

Oblivious, the cabaret continues with a dance-off and some group songs (including a four-part chorus of the Amy Winehouse classic 'they tried to dig another coal mine, but I said no, no, no').

The resident samba band headlines the show with a priceless two-hundred-person 'keep it in the ground' Coal Mine Conga.

A cabaret makes perfect sense in the expressive fluidity of protest and this is a kettle mobilising for its own entertainment. Energised with music, the kettle becomes a dance of particles and phonemes colliding into songs, jokes, and hugs. When the police finally let us go, we sing our way out of the mine.

I am reminded at the Coal Mine Cabaret that kettles are opportunities for movement building, gifted to us by the oppressive apparatus of the state. I once saw a Clown Army troupe at an anti-austerity demo (in 2012) bring a kettle to boil with singing, improvisation, and a few group games. When the police finally opened up the kettle, people refused to leave. At moments like these, both 'artist and audience regain a potency of creation and action that is denied to them by official society.'[28] Poetry becomes *voice* in the shadow of two-party 'austerity' politics, a means to subvert police repression and a catalyst for collective joy. As the poet James White writes, sometimes 'the only courage is joy', because the world so often conspires against it.[29]

In Chile, Adrienne Rich found 'radical happiness' at mass poetry festivals at the time of the arrest of the former dictator Augusto Pinochet. Lynne Segal uses this phrase as the title for her book, *Radical Happiness: Moments of Collective Joy*, in which she outlines the political ramifications of Durkheim's 'collective effervescence', where *carnivalesque* activities create contagions of hope and revelrous disobedience.[30] Segal builds on the work of Max Weber who, over a century ago, argued that capitalism leads to the individualisation of pathology.[31] Today this self-medication lives on in an epidemic of binge eating, a 'self-improvement industry' of relaxation therapies and personal development books, and a tsunami of pharmaceutical pellets; just some of many social sedatives to be found in a growing market of 'privatised stress'.[32]

Through public revelry, spoken word helps to cultivate a collective form of political expression. Its hallmark physicality speaks to the physical release of demos and actions, where spontaneous ecstatic participation is never far from the surface.

Carnival, that age-old dynamo of subversion, is a natural home for poetry, an arena where protest and poetry can expand their creative potency.

Part 4: 'Onstage. Without Permission. In Iambic Pentameter.'

Poetic acts of protest and mischief are not always surrounded by riot police and samba bands. Let's take a look at how this creative potency can spill into the halls of 'high culture'.

It is 23 April 2012, and the curtain is about to rise on *The Tempest*. It is being performed by the Royal Shakespeare Company (RSC) at its Stratford-upon-Avon theatre for the World Shakespeare Festival. A packed auditorium of theatregoers is rustling and whispering in hushed expectancy. Just seconds before the opening scene is due to commence, two uninvited 'actorvists' climb onstage in full Shakespearean attire. Helpless, the production and theatre staff exchange confused glances. The audience thinks the action has begun, and it has.

In the preceding weeks these 'anarcho-thespians' had scripted and rehearsed their performance. They even carried out a reconnaissance mission ('surely the most civilised in direct action history') which involved visiting a Shakespeare play to assess lighting, potential entry points and the position of staff and security.[33]

Their target is the petroleum giant BP who are sponsoring the festival and plastering their logo across its theatres and publicity materials. This sponsorship is an example of what is known as 'greenwashing' or 'artwashing', a tactic of hijacking the publicity of cultural institutions to legitimise a company's actions.[34] BP (whose slogan is 'Fuelling the Future') is one of the world's most destructive companies, and their sponsorship of repressive regimes in the pursuit of fossil fuels is creating ecological disfigurement and human dystopia for billions. BP is responsible for the worst environmental disaster in history (the Deepwater Horizon oil spill in the Gulf of Mexico) and is prospecting for further drilling in the fragile ecology of the Arctic. While working as a human rights observer in 2007,

I helped take testimonies from scared and grieving Colombians who were affected by BP's activities in the oil region of Casanare, Colombia. Their loved ones were just some of the twelve thousand people who were tortured, murdered, or disappeared in BP-sponsored violence against trade unionists and local residents.[35]

The Tempest has begun. The two guerrilla poets (Richard Howlett and Miranda Shaw) throw off long coats to reveal their Jacobean finery and launch into their poem:

> What country, friends, is this? [raises programme]
> Where the words of our most prized poet
> Can be bought to beautify a patron
> So unnatural as British Petroleum?
>
> Strange association! [Performer One unveils image
> of BP's Deepwater Horizon drilling disaster]
> They, who have incensed the seas and shores
> From a dark deepwater horizon
>
> Who have unleashed most foul destruction
> [Performer One unveils image of tar sands]
> Upon far Canada's aged forests,
> Clawing out the lungs of our sickening earth
>
> Who even now would bespoil the high, white Arctic
> [Performer One unveils image of untarnished Arctic]
> In desperate search of more black gold
> To make them ever richer.
> These savage villains!
>
> And yet –
>
> They wear a painted face of bright green leaves,
> Mask themselves with sunshine.
> And with fine deceitful words
> They steal into our theatres, and our minds.
> They would have us sleep.

But this great globe of ours is such stuff as
dreams are made on.
Most delicate, wondrous, to be nurtured
For our children and theirs beyond.

Let not BP turn these dreams to nightmares.

Fuelling the Future?
Thou liest malignant thing!
[holding up programme, looking at back page]
Do we sleep? I find not myself disposed to sleep.

Let us break their staff that would bewitch us!
Out damned logo! [rips out logo from programme]

[Audience starts to applaud]

As the poem concludes, many in the audience start to tear the BP logo from their programmes. The performers leave to be interviewed by local TV while others hand out leaflets to (and collect torn out logos from) departing theatregoers.

Reclaim Shakespeare's merry band of players went on to do a further eight performances during the festival, causing a storm in the press and on social media. During one stage invasion, a (legitimate) actor stepped in to prevent security from dragging them off stage. He later tweeted his support for the action during the interval backstage. The shamed RSC later dropped the sponsorship for their plays, though BP does still fund tickets for 16–25-year-olds (for now).[36]

Energised by their positive reception, Reclaim Shakespeare morphed into 'BP or Not BP'. The guerrilla theatre company that has, to date, staged seven years of interventions against BP sponsorship in some of Britain's most cherished cultural institutions: the British Museum, National Portrait Gallery, Royal Opera House and the Tate. Increasingly ambitious productions have involved elaborate props such as giant cardboard ships or fifty-metre oil slicks made of black fabric. They have commanded large casts, hundreds of participants, and audiences of many thousands. Through poetry and theatrics, they have achieved what often seems impossible—making activism fun. The 'part campaign group, part theatre troupe' have managed to combat activist 'burnout' and birth many new friendships.[37]

Part 5: Word is Bond, Community is Political

It is to these communities that I will now turn. Irina Garbatzky describes spoken word as a 'relational aesthetic', a medium for the circulation of ideas, feelings, and shared experiences.[38] This section will look at how poetry can occupy and hold space, and then galvanise the people inside it.

Two days after the re-election of the Tory Government in May 2015, a lively and unplanned demonstration poured onto the streets of central London. By late afternoon, two hundred of us were kettled (you can see a pattern emerging here) outside Downing Street. Once the jamming, singing, and chanting had petered out, people seemed impatient and frustrated at being detained. Then some poets started performing. Their words drew a crowd of disparate conversations into a unified body of feeling and soon everyone was taking part. We passed the mic and invited others to share their experiences. The average age in the kettle must have been only 21, and most were speaking in public for the first time. A nurse explained that funding cuts were turning her hospital into a dangerous farce. A girl of 14 spoke about her fears for the future, then a girl of 7 spoke while perched on the shoulders of her father. I don't remember what they said, but I remember being deeply moved. I wasn't alone, as the child spoke, a police officer wiped away a tear. The kettle burnt itself indelibly onto the emotional memory of all inside it. 'This has been one of the best days of my life,' an 18-year-old told me as we left the kettle. It was his first ever demo.

Live performance is a petri dish of human solidarity. This is true of the demo as it is with longer-term protests like university occupations, camps, or strike actions. In the context of exhaustion, mental health issues, and police violence, a simple stage made of pallets can give a much-needed release. In recognition of this, Danny Chivers took his 2015 spoken word show *Arrest that Poet* around fracking sites, squats, and social centres to tell the story of his 'ranting and polemical' mischief and other misdemeanours.

In an interview at Preston New Road fracking site, York-based poet Henry Raby told me that his job is often to celebrate embattled social struggles: 'Sometimes we just need something to tell us, actually *yeah*, we're not wrong.'[39] Poets often find themselves 'preaching to the choir' at protests, but this shouldn't be dismissed out of hand. As David Lee Morgan puts it:

> Why the fuck not preach to the choir? Are they saved already and they don't need to hear anything more? But also, it's not about preaching to the choir, it's about singing to them and *with* them.[40]

In a later conversation, Morgan added that it's also important to 'challenge the choir' and question their assumptions. To quote James Baldwin: 'The role of the artist is exactly the same as the role of the lover. If I love you, I have to make you conscious of the things you don't see.'[41]

Even when it doesn't celebrate or challenge, this love is still a political act. Poet Tim Wells set up the Picket Line Poets in London to mobilise poetic solidarity for striking workers. 'Poets would say, "well I don't have any political material"' he explained, 'I tell em' "It doesn't matter, what is important is *where* you are, and *who* you are with."'[42]

Society is fast losing spaces where it can *be*. At the time of writing, predatory real estate practices and bank bailouts are making casualties of community centres, venues, and libraries. The housing crisis is dislocating families and entire neighbourhoods. Along with other social problems like unemployment, increased childcare costs, and poverty among the elderly, many are caught in a toxic mix of *social exclusion* and *social isolation*.

Research published in 2009 found Britain to be 'the most individualistic society in the world.'[43] Another study in 2014 found us to be 'Europe's most lonely country'. Both reports link these findings with high levels of unhappiness and ill health.[44] Isolation increases our risk of mortality by 26 per cent[45] and is now a public health risk on a par with substance abuse and obesity. Those who suffer loneliness are 'more likely to have poor physical and mental health outcomes, including increased propensity to depression, sleep deprivation, problems with the cardiovascular and immune systems, early morbidity and even dementia.'[46] Today, perhaps more than ever, spoken word (and protest) have vital work to do.

Live poetry and protest actions are not, however, a panacea to loneliness. Just because people are not *alone*, this does not mean they are not *lonely*. The poet who is performing, for example, may well be developing their self-esteem and social support network, but the audience who are passively listening to the 'gobshite' on the mic may be withering from within. Even the speaker may not feel a genuine and intimate connection with the people applauding them.

Poetry and protest are, however, steps in the right direction. In reclaiming space, and repurposing it for creative participation, protest builds the *social capital* looked at in Chapter 4. In a 2018 bid to reduce pressure on health services, Prime Minister Theresa May vowed to roll out 'social prescribing', a low cost non-drug referral for patients to participate in communities (like art or gardening groups) to aid their health.[47] Indeed, mental health patients are being prescribed spoken word workshops in the West Country as part of a scheme run by Take Art.[48] If any readers of this book feel isolated or unwell, they may also consider joining an activist community to fight the savage cuts to the National Health Service (or the arts).

In summary, spoken word serves as a catalyst for *social-* movements to metabolise and grow. It can reclaim space, create moments of togetherness and generate 'radical friendship' to energise, motivate and heal. In short, spoken word *is* activism.

Part 6: The 'Emotional Mechanisms' of Protest

If poetry is a social glue, how does it succeed in holding us together? Let's now look at some examples of spoken word that use 'emotional mechanisms' to create 'moments of collective empathy' in spaces of protest.[49]

On 2 August 2014, hundreds of activists under the banner of Reclaim the Power arrived in rural Sussex for 'The Battle of Balcombe'. They came in solidarity with a blockade of hundreds more who were already camped outside the fracking rig being constructed by oil and gas company Cuadrilla Resources. It was a momentous weekend for the climate movement. Lines of activists, including many local, elderly, and even Conservative-voting residents, held off police incursions with lines of locked arms. Behind them, hundreds more activists were sat on the floor with linked arms to block lorries from entering the site. Among those arrested for doing this was the MP and sometime-leader of the Green Party, Caroline Lucas.

By evening, those working on the fracking site had left. A 'surreal stalemate' took hold of the camp between the 'protectors' (protestors) and the police.[50] As night fell, we gathered for a poetry open mic in a large canvas tent. After sharing a couple of poems, someone shouted up to me from the audience 'What are we doing in here?! Let's go and tell it to the police!' Everyone cheered and within minutes we re-formed at the gate of the fracking rig just metres away from the camp. Singer-songwriter Alex Etchart recalls what happened next:

> It was unanimous, we all walked out to face the nightly guard - a semi-circle of police officers holding the main gates of the fracking site... As we mirrored their semi-circle, they tensed, expecting a late night action. Instead, the two sides joined, forming a full circle...Together we generated a powerful, mystical space.

Etchart pierced the stand-off by delivering 'Remembering' (a poem written by the radical theatre maker Siobhán Knox) into the stiffened gaze of the dimly-lit police:

> I want to cry in front of you. I want to reach into
> your stomach and grab onto that uncomfortable

awkwardness that's grown inside you like a fungus
and rip it out from the root...inverting you inside out
explosion...you...firework screaming frenzy.

I want to take all of your insecurities and pain...
mix them with mine and turn it into a cocktail we
drink together [...] get wrecked on weeping, confess
ourselves to each other, hide away in fear, come back
round full circle to each other's arms. Hold. Have.
Love.

[...]

I DON'T want these clinical cliché cardboard cut-
outs of beauty that you tell me I should desire.

I don't want fleeting, greeting, gratuitous grunts of
gorgeousness.

I want you to see me as ugly

and I want you to LOVE it

I want to make love to the worst of you

Mid-poem, a 16-year-old kid in the crowd started to cry 'the
kind of sobs you can't control the volume or intensity of...cut-
ting through the poem, piercing the night'. The weeping was not,
says Etchart, brought on by a specific lyric, but by the sight of
activists offering their tenderness to 'these scared, paralysed
police officers'.

[...]
I want YOU.
I want you with me right now, I want us naked and
pure.
I want us stripped of uniform.

Uniform.

> I uniform me into sexy lady
> You uniform you into business suitsI uniform me into
> conscious hippy
> You uniform collars and truncheons and boots

As the poem climaxed 'the police officers' eyes became rab-bits-in-the-headlights' who were no longer able to maintain the 'awkward banter to disbelieve' and 'dispel' what was happening. Soon a couple of coppers began to cry, Etchart recalls. 'It was a haunting moment.'

> WE are a fucking comet with a face attached
> hurtling through infinity on FIRE

> WE need to stop pretending we are all strangers
> and start remembering that we are old friends.

By deploying the chemical weaponry of affect, Knox's poem made it impossible for the activists to be dismissed and pigeon-holed by the police. The officers appeared punctured and dis-armed by the event, dropping the 'emotional shields' and ad-versarial facades that had enabled them to commit so many dehumanising acts of brutality against the protesters. While Etchart doesn't hold the police to be entirely blameless and mis-guided, he does maintain that, that night, poetry 'transcended uniform'.[51]

Events like this give a new angle to what Julie Schmid calls the 'empathetic alliances' of spoken word.[52] Though rare, such alliances can prove pivotal. During the Arab Spring in 2011, officers of the Egyptian Army refused orders from dictator Hosni Mubarak to fire on protesters. This act of sympathy was a turning point that led to the collapse of the regime.[53] It is noteworthy that live poetry and music played a big role in the expression of dissent and solidarity that occupied Cairo's Tahrir Square and won global attention and sympathy.

Waist-deep in action, Knox's poem also defies the stereotype of 'navel gazing' poetry. Some researchers in the field of *poetry therapy* conclude that intensely personal poetry can be a barrier to group cohesion because it 'ignores important aspects of the world beyond the poet's doorstep.'[54] However, a rejection of poetry that 'remains cloistered in the prison of self'[55] risks implying that certain subject matters have no place in group processes like a protest. In practice, of course, all emotions are valid catalysts for 'collective empathy.'

*

We can see this in David Lee Morgan's performance in March 2018 at a people's blockade of the Preston New Road fracking site in Lancashire. The event was a carnival of speakers, poets, live music, and dance-offs. Halfway through a tag-team poetic interlude of doggerel, laughter, and call-and-response, Morgan brought the protest to silence with 'The Gift of Pain':

> [...]
> I am strong because I am weak, because I can be hurt
> Because I can give myself without reserve
> Holding nothing back, not even dignity or pride
> Because I can love, no matter what the cost
>
> If anyone ever reads this
> And feels a stab of recognition
> Listen to me
> You are powerful in ways
> that many can only dream of
> A path is open for you
> You are part of a communion of lost souls
> Who can find their way to a light that will shine
>
> only for those blinded by pain
> Welcome
> [...] [56]

Soft in volume and intensely personal, the poem bought many to tears, but it didn't come across as introspective. As is so often the case in spoken word, the piece speaks to the listener in a direct address. It was also amplified by a dodgy sound system on the side of an A Road to a crowd whose attention was flagging in the wind. Morgan enacted the poem with an intense physical poise that secured its connection with the audience. The performative poem, rather than that which we might associate with the reading or recital, seems better adapted to protest.

*

To further explore spoken word's 'emotional mechanisms' let's now turn to a poem performed by Kat François in October 2012 at a London demo for the United Family & Friends Campaign Against Deaths in Custody.

François starts by recounting how, as a young woman, she flagged down a police car shortly after being attacked by a drunken white male on the street. After misidentifying her as someone having a mental health issue (rather than as a victim of violence), the police brutalised her and took her to a mental health hospital to try and have her sectioned. François won a cheer from the audience when she explained that she successfully sued the police. This piece is called 'Does My Anger Scare You':

> Does my anger scare you?
> Does the darkness of my skin make you uncomfortable
> because of the safety of the whiteness that you sit in?
> Does the word comfort or protect, embrace or reject,
>
> Are you seen as an asset or a threat?
> [...]

François inhabits the 'angry black woman' stereotype and slings it back at the world in visceral detail:

> Does my anger scare you?
> Does my truth annoy and irritate you,
> that there are blacks dying with knees in their backs

and handcuffs round their wrists,
windpipes restricted and breath cut off,
lips turning blue, eyes bulging with fear and pain?
Does it make you shift in your seat,
the thought of flesh and feet
of fingers gnarled and desperate
trying so frantically to get free.

Or does it make you want to say
She's so aggressive. Her demeanour's so harsh
If I had to face that I would respect how the police behaved.

When I first saw her perform it, years earlier, I was deeply moved by the poem which succeeded in confronting and implicating my privilege. It is hard to imagine another scenario where François could say these things to an audience of white people in a way that could win her applause. She weaponised her anger by aestheticising it into something that was simultaneously disturbing and compelling. This time her voice is louder, her pace quicker, and her body more animated:

[…]

Yes, I'm meant to make you feel uncomfortable
I'm meant to make you squirm
I'm meant to make your stomach burn
I'm meant to make your conscience turn
I'm meant to make you cry, and I'm meant to make
you ask *why*.

The poem goes on to to invoke some of the 162 British BAME men and women who have died in police custody between 1990 and 2018 alone:[57]

[…]
Joy Gardner, killed July 1993.
In front of her 6-year-old son

> they wrapped their head and mouth
> in 13 feet of tape and placed her in a body bag
> complete with straps and chains.

Splicing factual material with the 'emotional mechanisms' of writing and performance, François creates different registers of experience. Indeed, art is often celebrated for its ability to synthesise facts with emotions. Julie Schmid points out that political spoken word is able to re-contextualise 'abstracted stats of headlines, talk shows, news items within life stories of individuals.'[58]

New research in *cognitive poetics* suggests that spoken word is particularly well placed to do this. In his study of rhetoric (persuasive speech), David Gruber shows how poetic devices (such as rhyme, metre, and figurative language) engage specialist areas of the brain, creating arousal in the listener and faster mental processing. The research draws on MRI scans of the brain, as well as *pupilometry* which detects emotional changes in listeners through fluctuations in their pupil size (see also Chapter 6, Part 5). Gruber notes that the study of rhetoric is moving away from the text towards the emotional impact of 'affective sounds' and 'the fluttering affects of bodies in environments swirling with rhetorical sounds'.[59] Strongly rhythmical, melodious, and physical, François brings performative powers of persuasion to the poem.

By the end of the piece François is half-singing, half-chanting 'how many more, how many many more / how many more how many many more'. The audience starts to sing along as the poem climbs across a fluid continuum of speaking, singing, shouting and crying—all valid forms of political (and poetical) expression.

On finishing the poem, she gives a near-tearful blessing to the victims' families in the audience:

> Guys, my heart goes out to you. I'm one of the lucky ones, I'm a survivor, I'm here. It can happen to anyone. Even I was a girl, it happened to me. Its something I find *very* hard to talk about. But the Ring sisters I met em', and they just inspired me. God bless everyone who didn't make it. My mum could be here

today talking about me who died in police custody,
and she's not. And girls, I'm just *here* for you. I know
I've got a voice, and I've never felt confident enough
or strong enough to talk about this stuff. I'm here,
and I'm ready. Thank you.

One of the victims' family members runs over to François and
gives her a long, hard hug. The audience and the djembe erupts,
and the video ends.[60]

The role of the poem here is one of solidarity and *catharsis*—a
term Aristotle coined in his *Poetics* to describe the sense of
'release' we get from dramatic theatre. Central to modern
thinking of catharsis (as it appears in ritual or art) is the concept
of *aesthetic distance*.[61] Too little aesthetic distance and the poem
can re-traumatise, too much and it may fail to resonate and
elicit emotions that can be shared and released. 'Does My Anger
Scare You?' gets this balance right. It has enough detail to bring
police brutality to life ('lips turning blue, eyes bulging') but then
transforms this emotion through the release of collective singing:
('How many more, how many many more?'). At moments
like this 'artists go to work' writes Toni Morrison: 'There is no
time for despair, no place for self-pity, no need for silence, no
room for fear. We speak, we write, we do language. That is how
civilisations heal.'[62]

*

Let's now bring together 'Remembering', 'The Gift of Pain' and
'Does My Anger Scare You?' to evaluate the 'emotional mechanisms' of poetry in protest.

Through its emotional sleight of tongue, poetry creates
'moments of collective empathy' that can hold protest
communities together. Emotion is the sticky substance of poetry
and, as the above poems show, it can make almost anything
adhere. Both protesters and armed officers of state repression can
be made to 'remember' when they were made to *feel*.

The poems also show us that poetry can widen the *emotional
spectrum* of protest by taking us to unexpected (and arguably

'unnecessary') places that can be the most *felt* moments of a protest. Spoken word excels at public acts of emotion and vulnerability. Morgan was able to present the raucous crowd of protesters with the gift of pain because it was spun in the elevated language of verse. François made her audience feel uncomfortable through the theatricality of her witness.

These testimonies cut through the sober and rational world of broadsheet articles and political punditry and challenge the dismissal of emotions as 'narrowly subjective' or 'irrational'. Indeed, it is through 'emotional reasoning' that the *truth of feeling* is conveyed.[63] Heart-based 'radical empathy' transcends the 'reasonable' and 'sensible' logic of opinion and debate. As poet Maya Angelou put it, 'people will forget what you said, people will forget what you did, but people will never forget how you made them feel'.

Part 7: The Muscles of Courage and Political Renewal

So far we have seen how spoken word gives us a way to communicate politics and take action. We have seen how it can occupy space, create community, and beguile us with its emotional trickery. Let's now bring some of these arguments together to see how poetry can intervene in the popular conversation and feed the stories we live by.

For journalist George Monbiot, there is no time to waste. In the wake of environmental and economic plunder, the resurgence of European fascism and nuclear threats bandied by politicians in 140 characters on Twitter, the time is ripe for *political renewal*. This *renewal* argues Monbiot is about changing the stories that control us and prevent us from recognising our own power. The principal story of our times is that of *neoliberalism*, which he describes as a vicious ideology of competitiveness, individualism, and patriarchy.[64] In its place, he posits a *Politics of Belonging*, which speaks to the cooperative nature of humanity— that ancient urge we all hold for community, togetherness, and connection. The *Politics of Belonging* recognises our primal need for our voice to be valued in a 'vibrant participatory culture' founded on nurture: the circular, the peaceful, and the feminine.

*

It is 14 March 2018, the *Politics of Belonging* spill onto the streets of London and spoken word is right at the centre of it. A century after the success of the suffragettes, over ten thousand people gather for the rally of the Women's March in Trafalgar Square, London. As part of a string of VIP speakers, Salena Godden walks on stage wearing a sweater that reads 'The Good Immigrant'. 'There's a lot of you, there's only one of me,' she says with a slight quiver in her voice. There are some whoops and cheers, then a charged silence. Godden rolls up her sleeves. 'OK let's do this'…

> Courage is the muscle we use when we speak
> When we're being talked over and told we're
> too weak
>
> And when we get weary and when it gets tough
> It's our united courage that says enough is enough
>
> Courage is the muscle we work night and day
> To get equal rights to get equal pay
>
> Our blood is taxed our blood is shame
> Our blood fury unites us because we all bleed
> the same
>
> Courage is the muscle we flex when we must
> Courage is the muscle for truth and for trust
>
> And when we get weary we march side by side
> A hundred years we're still marching with courage
> and with pride.[65]

Her delivery is a boisterous dignity; slow, shuddering, and sonorous. The heavy rhythmic pulse of the piece marches defiantly through a history of resistance, toward a triumph as certain as each coming rhyme. The poem engenders ripples of appreciation as it echoes through the white granite of Trafalgar Square.

The event of 'Courage is a Muscle' is a microcosm of Monbiot's political renewal. With reference to the suffragettes and the struggles for 'equal rights' and 'equal pay', the protest is placed within a history of resistance. Defiantly hopeful, the poem offers a positive proposition of unity that combats the oppositional reaction of nationalism and misogyny. Godden's 'blood fury' isn't racially superior, but universal. Unlike the speeches before and after, her poem conveys no information but the *emotional truth* of the moment. As Monbiot points out:

> A string of facts, however well attested, will not correct or dislodge a powerful story. The only response it is likely to provoke is indignation: people often angrily deny facts that clash with the narrative 'truth' established in their minds.[66]

By resonating with the fundaments of human desire and need, 'Courage is a Muscle' is an *affective* as well as an aesthetic act of public ideology. Not only that, but it contributes to a pretty significant moment in history. In the world of 'protest', this qualifies as one of the larger crowds a single voice can address. Beyond the ten thousand in the crowd, hundreds of thousands more were reached online. The poem manages to articulate the sentiment of a movement and energises it at one of its most tangible moments of action and expression. It is what Foucault would call a 'political technology'.[67]

Summary

Spoken word and protest are two strands of the same DNA. Both deal in stories and seek to put these stories in places where they would not otherwise be. Both have a vibrant sense of urgency and disobedience. Both recognise that expression exists in a matrix of power whose rules should be broken. Both believe that society is our canvas and are willing to deploy creative energies to make 'injustice' visible, communities powerful, and resistance beautiful. Both have an appetite for collective joy.

Spoken word can be entertaining, theatrical, and moving. Through performance, it is alive to the presence and voices of other protesters and lives comfortably in the high frequencies of carnivalesque behaviour. It can occupy space, steal the show, make the news, and even get you arrested—all classic traditions of verbal artistry. Indeed, the 'high art' of poetry has an ancient longing for marker pens, megaphones, and stages made of pallets, and this 'equipment for living' is renewed by each successive social movement.

The politics of spoken word lie not just in *what* it does, but also in *how* it does it. This chapter has looked at rallies, blockades, occupations, demos (and kettles), as well as guerrilla theatre troupes. The *togetherness* they are founded on has far-reaching political implications. These are not just communities of politics, they are political *because* they are communities. If power rests on networks of relationships,[68] then spoken word's greatest gift may not be *to inform* so much as *to involve*. This not only generates power, but provides a remedy for the pathological individualism of modern life.

The principal method of involvement is 'emotional participation'. With this super-power, poetry helps steer the emotional trajectories of activism. We are, after all, not wholly rational creatures, but volatile chemical organisms. Anxious and fearful, we are easily programmed by evocations of nation, race, and belonging.[69] In this context, poetry is not at the fluffy edges of activism, but a weapon in a battleground of feelings. Consciously or otherwise, spoken word is in combat with the subliminal messages of every advert, headline, political broadcast, and meme.

Whether or not poets wear their politics with a capital or a lower case 'p', it is hard to extricate their work from the broader struggle for a more equitable and just world. When grants turn into bank bailouts, scholarships turn into lifelong debts, and visiting artists turn into empty chairs, it is not just poetry that is being silenced. This is as much about *power* as it is about creativity, and spoken word can enchant and galvanise both these things.

Notes

1   I first came across this brilliant concept years ago through John
     Jordan of CIRCA (Clandestine Insurgent Rebel Clown Army)
     and the Laboratory of Insurrectionary Imagination. It is unclear
     who coined the phrase, though it has been used by others including
     Christian religious organisations.

2   See Chapter 1 of Couldry, *Why Voice Matters* (2010).

3   Rancière, *The Politics of Aesthetics* (2006), p.10.

4   Osborne, "'Set in Stone'" (2011), p.199.

5   Fenton, 'A Voice of His Own', 3 Feb. 2007, https://www.
     theguardian.com/books/2007/feb/03/poetry.whauden

6   Parini, *Why Poetry Matters* (2008), ix.

7   Coates, 8 Feb. 2017, https://davepoems.wordpress.
     com/2017/02/08/kate-tempest-let-them-eat-chaos.

8   Swift, 'Whose Streets? The Clampdown on Popular Rights'
     (2017), p.13.

9   Liberty, 'Protest around Parliament', https://www.
     libertyhumanrights.org.uk/human-rights/free-speech-and-protest/
     protest/protest-around-parliament.

10   Travis, 30 Jan. 2018, https://www.theguardian.com/uk-
     news/2018/jan/30/uk-mass-digital-surveillance-regime-ruled-
     unlawful-appeal-ruling-snoopers-charter.

11   Liberty, https://www.libertyhumanrights.org.uk/human-rights/
     human-rights-uk-after-brexit.

12   Carlo & Krueckeberg, 24 Sept. 2018, https://bigbrotherwatch.
     org.uk/wp-content/uploads/2018/09/The-State-of-Surveillance-
     in-2018.pdf, p.3.

13   Assange, "'This Generation Is the Last Free Generation'", https://
     www.youtube.com/watch?v=4vB05rZ6AMk&t=35s.

14   Some good texts on this are: Schmid, 'Performance, Poetics and
     Place' (2000); Somers-Willett, 'The Cultural Politics of Slam
     Poetry' (2009); Johnson, *Killing Poetry* (2017); and Fields, et al,
     'Youth Voices and Knowledges' (2014).

15   See Bearder, 'Liberating Tongues?' (2015); Burr, 'Springsteen,
     Spoken Word, and Social Justice' (2017); Camangian, 'Untempered
     Tongues' (2008); and Fiore, 'Pedagogy for Liberation' (2015).

16   A variety of texts on performance poetry in places of protest around the world can be found in Gräbner & Casas, *Performing Poetry* (2011).

17   Chivers, 'Shop a Scrounger', 2011, https://vimeo.com/17295443.

18   O'Hagan, 'The Fortnum & Mason Protest Verdict', 17 Nov. 2011, https://www.theguardian.com/commentisfree/2011/nov/17/fortnum-mason-verdict-uk-uncut-protesters.

19   Danny Chivers, unpublished text of stage show Arrest That Poet!

20   Cited in Burgum, *Occupying London* (2018), p.8.

21   Cited in Scott, *Domination and the Arts of Resistance* (1990), p.122.

22   Graeber, *The Democracy Project* (2014).

23   James McKay Interview, Stage Invasion, Vimeo, (00:20:30).

24   Al Jazeera, 31 Jul. 2018, https://www.aljazeera.com/news/2018/07/dareen-tatour-sentenced-months-prison-poem-180731084215893.html.

25   For more on the controversy of 'ranting poetry', see Damon, 'Was That "Different," "Dissident" or "Dissonant"?' (1998); and Blitefield, 'Populist Poetry or Rantum-Scantum' (2003).

26   Bee Powers, untitled and unpublished poem.

27   Getting dragged around by police is not big or clever. Poetry, on the other hand, is.

28   I have borrowed the phrase from Pijpers, 'Artimanha, the Precise Moment of Being' (2011) p.63, which looks at live poetry as it appeared in radical carnivals in Brazil during its dictatorship of the 1970s.

29   Quoted in Stein, *Poetry's Afterlife* (2010), p.37.

30   Segal, *Radical Happiness* (2017).

31   Novara Media, 11 Dec. 2017, https://novaramedia.com/2017/12/11/radical-happiness-lynne-segal.

32   Fisher, 'The Privatisation of Stress' (2011).

33   Howlett, 11 Jan. 2013, https://bp-or-not-bp.org/2013/01/11/how-we-reclaimed-the-bard-from-bp.

34   Contrary to what is often claimed, corporate sponsorship is not essential to the upkeep of artistic institutions. The British Museum and the Royal Opera House for example, get just 1% of their income from BP. As with the banning of tobacco sponsorship of events like the Grand Prix, events and institutions are able to continue without the sponsorship of individual companies. See BP

or Not BP, https://bp-or-not-bp.org/problems-with-bp.

35   BP or Not BP, as above.

36   Reclaim Shakespeare's stage invasions made literary history, appearing in the recent publication: Findlay, *Twelfth Night: A Critical Reader* (2013), p.7.

37   Howlett, as above.

38   Garbatzky, 'Roberto Echavarren's Atlantic Casino and Oír no es ver' (2011), p.182.

39   Henry Raby Interview, Stage Invasion, Vimeo, (00:01:50).

40   David Lee Morgan Interview, Indiefeed, 6 Jan. 2014. (00:07:30). http://indiefeedpp.libsyn.com/david-lee-morgan-music-by-michael-harding-east-market-capital-by-karl-marx-chapters-1-4-the-beast-speaks.

41   Cited in Popova, 'James Baldwin on the Creative Process and the Artist's Responsibility to Society', 20 Aug. 2014, https://www.brainpickings.org/2014/08/20/james-baldwin-the-creative-process.

42   Tim Wells Interview, Stage Invasion, Vimeo.

43   Alleyne, 6 Nov. 2009, https://www.telegraph.co.uk/news/science/science-news/6514956/Britains-me-culture-making-us-depressed.html.

44   Bingham, 18 Jun. 2014, https://www.telegraph.co.uk/lifestyle/wellbeing/10909524/Britain-the-loneliness-capital-of-Europe.html.

45   Harris, 30 Mar. 2015, https://www.independent.co.uk/life-style/health-and-families/features/the-loneliness-epidemic-more-connected-than-ever-but-feeling-more-alone-10143206.html.

46   Shorthouse, 26 Feb. 2014, https://www.theguardian.com/commentisfree/2014/feb/26/loneliness-signal-poverty-britain-iain-duncan-smith.

47   Marsh, 14 Oct. 2018, https://www.theguardian.com/society/2018/oct/14/loneliness-social-prescribing-theresa-may.

48   Take Art, 'Word/Play', https://takeart.org/word-play.

49   I have borrowed the phrase 'emotional mechanisms' from Cebreiro & Villar, 'Politics of Sound' (2011), p.117.

50   Alex Etchart email to Peter Bearder, 5 Dec. 2018.

51   Alex Etchart, as above.

52   Schmid, 'Performance, Poetics and Place' (2000), p.46.

53   BBC News, 31 Jan. 2011, https://www.bbc.co.uk/news/world-

middle-east-12330169.

54   Sontag & Graham cited in Bowman, 'Potential Misuses of Poetry Therapy' (2004), p.228.

55   As above.

56   Morgan, 'THE GIFT OF PAIN', 25 Dec. 2015, https://www. youtube.com/watch?v=liCARIpQk1o&feature=youtu.be.

57   People of colour who are forced or restrained in the custody of British police are over twice as likely to die than white people in the same situation. See INQUEST, 'BAME Deaths in Police Custody', Updated 10 Jan. 2019, https://www.inquest.org.uk/bame-deaths-in-police-custody.

58   Julie Schmid gives an excellent dissection of political spoken word and the 'poetic of witness' which uses 'testimonial form' to make affect dance with information, see chapter 'Hearing Between the Lines' of 'Performance, Poetics and Place' (2002),

59   Gruber, 'Suasive Speech' (2016), p.41.

60   François, 'Does My Anger Scare You', 31 Oct. 2012, https://www. youtube.com/watch?v=kCOWzMnA3EU.

61   Kirmayer, 'Cultural Psychiatry: Lecture #10 Healing, Ritual and Psychotherapy Pt 1', 19 Apr. 2013, (00:44:00). https://www. youtube.com/watch?v=JnxcMhH_-n4&t=4379s.

62   Morrison, 'No Place for Self-Pity, No Room for Fear', 23 Mar. 2015, https://www.thenation.com/article/no-place-self-pity-no-room-fear/.

63   These quotes are taken from Phil Mizen, who argues that the public emotions of the Occupy movement succeeded in infiltrating the national debate. See Mizen, 'The Madness that is the World' (2015).

64   Monbiot, *Out of the Wreckage* (2017).

65   Godden, 'Salena Godden | March 4 Women | "Courage Is A Muscle" | "Pessimism Is For Lightweights"', 16 Mar. 2018, https:// www.youtube.com/watch?v=wjTVyBcJR7I

66   Monbiot, 'How Do We Get out of This Mess?', 9 Sept. 2017, https://www.theguardian.com/books/2017/sep/09/george-monbiot-how-de-we-get-out-of-this-mess.

67   Foucault, 'Afterword by Michel Foucault: The Subject and Power' (1982), p.211.

68   Foucault, as above.

69   Ahmed, *Feel Your Way* (2014).

Conclusion

*'how people find their pleasure, entertainment and celebration
is how they find their sexual identity, their political courage
and their strength to change.'*
—Dave Randall

At the beginning of this book, I invited you to see yourself as part
of a democratic literary movement made up of audiences, artists,
and organisers. If you have seen yourself in this picture, then you
are in possession of a toolkit for cultural, spiritual, and political
renewal. Let's now bring these findings together to see how, in an
age of collapse, spoken word serves us as a *remedial aesthetic*.

*

In Chapter 1 we saw how play and collective joy can find a home
in poetry through slam. Slam is a way to bring people in, and,
through the ceremony of competition, empower them to con-
secrate art. By treating the crowd as if it matters, slam creates
'democracy' (and all the controversies that come with it). On the
other side of the mic, slam offers a rite of passage. It invites poets
to grow and gain credentials as performers in the volatile arena
of the live event.

It remains to be seen if slam will keep its current form, or if it
will spill into new formats, gimmicks, and poetic rituals. Slam is
now a mature and accepted part of poetry. Its challenge now is
to continue to bring new voices and audiences to the verbal arts,
and to avoid becoming the new normal. Whatever happens, the
ancient practice of live poetic contest is unlikely to disappear as it
is simply part of what humans do.

*

Given how central oral poetry has been (and still is) to humanity,
it is hard to account for the relative lack of attention has received
from academia. As we emerge from the page-centric poetic tra-

dition, a clearer picture of spoken word appears and it is possible to see it a distinct and categorisable sphere of artistry.

The audibility and visibility of the Spoken Word Renaissance returns us to the taproots of poetry—the social and the somatic. It is not composed of artefacts so much as people, places, and events. As such, it comes with a raft of values, beliefs, and practices, which are nothing if not communitarian and implicitly (if not explicitly) leftist.

Spoken word is also a mercurial entity. It absorbs the flow of rap, the banter of comedy, and the movement of theatre. This leaves us with an amorphous mass from which it is hard to reliably pin down many stylistic features. It is not 'slam poetry' but a large and evolving family of styles and techniques.

We now see a blurring of worlds: the wild and irreverent, and the quiet and reflective. Indeed, it may be that we are approaching a *post spoken word era*. With so many performers becoming central figures in the literary world, it is easier for those who identify with performance to own the name 'poet'. 'Poetry' is being remade. It is a matter of opinion as to whether this is a denigration, a maturation, or the 'revenge of the normal'.[1]

Things could also swing in the other direction. I have found considerable appetite in the UK live poetry circuit for a return to the cabaret experimentation of props, character poets, and comedic variety. People may well decide there is too much 'poetry' in spoken word.

In addition to these changes, new technologies, formats, and performance spaces are altering the way we interface with poetry. In a digitally mediated world, concepts like 'live' and 'performance' seem increasingly unstable.

As the art form grows, so too does its complexity and variety. The Spoken Word Renaissance is now at an intersection. Will the spoken word community provide a home to the avant-garde experimental fringes with which it has often shared a stage? Can the spirit of inclusion live alongside a growing desire to raise standards? Can spoken word be on TV adverts and still be countercultural?

*

Arguments over who gets to wear the beret are not new. The People's Republic of Poetry (as with The Kingdom) has always been disputed territory. The last two centuries alone have been a dynamic historical process of reconfiguring the poet's place in society. Successive movements have tried to permission new cultural influences from outside 'the canon' and 'high culture'.

Each of these movements has emerged from unique historical confluences. On the one hand, they were fed by evolving technologies and formats (like radio, vinyl, cabaret, and slam). On the other, they were fed by new people and ideas (through, for example, migration, postcolonialism and multiculturalism). The result each time has been a modern poetic sensibility that captures the language and the mood of its times. Spoken word is another exciting moment in history when a people's desire to express itself falls in love with an art form; the energy of life articulated anew.

Art forms, says Norman Finkelstein, are 'socially-inherited materials for reflecting reality'.[2] Yet these materials also change reality, and if we are talking words, we are talking power. For centuries, official culture has sought to suppress people by delegitimising their speech. For this reason, poetic movements have always shared chromosomes with social ones. You have to fight for your right to poetry. As a social algorithm of embodied testimonies, spoken word is one way we can do this.

*

Chapter 4 looked at spoken word as a form of *cultural renewal*; a grass-roots artistic practice that self-creates (auto-poetically) in the manner of a rhizome. Key to its success in doing this are its horizontal networks, not just of poets, but of 'poetry activists' generally. To repeat the words of slam founder Marc Smith 'slam is not about poets, it's about organisers'.[3] But it is also about audiences and the reviewers and bloggers who disseminate the art. The result is a cultural matrix, a dynamic flux of interactions. In the words of Ernst Fischer, art is 'commissioned by society',[4] and this is undoubtedly true of spoken word.

This process has enabled new voices to participate in the conversation, prompting some to call spoken word a 'devolution of poetry'.[5] Yet as spoken word grows in profile, it connects vertically to theatres, mainstream publishers, and broadcasting companies. It is still to be seen if spoken word will keep its current constellation and remain democratically controlled. However the scene organises itself, it faces considerable challenges. In the wake of cuts to public funding and the growing paywall that surrounds education, spoken word must find new ways to bring people into the conversation.

In Chapter 5 we examined the 'poem' as a *physical process*. Spoken word's focus on performance re-connects poetry to the articulatory power of movement, breath, and the spoken voice. What I call *biodynamic poetry* looks at the poem as a process of physical stimulus, charge, and expression. Spoken word incorporates this into the poem's design, allowing the text and the flesh to interanimate. Poetry here occupies a centre ground between the immaterial realm of language and the tangible body of the author. In this way, it achieves its authenticity. Spoken word, then, is a *somatic renegotiation of literature*. This is not just an artistic position but a philosophical one. In our high-tech society, many have argued we are in a state of 'tactile deprivation', ungrounded from physical sensation.[6] 'The body,' in the words of Morris Berman, 'is (literally) beneath our consideration.'[7]

Spoken word's recognition of the author's body also extends to those of the audience. In Chapter 6 we examined the live setting as a space of intersecting bodily rhythms. It is here, beyond the private communion of page and reader, that affect is circulated and amplified. Performer and audience are submerged in streams of non-verbal exchanges, and the craft of live poetry is to develop a literacy for these codes and harness them in the cause of emotional contagion.

As audience members, we are able to detect many of these techniques. We can see it in audience participation, banter, or the way the performer uses jokes to send us into collective spasms. Some will be less detectable, like the way a performer uses the music of their voice or well-timed pauses. Still harder to detect is the way the poem passes through us subconsciously. A poem can make our hearts race, our pores open, and our hair stand on end. It can even knock the air out of us. Subliminal though this may be, performers deserve credit for orchestrating these processes into their performances. Experienced performers are paying keen attention to interlocking rhythms: silence and noise, tension and release, suspense and surprise.

Yet live poetry cannot be controlled in the same way that a poem on the page can be. The performer is affected by the reflective consciousness of those around them, and the live setting is a field of electrochemical signals where we converse without taking. As laughter, noise, or even pheromones pass between us, we conspire (unwittingly) to support or deaden the performance.

The MC or performer can tune into this 'vibe' with a full-bodied, multi-sensory awareness and react to make the crowd more conductive. The intimate and highly personal setting of poetry is well lubricated for this. Poetry audiences are notoriously supportive and well versed in the skill of *transformational listening*. I believe this to be the result of a culture that has grown over time. While unconditional supportiveness should never come at the expense of discernment and criticism, this respect and empathy does deserve celebration.

*

The togetherness of spoken word also presents other opportunities. If we see audiences as *participants* in the poem, we can conceive of them as *filaments* that are connected by a trans-personal circuitry of energy. This has spiritual implications that invite us to understand spoken word as an 'implicit religion' (a secular activity that has religious qualities).[8]

Live poetry can induce semi-trance states that enable us to transcend individual and rational cognition to states of 'collective effervescence'[9] or hypnotic dissociation. Performance is right at the centre of this. The musical qualities of the voice can be used to create flow states in listeners, and the contours and connotations of the spoken voice can trigger feelings of ecstasy. Poets, then, are using frequencies to manipulate your brain and alter your consciousness.

*

I have closed the book by analysing how these 'techniques of controlled ecstasy'[10] can contribute to political renewal. We have seen how spoken word crosses over from the private and the self-reflective, to the rhetorical and the public. Often loud and theatrical, the art form is well suited to spaces of protest not always associated with poetry. In *carnivalesque* moments of riotous joy, spoken word becomes a form of creative disobedience (or non-violent direct action). In so doing, it counters what Bourdieu calls 'the intellectualist philosophy which makes language an instrument of understanding rather than an instrument of action (or power)'.[11]

It is not my intention here to instrumentalise spoken word as a mere tool of activism. In fact, much of what the art can offer social movements has less to do with *what* it does, and more with *how* it does. Spoken word is a social process that creates community and gives those communities a way to metabolise ideas and experiences. By interfacing testimonies and 'moments of collective empathy', spoken word energises social change.

Its success in doing this lies in the fact that it is (in one sense) a way to *aestheticise* our testimonies. Though it can convince, it's not just rhetoric; and though it can entertain, it's not just entertainment. It is art. Like all art forms, it has an armoury of techniques to beguile us into feeling and thinking simultaneously. These *feely-thinks* are the sticky substance of poetry and politics alike. With spoken word, we can weaponise information and affect in ways that can be applauded.

In the combative arena of activism, protest and civil disobedience, the human voice is weapon *par excellence.* It is low-tech, high-impact, widely available, and thousands can be used simultaneously (see the antiphonal poetry of call-and-response or the 'mass declamations' of the Popular Front). Conceptions of poetry as private and reflective deny the sermonic and collective-ecstatic tradition of oral poetry.

Given the scale of the challenges we face, there is no time to retreat into the inner sanctum. The coalescing tidal waves of social, political, and ecological collapse are bearing down on us. I believe spoken word can help. For a social movement to grow, it needs new—and preferably young—people. For them to join in sufficient numbers, they must be able to make friends and feel part of an exciting new vision of global change. Ideally, the movement should offer the opportunity for them to express themselves, sing, dance, laugh, and make noise. Spoken word lives comfortably alongside all of these activities.

*

It has been fascinating to investigate some of what can happen in the force field of the voice. The Spoken Word Renaissance looks to the audience with an accepting smile and in them recognises opportunity. In doing this, it returns poets to their role as orators, activists, and ecstatic preachers. This is a three-dimensional poetic, made not just of poetry, but the living fabric of culture; the heterogeneous flux of life. Dotted across the land, these nodes of empathy and creativity are part of society's immune system.

You don't have to be a poet or a poetry activist to be part of this movement. You only need to have been moved by it, whether inwardly (as an emotional transaction) or outwardly (as a social one). There is much to be excited about. Spoken word is not an emerging, marginal, or amateur practice, but a mature and complex cultural asset with its own canon and fields of expertise. My hope is that you feel it belongs to you. If it does not, then it may be time to remake it.

Notes

1   'revenge of the normal': Jem Rolls Interview, Stage Invasion, Vimeo.

2   Finkelstein, 'Art as Humanization' (1979).

3   'SlamCulture 2011 - Marc Smith Interview', 5 Apr. 2013,
        https://www.youtube.com/watch?v=MmH_ePoYCOM&t=2s.

4   Fischer, *The Necessity of Art* (2010), p.4.

5   Beasley, 'Performance Poetry or Sub-verse' (1999). See also: Pearce, Fowler
        & Crawshaw, *Postcolonial Manchester* (2013).

6   Fleming, *Surviving the Future* (2006), p.64.

7   Berman, *Coming to Our Senses* (1990), p.59.

8   Bailey, 'Implicit Religion' (2010).

9   Durkheim, *The Elementary Forms of Religious Life* (2012).

10   Karafistan, '"The Spirits Wouldn't Let Me Be Anything Else"' (2003), p.162.

11   Bourdieu, 'The Economics of Linguistic Exchange' (1997), p.647.

Appendix:
Hammer & Tongue National Slam Final, Royal Albert Hall, January 2018

The following statistics were gathered through observation, rather than by survey. Contestants were previous slam winners from around the UK including regional Hammer & Tongue events and slams hosted by other organisations. Each poem was considered against a range of writing and performance characteristics in order to illuminate different facets of what was performed.

These figures cannot be said to be representative of UK spoken word as a whole. Most 'established' spoken word artists did not take part in the competition. The event also may not represent Hammer & Tongue Slam Finals, since there is no data on previous years with which to compare it. Despite these limitations they provide an illuminating insight into how this slam, in practice, compared to both certain expected tropes of spoken word and oral poetry more broadly. For a complementary discussion of these themes see Chapter 2.

Writing

Rhyme: The largest category (41%) made 'no use of rhyme'. This figure is balanced at the other end of the spectrum with 'heavy, end-of-line rhymes' (37%). The remaining poems used 'sporadic, syncopated or internal rhyming' (17%), and 'occasional rhyming' (5%).

Metre: An overriding contingent (63%) had a 'heavy rhythmic structure' which would suggest an adherence to a metric structure of regular stressed and unstressed syllables. The rest leaned towards the natural rhythms of speech, with a quarter showing 'light' to 'medium' rhythmic characteristics, and 13% with none.

Prose: Around a quarter of all poems could be described as 'prose' as they were not densely packed with figurative language, rhyme, or predictable (or at least noticeable) metre. As performance poems, all were long-form (which is customary of three-minute slam poems and spoken word more generally). As such, they were less distilled than some might qualify as 'poetry'. It is, however, impossible to give a reliable definition of 'poetry' or 'prose' since conventions of identifying those categories rely on page-based definitions. In performance, it is impossible to see how form and lineation are used. What is more, the word 'poetry' itself is an unstable definition and changes throughout time and arena of discourse.

Repetition: Around 30% of poems had a medium-to-high amount of repetition, and around 16% of poems could be described as 'list poems' as this was their primary form.

Figurative Language: Imagery, metaphor, and simile were commonplace, with only 10% of poems making no use of them.

Narrative: I understood around 35% of poems in the competition to be principally 'stories', though what constitutes narrative is open to interpretation.

Characterisation: 20% of all poems inhabited the voice of a persona.

Biography: Around 50% of poems were explicitly about the poets' own lives or about friends and family (though this can be hard to gauge in fictionalised pieces).

Humour: 80% of poems made 'medium' to 'heavy' use of humour; that is to say that they had many jokes, or were primarily comic poems. This characteristic stood out most noticeably from all the data collected.

Subject Matter: A majority of the poetry was 'conscious' or political. For a full breakdown of subject matters see Chapter 2, Part 3.1.

Diction: The majority of the poems used accessible, everyday language.

Performance

Interaction: This was abandoned as a performance indicator since innumerable interactions appeared in a variety of ways (such as subtle facial gestures or pauses for laughter), as well as more apparent breaks in the poem to make asides to the audience. No poets used call and response, though one poet did get the audience to give a special laugh on the cue of a hand signal.

Vocal Performance: The overwhelming majority of poems (80%) made dynamic shifts between loud and soft for surprise and poetic effect, as well as significant musical patterning of stress and intonation. Of those delivered in a flat, monotone voice, many did so purposefully for dramatic effect. For more on prosody, see **Metre** above.

Without seeing the text of the pieces, it is impossible to know whether these performed characteristics relate to the poems as they were written down. This area of study deserves more attention, since many of these dynamics would be impossible to represent on the page, or would have to be represented in ways that diverge from the usual conventions on arranging verse as text. Though most attempts to transcribe vocal performance to the written word belong to the experimental fringes of sound poetry, Novak (2011) is one author who integrates phonetics into her study of performed poetry more generally.

Memorisation: Surprisingly, only 20% of pieces were committed to memory (this increased in the final qualifying rounds). For the majority of those read from the page, there was still a strong performance element and attention to delivery.

Physical Gestures: 27.8% of poems made heavy use of gestures, 40.8% made notable use, while a full 31.3% had almost no gestures, or restricted their gesticulation to the face. For a discussion on this see Chapter 5.

The Poets

Age: Since poets were not surveyed on their age, it is impossible to give a reliable third-party assessment. These estimates are based on my perception:

Teens:	9%
20s:	31%
30s:	31%
40s:	20%
50s and above:	8%

Gender: Since poets were not surveyed on their sex or gender, it is impossible to give a reliable third-party assessment. Based on my perception, 40–43% of the slammers presented as typically female and 57–60% presented as typically male, but this records perception only, and in particular does not account for gender non-conformity or non-binary and other genders.

Ethnicity: Since poets were not surveyed on their race or ethnicity, it is impossible to give a reliable third-party assessment. Based on the perception of the researcher, between 10–13% of competitors might be described as poets 'of colour' in the widely used sense of not belonging exclusively to white European heritage, but this records perception only. By way of context, government figures class 13% of the UK population belonging to a black, Asian, mixed or other non-white ethnic group.

Bibliography

A

Abrahams, R. D., '"Playing the Dozens"', *The Journal of American Folklore*, 75(297) (1962), 209–220.

Abram, D., *The Spell of the Sensuous: Perception and Language in a More-Than-Human World* (New York: Pantheon Books, 1996).

Ahearn, E. J., 'Toward a Model of Ecstatic Poetry: Coleridge's "Kubla Khan" and Rimbaud's "Villes I" and "Barbare"', *Modern Language Studies*, 12(3) (Summer 1982), 42–58.

Ahmed, S., *Feel Your Way: The Cultural Politics of Emotion* (2nd edn., Edinburgh: Edinburgh University Press, 2014).

Akbar-Williams, T., 'Poetry Jams', in Smith, C. J. (ed.), *Encyclopedia of African American Popular Culture* (Santa Barbara, CA: Greenwood Press, 2010).

Alexander, M., *Women in Romanticism: Mary Wollstonecraft, Dorothy Wordsworth and Mary Shelley* (Lanham, MD: Rowman & Littlefield, 1989).

Alvarez, N. & Mearns, J., 'The Benefits of Writing and Performing in the Spoken Word Community', *The Arts in Psychotherapy*, 41(3) (2014), 263–268.

Anderson, L., 'Uncomfortable Conversations in Black British Arts Practice Now – Who, Where, What, Why?' at *'On Whose Terms?': 10 YEARS ON… Critical Negotiations in Black British Literature and the Arts* (Goldsmiths University of London, 22 March 2018).

Andreasen, N. C., 'Creativity and Mental Illness: Prevalence Rates in Writers and their First-Degree Relatives', *American Journal of Psychiatry*, 144(10) (1987), 1288–1292.

Anonymous, 'In Memoriam: Keorapetse W. Kgositsile: Poet Laureate of South Africa', *The Journal of Pan African Studies*, 11/3 (2018), 1-3.

Appel, A., 'Nabokov's Puppet Show, Part II', *The New Republic* (21 January 1967).

Aptowicz, C. O., *Words in Your Face: A Guided Tour Through Twenty Years of the New York City Poetry Slam* (New York: Soft Skull Press, 2007).

Auslander, P., *Liveness: Performance in a Mediatized Culture* (2nd edn., London: Routledge, 2008).

Austin, J. L., *How to do Things with Words* (1962, Reprint, Cambridge, MA: Harvard University Press, 2005).

Avorgbedor, D. K., 'Freedom to Sing, License to Insult: The Influence of Haló Performance on Social Violence Among the Anlo Ewe', *Oral Tradition*, 9 (1994), 83–112.

A.W., 'To The Sons of Toil', *Northern Star and Leeds General Advertiser*, (3 April 1841), cited in Scheckner. P. (ed.), *An Anthology of Chartist Poetry: Poetry of the British Working Class 1830s–1850s* (Rutherford, NJ: Fairleigh Dickinson Univ Press, 1989), 88–89.

B

Bailey, E., 'Implicit Religion', *Religion*, 40 (2010), 271–278. doi:10.1016/j.religion.2010.07.002

Bakhtin, M. M., 'Discourse in the Novel' in Holquist, M. (ed.) & Emerson, C. (trans.), *The Dialogic Imagination: Four Essays* (New edn., Austin: University of Texas Press, 1982).

Banks, D., 'From Homer to Hip Hop: Orature and Griots, Ancient and Present', *The Classical World*, 103(2) (Winter 2010), 238–245.

Battle, J., *Free at Last?: Black America in the Twentieth-Century* (New Brunswick, NJ: Transaction Publishers, 2006).

Bauman, R., *Verbal Art as Performance* (Prospect Heights, IL: Waveland Press, 1977).

Bauman, R. & Briggs, C. L., 'Poetics and Performance as Critical Perspectives on Language and Social Life', *Annual Review of Anthropology*, 19 (1990), 59–88.

Bearder, P., 'Communities of Words: Developing Voices through Spoken Word Education', *Teaching English*, NATE, Issue 8 (2015), 53–56.

Bearder, P., 'Liberating Tongues?: A Theoretical Analysis of the Work of a full-time Embedded Spoken Word Educator in a Secondary School', *English in Education*, 49/3 (2015), 233–251.

Beasley, P., 'Performance Poetry or Sub-verse', in Munden, P. & Wade, S. (eds.), *Reading the Applause: Reflections on Performance Poetry by Various Artists* (York: Talking Shop, 1999).

Belle, F., 'The Poem Performed', *Oral Tradition*, 18(1) (2003), 14–15.

Bennett, A., 'Rappin' on the Tyne: White Hip Hop Culture in Northeast England – an Ethnographic Study', *The Sociological Review*, 47(1) (1999), 1–24.

Bennett, T., *Outside Literature* (Routledge, 1990).

Berman, M., *Coming to Our Senses: Body and Spirit in the Hidden History of the West* (London: Unwin, 1990).

Berman, M., *The Reenchantment of the World* (Ithaca, NY: Cornell University Press, 1981).

Bernstein, C. (ed.), *Close Listening: Poetry and the Performed Word* (New York: Oxford University Press, 1998).

Bernstein, C., 'Introduction', in Bernstein, C. (ed.), *Close Listening: Poetry and the Performed Word* (New York: Oxford University Press, 1998).

Bey, H., *The Temporary Autonomous Zone* (1991, Reprint, New York: Autonomedia, 2017).

Birkerts, S., *The Gutenberg Elegies: The Fate of Reading in an Electronic Age* (New York: Faber and Faber, 2006).

Blitefield, J., 'Populist Poetry or Rantum-Scantum? The Civil Disobedience of Poetry Slams', in Hauser, G. & Grim, A. (eds.), *Rhetorical Democracy: Discursive Practices of Civic Engagement* (London: Routledge, 2003).

Bolinger, D., *Language, the Loaded Weapon: The Use and Abuse of Language Today* (London: Longman, 2014).

Boos, F. S., *Working-Class Women Poets in Victorian Britain: An Anthology* (Peterborough, Ont.: Broadview Press, 2008).

Boos, F. S., 'The Poetics of the Working Classes', *Victorian Poetry*, 39(2) (2001), 103–110.

Bourdieu, P., 'The Economics of Linguistic Exchanges', *Social Science Information*, 16(6) (1977), 645–668.

Bourdieu, P., *The Rules of Art: Genesis and Structure of the Literary Field* (Stanford: Stanford University Press, 1996).

Bowman, T., 'Potential Misuses of Poetry Therapy: A Process for Reflecting on Practice', *Journal of Poetry Therapy*, 17(4) (2004), 223–230.

Boyle, C., 'Lord Byron', in Jones, D. (ed.), *Censorship: A World Encyclopedia*, Vol 1–4, (Routledge, 2015), 392–393.

Brennan, T., *The Transmission of Affect* (London: Cornell University Press, 2004).

Brogan, T. V. F., 'Invective', in Preminger, A. & Brogan, T. V. F. (eds.), *The New Princeton Encyclopedia of Poetry and Poetics* (Princeton, NJ: Princeton University Press, 1993), 627–628.

Brogan, T. V. F., 'Iambic', in Preminger, A. & Brogan, T. V. F. (eds.), *The New Princeton Encyclopedia of Poetry and Poetics* (Princeton, NJ: Princeton University Press, 1993), 548–550.

Bronte, J., 'Health Benefits of Going to Musicals, Theatre Touted', *Daily Gleaner, Fredericton, New Brunswick* (24 June 2014).

Brown, W., *Politics Out of History* (Princeton, NJ: Princeton University Press, 2001).

Bruce, S., 'The Sociology of Late Secularization: Social Divisions and Religiosity', *British Journal of Sociology*, 67(4) (December 2016), 613–631.

Burgum, S., *Occupying London: Post Crash Resistance and the Limits of Possibility* (London: Routledge, 2018).

Burr, J. C., 'Springsteen, Spoken Word, and Social Justice: Engaging Students in Activism through Songs and Poetry', *English Journal*, 106(6) (2017), 61–66.

Byron, G. G., 'Epigram', in *The Complete Works of Lord Byron* (Paris: A&W Galignani, 1831), 722.

C

Camangian, P., 'Untempered Tongues: Teaching Performance Poetry for Social Justice', *English Teaching: Practice and Critique*, 7(2) (Sept. 2008), 35–55.

Cebreiro, M. D. & Villar, R., 'Politics of Sound: Body, Emotion and Sound in the Contemporary Galician Poetry Performance', in Gräbner, C. & Casas, A. (eds.), *Performing Poetry: Body, Place, Rhythm in the Poetry of Performance* (Amsterdam: Rodopi, 2011).

Cervellin, G. & Lippi, G., 'From Music-Beat to Heart-Beat: A Journey in the Complex Interactions Between Music, Brain and Heart', *European Journal of Internal Medicine*, 22(4) (2011), 371–374.

Chang, J., *Can't Stop, Won't Stop: A History of the Hip-hop Generation* (New York: Picador, 2006).

Chappell, Z., *Deliberative Democracy: A Critical Introduction* (Basingstoke: Palgrave Macmillan, 2012).

Chivers, T. (ed.), *Stress Fractures: Essays in Poetry* (London: Penned in the Margins, 2010).

Churchich, N., *Marxism and Alienation* (Rutherford, NJ: Fairleigh Dickinson University Press, 1990).

Claxton, G., *What's the Point in School: Rediscovering The Heart Of Education* (Oxford: Oneworld Publications, 2008).

Clare, T., 'Slam: A Poetic Dialogue', in Chivers, T. (ed.), *Stress Fractures: Essays in Poetry* (London: Penned in the Margins, 2010).

Clarke, J. C., 'Evidently Chicken Town', in *Ten Years in an Open Necked Shirt* (London: Vintage Books, 2012), 49–50.

Coleman, J. L., *Words of Protest, Words of Freedom: Poetry of the American Civil Rights Movement and Era* (Durham, NC: Duke University Press, 2012).

Collins, L., 'Rude Bwoys, Riddim, Rub-a-Dub, and Rastas', in Morris, A. (ed.), *Sound States: Innovative Poetics and Acoustical Technologies* (Chapel Hill: University of North Carolina Press, 1997).

Colón, D. A., 'Siempre Pa'l Arte: The Passions of Latina/o Spoken Word', in Aldama, F. L. (ed.), *The Routledge Companion to Latina/o Popular Culture* (New York: Routledge, 2016).

Couldry, N., *Why Voice Matters: Culture and Politics After Neoliberalism* (Los Angeles: Sage Publications, 2010).

Coutinho, E. & Dibben, N., 'Psychoacoustic Cues to Emotion in Speech Prosody and Music', *Cognition & Emotion*, 27(4) (2012), 1–27.

C Q Researcher, *Issues for Debate in American Public Policy: Selections from CQ Researcher* (Sage Publications, 2013).

Csikszentmihalyi, M. *Flow: The Psychology of Optimal Experience* (New York: Harper Collins, 1990).

D

Damon, M., 'Was That "Different," "Dissident" or "Dissonant"? Poetry (n) the Public Spear: Slams, Open Readings, and Dissident Traditions', in Bernstein, C. (ed.) *Close Listening: Poetry and the Performed Word* (New York: Oxford University Press, 1998).

Darlington, A., 'The Ranters, 18 years on', in Munden, P. & Wade, S. (eds.), *Reading the Applause: Reflections on Performance Poetry by Various Artists* (York: Talking Shop, 1999).

Derrida, J., *Of Grammatology*, Gayatri Chakravorty Spivak (trans.), (1967, Reprint, Baltimore: John Hopkins University Press, 1997).

Davies, L. I., 'Orality, Literacy, Popular Culture: An Eighteenth-Century Case Study', *Oral Tradition*, 25/2 (2010), 305–323.

De Quincey, T., *Recollections Of The Lakes And The Lake Poets: Coleridge, Wordsworth, And Southey* (Edinburgh: A & C Black, 1863).

Diepeveen, L., *The Difficulties of Modernism* (London: Routledge, 2002).

Dobson, J., *How to Save Our Town Centres: A Radical Agenda for the Future of High Streets* (Bristol: Policy Press, 2015).

Dobyns, S., *Next Word, Better Word: The Craft of Writing Poetry* (London: Palgrave MacMillan, 2011).

Double, O., *Stand Up: On Being a Comedian* (London: Methuen, 1997).

Dowdy, M., 'Live Hip Hop, Collective Agency, and "Acting in Concert"', *Popular Music and Society*, 30(1) (Feb 2007), 75–91.

DuBois, T. A., 'Oral Tradition', *Oral Tradition*, 18(2) (2003), 225–257.

Durkheim, E., *The Elementary Forms of Religious Life*, Swain, J. W. (trans.) (1920, Reprint: Courier Corporation, 2012)

Dworkin, C., 'The Stutter of Form', in Perloff, M. & Dworkin, C. (eds.), *The Sound of Poetry: The Poetry of Sound* (Chicago: University of Chicago Press, 2009).

Dymoke, S. & Spiro, J. (eds.), 'Poet-Academics and Academic-Poets: Writing Identities, Practices and Experiences within the Academy', *Writing in Education: Writing in Practice*, 3 (March 2017), https://www.nawe.co.uk/DB/current-wip-edition-2/articles/poet-academics-and-academic-poets-writing-identities-practices-and-experiences-within-the-academy.html [accessed 22 March 2019].

Dyson, A. H., 'Crafting "The Humble Prose of Living": Rethinking Oral/Written Relations in the Echoes of Spoken Word', *English Education*, 37(2) (2005), 149–164.

E

Effiong, P. U., *In Search of a Model for African-American Drama* (Lanham, MD: University Press of America, 2000).

Ehrenreich, B., *Dancing in the Streets: A History of Collective Joy* (London: Granta Books, 2015).

Ellis, L., Gere, A. R. & Lamberton, J., 'Out Loud: The Common Language of Poetry', *English Journal*, 93(1) (Sept. 2003), 44–49.

Emmerson, P., 'Thinking Laughter Beyond Humour: Atmospheric Refrains and Ethical Indeterminacies in Spaces of Care', *Environment and Planning A: Economy and Space*, 49(9) (2017), 2082–2098.

Estés, C. P., *Women Who Run With the Wolves: Myths and Stories of the Wild Woman Archetype* (1992, reprint, New York: Ballantine Books, 1997).

Evans, R. O., 'Incantation', in Preminger, A. & Brogan, T. V. F. (eds.), *The New Princeton Encyclopedia of Poetry and Poetics* (Princeton, NJ: Princeton University Press, 1993).

Evaristo, B. & Astley, N., 'Head to Head' in *Free Verse Report: Publishing Opportunities for Black and Asian Poets* (London: Spread the Word, 2007), in Danuta, K. (ed.), *The Complete Works Poetry* (London: Spread the Word, 2007). 14–17. <https://www. spreadtheword.org.uk/wp-content/uploads/2016/11/Free-Verse-Report.pdf> [accessed 22 March 2019]

F

Falletti, C., 'Introduction', in Falletti, C., Sofia, G. & Jacono, V. (eds.), *Theatre and Cognitive Neuroscience: Performance and Science: Interdisciplinary Dialogues* (London: Bloomsbury, 2016).

Featherstone, M., Lash, S. & Robertson, R. (eds.), *Global Modernities* (London: Sage Publications, 1995).

Fields, A., Snapp, S., Russell, S. T., Licona, A. C. & Tilley, E. H., 'Youth Voices and Knowledges: Slam Poetry Speaks to Social Policies', *Sexuality Research and Social Policy*, 11(3) (2014), 310–321.

Fiore, M., 'Pedagogy for Liberation: Spoken Word Poetry in Urban Schools', *Education and Urban Society*, 47(7) (2015), 813–829.

Findlay, A., *Twelfth Night: A Critical Reader* (Bloomsbury, 2013).

Finkelstein, S., 'Art as Humanization' in Solomon, M. (ed.), *Marxism and Art* (Wayne State University Press, 1979).

Finnegan, R., 'The How of Literature', *Oral Tradition*, 20(2) (2005), 164–87.

Finnegan, R., *Oral Poetry* (London: Cambridge University Press, 1977).

Fischer, E., *The Necessity of Art* (Reprint, London: Verso, 2010).

Fischer-Lichte, E., 'Appearing as Embodied Mind: Defining a Weak, a Strong and a Radical Concept of Presence', in Giannachi, G., Kaye, N. & Shanks, M. (eds.), *Archaeologies of Presence* (London: Routledge, 2012).

Fisher, M., 'The Privatisation of Stress', *Soundings: A Journal of Politics and Culture*, 48 (2011), 123–133.

Fleming, D., *Surviving the Future: Culture, Carnival and Capital in the Aftermath of the Market Economy* (White River Junction, VT: Chelsea Green, 2006).

Flynn, C. & Mitchell, C., '"It may be verifyit that thy wit is thin": Interpreting Older Scots Flyting through Hip Hop Aesthetics', *Oral Tradition*, 29(1) (2014), 69–86.

Foley, J. M., *How to Read an Oral Poem* (Chicago: University of Illinois Press, 2002).

Foucault, M., 'Afterword by Michel Foucault: The Subject and Power' in Dreyfus, H. L & Rabinow, P., *Michel Foucault: Beyond Structuralism and Hermeneutics* (London: Harvester Press, 1982).

Fowler, C., 'Publishing Manchester's Black and Asian Writers', in Pearce, L. Fowler, C. & Crawshaw, R. (eds.), *Postcolonial*

Manchester: Diaspora Space and the Devolution of Literary Culture (Manchester: Manchester University Press, 2013).

Fowler, K. D., 'The Anatomy of Joy: Transforming Perceptions of Mysticism in the Early Modern Period', PhD dissertation, The University of North Carolina at Greensboro, 2016.

Fox, K., *Watching the English: The Hidden Rules of English Behaviour* (London: Hodder & Stoughton, 2004).

Freire, P., *Pedagogy of the Oppressed* (Reprint, London: Penguin, 1996).

Fusetti, G. & Willson, S., 'The Pedagogy of the Poetic Body', in Bradby, D. & Delgado, M. M. (eds.), *The Paris Jigsaw: Internationalism and the City's Stages* (Manchester: Manchester University Press, 2015).

Fussell, P., *Class: A Guide Through the American Status System* (New York: Summit Books, 1983).

G

Garbatzky, I., 'Roberto Echavarren's Atlantic Casino and Oír no es ver: The "Neobarocker" Body in Performance', in Gräbner, C. & Casas, A. (eds.), *Performing Poetry: Body, Place, Rhythm in the Poetry of Performance* (Amsterdam: Rodopi, 2011).

Gilchrist, A., *The Life of William Blake* (Hesperides Press, 2008).

Gioia, D., *Disappearing Ink: Poetry at the End of Print Culture* (Saint Paul, MN: Graywolf Press, 2004).

Glazner, G. M., *How to Make a Living as a Poet* (New York: Soft Skull Press, 2005).

Glazner, G. M. (ed.), *Poetry Slam: The Competitive Art of Performance Poetry* (San Francisco: Manic D. Press, 2000).

Goffman, E., *The Presentation of Self in Everyday Life* (1956, Reprint: Penguin, 1990).

Goodman, F. D., *Ecstasy, Ritual and Alternative Reality: Religion in a Pluralistic World* (Bloomington and Indianapolis: Indiana University Press, 1988).

Gordon, L. R., 'The Problem of Maturity in Hip Hop', *The Review of Education, Pedagogy, and Cultural Studies*, 27 (2005), 367–389.

Graeber, D., *The Democracy Project* (London: Penguin, 2014).

Gräbner, C. & Casas, A. (eds.), *Performing Poetry: Body, Place, Rhythm in the Poetry of Performance* (Amsterdam: Rodopi, 2011).

Gräbner, C., 'Hurricanes don't Roar in Pentameters', in Gräbner, C. & Casas, A. (eds.), *Performing Poetry: Body, Place, Rhythm in the Poetry of Performance* (Amsterdam: Rodopi, 2011).

Gräbner, C., 'Is Performance Poetry Dead?', *Poetry Review*, 92(2) (2007), 78–82.

Grace, N. M., 'The Beats and Literary History: Myths and Reality', in Belletto, S. (ed.), *The Cambridge Companion to the Beats* (Cambridge: Cambridge University Press, 2017).

Greenblatt, S., *Will in the World: How Shakespeare became Shakespeare* (London: Pimlico, 2005).

Gregory, H., '(Re)presenting Ourselves: Art, Identity, and Status in U.K. Poetry Slam', *Oral Tradition*, 23(2) (2008), 201–217.

Gregory, H., 'Texts in Performance: Identity, Interaction and Influence in U.K. and U.S. Poetry Slam Discourses', unpublished thesis for PhD in Sociology, University of Exeter, 2009.

Grenfell, M. J., *Pierre Bourdieu: Key Concepts* (London: Routledge, 2012).

Gruber, D. R., 'Suasive Speech: A Stronger Affective Defence of Rhetoric and the Politics of Cognitive Poetics', *Language and Communication*, 49 (2016), 36–44.

Gunster, S., 'Gramsci, Organic Intellectuals, and Cultural Studies: Lessons for Political Theorists', in Frank, J. A. & Tambornino, J. (eds.), *Vocations of Political Theory* (Minneapolis: University of Minnesota Press, 2000), 238–262.

H

Habekost, C., *Verbal Riddim: The Politics and Aesthetics of African-Caribbean Dub Poetry* (Amsterdam: Rodopi, 1993).

Hagedorn, K., '"From This One Song Alone, I Consider Him to be a Holy Man": Ecstatic Religion, Musical Affect, and the Global Consumer', *Journal for the Scientific Study of Religion*, 45(4) (2006), 489–496.

Hall, P. M., 'Interactionism and the Study of Social Organization', *The Sociological Quarterly*, 28(1) (Spring 1987), 1–22.

Harker, B., '"Communism is English": Edgell Rickword, Jack Lindsay and the Cultural Politics of the Popular Front', *Literature & History*, 20(2) (Oct 2011), 16–34.

Harrington, J., *Poetry and the Public: The Social Form of Modern U.S. Poetics* (Middletown, CT: Wesleyan University Press, 2002).

Harrison, N. A., Wilson, C. E. & Critchley, H. D., 'Processing of Observed Pupil Size Modulates Perception of Sadness and Predicts Empathy', *Emotion*, 7(4) (2007), 724–729.

Harvey, M., 'Curtains', in *The Hole in the Sum of My Parts* (The Poetry Trust, 2005).

Harvie, J., *Fair Play: Art, Performance and Neoliberalism* (Basingstoke: Palgrave Macmillan, 2013).

Hastings, R. P., *Chartism in the North Riding of Yorkshire and South Durham, 1838-1848* (York: Borthwick Institute, University of York, 2004).

Hatfield, E., Bensman, L., Thornton, P. D. & Rapson, R. L., 'New Perspectives on Emotional Contagion: A Review of Classic and Recent Research on Facial Mimicry and Contagion', *Interpersona*, 8(2) (2014), 159–179.

Hearne, C., 'A Comparison between the Concept of Western Hypnosis and African Trance', MA dissertation, University of Johannesburg, 2012.

Hegley, J., *The Family Pack* (Reprint, London: Methuen, 1996).

Heidegger, M., 'Letter on Humanism', *Global Religious Visions*, 1(1) (July 2000),

Henri, A., 'I Want to Paint' in Henri, A., McGough, R. & Patten, B., *The Mersey Sound* (Harmondsworth: Penguin, 1967), 24–25.

Henriques, J., 'The Vibrations of Affect and their Propagation on a Night Out on Kingston's Dancehall Scene', *Body and Society*, 16(1) (2010), 57–89.

Hoffman, T., *American Poetry in Performance: From Walt Whitman to Hip Hop* (Ann Arbor, MI: University of Michigan Press, 2013).

Hoffman, T., 'Treacherous Laughter: The Poetry Slam, Slam Poetry and the Politics of Resistance', *Studies in American Humour*, New Series 3, No. 8 (2001), 49–64.

Holman, B., 'DisClaimer', in Glazner, G. M. (ed.), *Poetry Slam: The Competitive Art of Performance Poetry* (San Francisco: Manic D. Press, 2000).

Howe, J., *Crowdsourcing: How the Power of the Crowd is Driving the Future of Business* (New York: Crown Business, 2009).

Howell, R., *The Analysis of Performing Art: A Guide to Theory and Practice* (Amsterdam: Harwood Academic Publishers, 1999).

Hoyles, A & Hoyles, M., *Moving Voices: Black Performance Poetry* (London: Hansib, 2002).

Hublin, J. J., Abdelouahed Ben-Ncer, Bailey, S. E., Freidline, S. E. Neubauer, S., Skinner, M. M., and others, 'New Fossils from Jebel Irhoud, Morocco and the Pan-African Origin of Homo Sapiens', *Nature*, 546 (7647), (2017), 289–92 <https://doi.org/10.1038/nature22336>

Hughes, J., *An Encyclopedia of Swearing: The Social History of Oaths, Profanity, Foul Language, and Ethnic Slurs in the English-Speaking World* (London: Routledge, 2006).

Hughes, L., 'Harlem', Reprinted by permission of Harold Ober Associates. Copyright 1994 by the Langston Hughes Estate.

Hymes, D., *I Tried in Vain to Tell You: Essays in Native American Ethnopoetics* (University of Nebraska Press, 2004).

J

Jameson, F., *The Prison-House of Language: A Critical Account of Structuralism and Russian Formalism* (Princeton, NJ: Princeton University Press, 1974).

Jamison, K. R., *Touched with Fire*, (New York: Free Press, 1993).

Johnson, J., *Killing Poetry: Blackness and the Making of Slam and Spoken Word Communities* (New Brunswick: Rutgers University Press, 2017).

Johnson, L. K., 'Reggae Sounds', in *Selected Poems: Linton Kwesi Johnson* (London: Penguin, 2006).

K

Kahn, D., 'Noises of the Avant-Garde', in Sterne, J. (ed.), *The Sound Studies Reader* (New York: Routledge, 2012).

Kapchan, D., 'Listening Acts: Witnessing the Pain (and Praise) of Others', in Kapchan, D. (ed.), *Theorizing Sound Writing* (Middletown, CT: Wesleyan University Press, 2017).

Karafistan, R., '"The Spirits Wouldn't Let Me Be Anything Else": Shamanic Dimensions in Theatre Practice Today', *New Theatre Quarterly*, 19(2) (May, 2003), 150–168.

Kennaway, J., 'Musical Hypnosis: Sound and Selfhood from Mesmerism to Brainwashing', *Social History of Medicine*, 25(2) (May, 2012), 271–289.

Kinney, P., *Welsh Traditional Music* (Cardiff: University of Wales Press, 2011).

Kraemer, W. G., 'The Hypnotic Literary Genre: Poetry Trance and Hypnotext', PhD dissertation, Indiana University of Pennsylvania, 2009.

L

Labov, W., 'The Logic of Nonstandard English', in Cashdan, A. & Grugeon, E. (eds.), *Language in Education: A Source Book* (London: Routledge & Kegan Paul in assoc. with the Open University Press, 1972).

Laing, J. & Mair, J., 'Music Festivals and Social Inclusion – The Festival Organizers' Perspective', *Leisure Sciences*, 37(3) (May/Jun 2015), 252–268.

Landau, J., 'The Flesh of Raving: Merleau-Ponty and the "Experience" of Ecstasy', in St John, G. (ed.), *Rave Culture and Religion* (London: Routledge, 2004).

Lee, B., 'Avant-Garde Poetry as Subcultural Practice: Mailer and Di Prima's Hipsters', *New Literary History*, 41(4) (2010), 775–794.

Lee, E., 'Spoken Word as a Way of Dismantling Barriers and Creating Space for Healing', in Trévien, C. (ed.), *Verbs that Move Mountains: Essays and Interviews on Spoken Word Cultures Around the World* (Sabotage Reviews, 2018).

Lee, J., *Writing from the Body* (London: St Martin's Press, 1994).

Leeuwen, T. van, *Speech, Music, Sound* (Basingstoke: Macmillan, 1992).

Lefebvre, H., *Rhythmanalysis: Space, Time and Everyday Life* (London: Continuum, 2004).

Lefever, H. G., '"Playing the Dozens": A Mechanism for Social Control', *Phylon*, 42(1) (1981), 73–85.

Lindsay, J., *Who are the English: Selected Poems: 1935-1981* (Smokestack Books, 2014).

Lord, A. B., *The Singer of Tales* (1960, reprint, Cambridge, MA: Harvard University Press, 2019).

Louv, R., *Last Child in the Woods* (London: Atlantic Books, 2005).

Lucie-Smith, E., *The Liverpool Scene* (London: Donald Carroll, 1967).

Ludwig, A. M., 'Mental Illness and Creative Activity in Women Writers', *American Journal of Psychiatry*, 151(11) (1994), 1650–1656.

Lynch, K. A., 'The Minstrelization of Hip Hop and Spoken Word Authenticity: Expressions of Postmodern Blackness', MA thesis, NC State University, 2005.

M

Maher, G. C., 'Brechtian Hip Hop: Didactics and Self-Production in Post-Gangsta Political Mixtapes', *Journal of Black Studies*, 36(1) (2005), 129–60.

Mahood, M. M., *Poetry and Humanism* (Camelot Press, 1950).

Makdisi, S., *William Blake and the Impossible History of the 1790s* (Chicago: University of Chicago Press, 2007).

Maxwell, W. J., 'Claude McKay' in Chinitz, D. E. & McDonald, G., *A Companion to Modernist Poetry* (John Wiley & Sons, Incorporated, 2014). ProQuest Ebook Central, https:// ebookcentral.proquest.com/lib/swansea-ebooks/detail. action?docID=1666475

Marsh, N., Middleton, P. & Sheppard, V., '"Blasts of Language": Changes in Oral Poetics in Britain since 1965', *Oral Tradition*, 21(1) (2006), 44–67.

Mayakovsky, V., *How are Verses Made?* (1926, reprint, London: Jonathan Cape, 1970).

McCaffery, S., 'Cacophony, Abstraction, and Potentiality: The Fate of the Dada Sound Poem', in Perloff, M. & Dworkin, C. (eds.), *The Sound of Poetry: The Poetry of Sound* (Chicago: University of Chicago Press, 2009).

McCrum, R., 'The Ties that Bind Us: Communities of Practice in Grass Roots Spoken Word in the Scottish Central Belt', in, Trévien C. (ed.), *Verbs that Move Mountains: Essays and Interviews on Spoken Word Cultures Around the World* (Create Space, 2018).

McDaniel, J., 'Slam and the Academy', in Glazner, G. M. (ed.), *Poetry Slam: The Competitive Art of Performance Poetry* (San Francisco: Manic D. Press, 2000).

McGilchrist, I., *The Master and His Emissary: The Divided Brain and the Making of the Western World* (New Haven: Yale University Press, 2012).

McGowan, J., 'Slam the Book: The Role of Performance in Contemporary UK Poetics', wrap.warwick.ac.uk/89799/, PhD thesis, University of Warwick, 2016.

McGuigan, J., *Cool Capitalism* (London: Pluto Press, 2009).

McKay, C., 'If We Must Die', in Maxwell, W. J. (ed.), *Complete Poems Claude McKay* (Urbana, IL: Univerity of Illinois Press, 2014), 177–178.

McLane, M. N., 'On the Use and Abuse of "Orality" for Art: Reflections on Romantic and Late Twentieth-Century *Poiesis*', *Oral Tradition*, 17(1) (2002), 135–164.

Mee, J. & Crosby, N., '"This Soldierlike Danger": The Trial of William Blake for Sedition', in Philp, M. (ed.), *Resisting Napoleon: The British Response to the Threat of Invasion, 1797-1815* (Abingdon, Oxon: Routledge, 2016).

Middleton, P., 'The Contemporary Poetry Reading', in Bernstein, C. (ed.), *Close Listening: Poetry and the Performed Word* (New York: Oxford University Press, 1998).

Middleton, P., *Distant Reading: Performance, Readership and Consumption in Contemporary Poetry* (Tuscaloosa: University of Alabama Press, 2005).

Miller, K., *Writing Down the Visions: Essays & Prophesies* (Peepal Tree Press, 2013).

Mills, C. W., *White Collar: The American Middle Classes* (New York: Oxford University Press, 1957).

Miner, E., 'Poetic Contests', in Preminger, A. & Brogan, T. V. F. (eds.), *The New Princeton Encyclopedia of Poetry and Poetics* (Princeton, NJ: Princeton University Press, 1993), 925–927.

Mitchell, V. D. & Davis, C. (eds.), *An Encyclopedia of the Black Arts Movement* (Rowman & Littlefield, 2019).

Mizen, P., 'The Madness that is the World: Young Activists' Emotional Reasoning and their Participation in a Local Occupy Movement', *Sociological Review*, 32(sup, 2) (June 2015), 167–182.

Monbiot, G., *Out of the Wreckage: A New Politics for an Age of Crisis* (New York: Verso, 2017).

Monson, J., *British Prose Poetry: The Poems Without Lines* (Cham, Switzerland: Springer, 2018).

Morgan, W. J., 'Social capital, citizenship and continuing education: What are the connections?', *International Journal of Continuing Education and Lifelong Learning*, 1(1) (2008), 35–45.

Morris, A. (ed.), *Sound States: Innovative Poetics and Acoustical Technologies* (Chapel Hill: University of North Carolina Press, 1997).

Muller, L. & The Blueprint Collective (eds.), *June Jordan's Poetry for the People: A Revolutionary Blueprint* (New York: Routledge, 1995).

Mulvey, L., 'Visual Pleasure and Narrative Cinema', *Screen*, 16(3) (1975), 6–18.

Munden, P. & Wade, S. (eds.), *Reading the Applause: Reflections on Performance Poetry by Various Artists* (York: Talking Shop, 1999).

N

Naess, A., *The Ecology of Wisdom: Writings by Arne Naess*, Drengson, A. & Devall, B. (eds.) (London: Penguin, 2016).

Nathanson, D. L., *Knowing Feeling: Affect, Script, and Psychotherapy* (New York: Norton, 1996).

Nealon, J., *Post-Postmodernism: Or the Cultural Logic of Just-in-Time Capitalism* (Stanford, CA: Stanford University Press, 2012).

Nelson, R. S. & Shiff, R. (eds.), *Critical Terms for Art History* (2nd edn., Chicago: University of Chicago Press, 2003).

Niles, J. D., *Homo Narrans: The Poetics and Anthropology of Oral Literature* (University of Pennsylvania Press, 2010).

Noel, U., 'The Body's Territories: Performance Poetry in Contemporary Puerto Rico', in Gräbner, C. & Casas, A. (eds.), *Performing Poetry: Body, Place, Rhythm in the Poetry of Performance* (Amsterdam: Rodopi, 2011).

Novak, J., *Live Poetry: An Integrated Approach to Poetry in Performance* (Amsterdam: Rodopi, 2011).

Nussbaum, C. O., *The Musical Representation: Meaning, Ontology, and Emotion* (Cambridge, MA: MIT Press, 2012).

O

Oliver, M., *Rules for the Dance: A Handbook for Reading Metrical Verse* (New York: Mariner Books, 1998).

Ong, W. J., *Orality and Literacy: The Techologizing of the Word* (London: Methuen, 1982).

Osborne, D. '"Set in Stone": Lemn Sissay's and SuAndi's Landmark Poetics', in Gräbner, C. & Casas, A. (eds.), *Performing*

Poetry: Body, Place, Rhythm in the Poetry of Performance (Amsterdam: Rodopi, 2011).

P

Pagliai, V., 'The Art of Dueling with Words: Toward a New Understanding of Verbal Duels across the World', *Oral Tradition*, 24 (1) (2009), 61–88.

Pais, A., 'Re-Affecting the Stage: Affective Resonance as the Function of the Audience', *Humanities*, 5 (2016), 79.

Parini, J., *Why Poetry Matters* (New Haven, CT: Yale University Press, 2008).

Parks, W., 'Flyting, Sounding, Debate: Three Verbal Contest Genres', *Poetics Today*, 7(3) (1986), 439–458.

Pearce, L., Fowler, C. & Crawshaw, R. (eds.), *Postcolonial Manchester: Diaspora Space and the Devolution of Literary Culture* (Manchester: Manchester University Press, 2013).

Penman, J. & Becker, J., 'Religious Ecstatics "Deep Listeners," and Musical Emotion', *Empirical Musicology Review*, 4(2) (2009), 49–70.

Perloff, M. & Dworkin, C. (eds.), *The Sound of Poetry: The Poetry of Sound* (Chicago: University of Chicago Press, 2009).

Pettitt, T., 'Ballads and Bad Quartos: Oral Tradition and the English Literary Historian', *Oral Tradition*, 18(2) (2003), 182–185.

Phelan, P., *Unmarked: The Politics of Performance* (London: Routledge, 1993).

Pijpers, J. M., 'Artimanha, the Precise Moment of Being: Performance and Carnival in the Poetry of Brazil's Nuvem Cigana', in Gräbner, C. & Casas, A. (eds.), *Performing Poetry: Body,*

Place, Rhythm in the Poetry of Performance (Amsterdam: Rodopi, 2011).

Pike, R., 'History of Poetry in Bristol', lecture at Lyra Poetry Festival, Wills Memorial Hall, Bristol, 20 March 2019.

Pinsker, S., 'An Appreciation: Allen Ginsberg defined his age - and its attitude', *Jewish Exponent*, Philadelphia 24 April 1997: 9.

Potash, J. L., *Drugs as Weapons Against Us: The CIA's Murderous Targeting of SDS, Panthers, Hendrix, Lennon, Cobain, Tupac, and Other Leftists* (Walterville, OR: Trine Day, 2015).

Preminger, A. & Brogan, T. V. F. (eds.), *The New Princeton Encyclopedia of Poetry and Poetics* (Princeton, NJ: Princeton University Press, 1993).

Primeau, R., 'Frank Horne and the Second Echelon Poets of the Harlem Renaissance', in Wintz, C. D. (ed.), *Remembering the Harlem Renaissance* (New York: Garland Publishing, 1996), 249–251.

Prochazkova, E. & Kret, M. E., 'Connecting Minds and Sharing Emotions Through Mimicry: A Neurocognitive Model of Emotional Contagion', *Neuroscience & Biobehavioral Reviews*, 80 (Sept 2017), 99–114.

Q

Quartermain, P., 'Sound Reading', in Bernstein, C. (ed.), *Close Listening: Poetry and the Performed Word* (New York: Oxford University Press, 1998).

R

Rancière J., *The Politics of Aesthetics* (London: Continuum, 2006).

Rancière, J., 'The Emancipated Spectator', *Artforum*, (March 2007), 271–280.

Randall, D., *Sound System: The Political Power of Music* (London: Pluto Press, 2017).

Reed, S., *The Necessity of Experience* (New Haven: Yale University Press, 1996).

Reinink, G. J. & Vanstiphout, H. L. J. (eds.), *Dispute Poems and Dialogues in the Ancient and Mediaeval Near East* (Leuven: Peeters, 1991).

Rennie, S., 'The Poetic Negotiations of a Gentleman Radical: Ernest Jones and the "Mighty Mind"', *Victorian Poetry*, 53(1) (2015), 57–76.

Révész, G., *Introduction to the Psychology of Music* (Mineola, NY: Dover Publications, 2015).

Reyes, G. T., 'Finding the Poetic High: Building a Spoken Word Poetry Community and Culture of Creative, Caring, Critical Intellectuals.', *Multicultural Education*, 14(2) (2006), 10–15.

Richardson, L. in Dymoke, S. & Spiro, J. (eds.), 'Poet-Academics and Academic-Poets: Writing Identities, Practices and Experiences within the Academy', *Writing in Education: Writing in Practice*, 3 (March 2017), https://www.nawe.co.uk/DB/current-wip-edition-2/articles/poet-academics-and-academic-poets-writing-identities-practices-and-experiences-within-the-academy.html [accessed 22 March 2019].

Ridout, N., 'Welcome to the Vibratorium', *The Senses and Society*, 3(2) (2008), 221–232.

Rilke, R. M., 'Rome, December 23rd 1903', in Herter Norton, M. D. (ed.), *Letters to a Young Poet* (New York: Norton & Company, New edn. 1993).

Roberts, J. M., *Digital Publics: Cultural Political Economy, Financialisation and Creative Organisational Politics* (London: Routledge, 2014).

Roberts, P., *How Poetry Works* (London: Penguin, 2000).

Robertson, R., 'Glocalization: Time-Space and Homogeneity-Heterogeneity', in Featherstone, M., Lash, S. & Robertson, R. (eds.), *Global Modernities* (London: Sage Publications, 1995).

Robinson, R., *Music Festivals and the Politics of Participation* (London: Routledge, 2015).

Robson, J. (ed.), *Poetry and Jazz in Concert* (London: Panther, 1969).

Rogers, C., *Freedom to Learn for the 80's* (1969, reprint, Columbus, OH: Merrill, 1983).

Rose, T., *Black Noise: Rap Music and Black Culture in Contemporary America* (Hanover, NH: Wesleyan University Press, 1994).

Rosen, M., 'Writer-in-Inner-City-Residence', in The Talk Workshop Group, *Becoming Our Own Experts: The Vauxhall Papers: Studies in language and learning made by the Talk Workshop Group at Vauxhall Manor School 1974 – 1979* (2nd edn., London: Talk Workshop Group, 2011).

Rossi, E. L., 'Mind/Body Communication and the New Language of Human Facilitation', in Zeig, J. (ed.), *The Evolution of Psychotherapy* (New York: Brunner/Mazel, 1987).

Roubaud, J., 'Prelude: Poetry and Orality' in Perloff, M. & Dworkin, C. (eds.), *The Sound of Poetry: The Poetry of Sound* (Chicago: University of Chicago Press, 2009).

S

Sachs, C., *The Rise of Music in the Ancient World, East and West* (London: Dent, 1944).

Sales, A. de, 'The Sources of Authority for Shamanic Speech: Examples from the Kham-Magar of Nepal', *Oral Tradition*, 30(2) (2016), 243–262.

Samy Alim, H., Lee, J. & Mason Carris, L., 'Moving the Crowd, "Crowding" the Emcee: The Coproduction and Contestation of Black Normativity in Freestyle Rap Battles', *Discourse & Society*, 22(4) (2011), 422–439.

Sanders, M., *The Poetry of Chartism: Aesthetics, Politics, History* (Cambridge: Cambridge University Press, 2009).

Sapir, E., *Language: An Introduction to the Study of Speech* (New York: Harcourt, Brace, 1921).

Saussy, H., *The Ethnography of Rhythm: Orality and Its Technologies* (New York: Fordham University Press, 2016).

Scheckner. P. (ed.), *An Anthology of Chartist Poetry: Poetry of the British Working Class 1830s–1850s* (Rutherford, NJ: Fairleigh Dickinson Univ Press, 1989).

Scheve, C. V., 'Collective Emotions in Rituals: Elicitation, Transmission and a "Matthew effect"', in Michaels, A. & Wulf, C. (eds.), *Emotions in Rituals and Performances* (London: Routledge, 2012).

Schmid, J. M., 'Performance, Poetics and Place: Public Poetry as Community Art', PhD in English thesis, University of Iowa, 2000.

Schmidgall, G., 'Triangulating Blake, Whitman, and Ginsberg', *Walt Whitman Quarterly Review*, 32(3) (2015), 131–143.

Scholes, R., *The Crafty Reader* (Yale University Press, 2011).

Schore, A. N., *Affect Dysregulation and Disorders of the Self* (New York: Norton, 2003).

Scott, J. C., *Domination and the Arts of Resistance* (New Haven and London: Yale University Press, 1990).

Segal, L., *Radical Happiness: Moments of Collective Joy* (New York: Verso Books, 2017).

Shelley, P. B., *The Masque of Anarchy, A Poem* (London: Edward Moxton, 1832).

Sigg, A., 'Therapeutic Theatre: Trauma and Bodily Articulation in Post-War European Drama', PhD thesis, McGill University, Montreal, 2015.

Silva, H., 'Live Writing: A Psychophysical Approach to the Analysis of Black British Poetry in Performance', PhD in English Literature, Stirling University, 2018.

Silva, H., 'Composing Speech', in Chivers, T. (ed.), *Stress Fractures: Essays in Poetry* (London: Penned in the Margins, 2010).

Silva, H., 'The Craft of Poetry in Performance', in Teitler, N. (ed.), *Freed Verse: Diversity in British Poetry 2015 – 2017* (London: The Complete Works, 2017).

Smethurst, J. E., *The Black Arts Movement: Literary Nationalism in the 1960s and 1970s* (Chapel Hill, NC: University of North Carolina Press, 2006).

Smethurst, J. E., '"Pat Your Foot and Turn the Corner": Amiri Baraka, the Black Arts Movement, and the Poetics of a Popular Avant-Garde', *African American Review*, 37(2/3) (2003), 261–270.

Smith, C. J. (ed.), *Encyclopedia of African American Popular Culture* (Santa Barbara, CA: Greenwood Press, 2010).

Smith, M. K. & Eleveld, M. (eds.), *The Spoken Word Revolution: Slam, Hip Hop & the Poetry of a New Generation* (Naperville, IL: Sourcebooks, 2003).

Smith, M. K. & Kraynak, J., *The Complete Idiot's Guide to Slam Poetry* (Indianapolis, IN: Alpha Books, 2004).

Snyder, E. D. & Shor, R. E., 'Trance-Inductive Poetry: A Brief Communication', *The International Journal of Clinical and Experimental Hypnosis*, 31(1) (1983), 1–7.

Somers-Willett, S., *The Cultural Politics of Slam Poetry: Race, Identity, and the Performance of Popular Verse in America* (Ann Arbor: University of Michigan Press, 2009).

St John, G., 'Electronic Dance Music Culture and Religion: An Overview', *Culture and Religion*, 7(1) (2006), 1–26.

St John, G. (ed.), *Rave Culture and Religion* (London: Routledge, 2004).

Stein, K., *Poetry's Afterlife: Verse in the Digital Age* (Ann Arbor, MI: University of Michigan Press, 2010).

Stern, F., 'The Formal Poetry Reading', *The Drama Review*, 35(3) (Fall 1991), 67–84.

Stiles, K., 'Performance', in Nelson, R. S. & Shiff, R. (eds.), *Critical Terms for Art History* (2nd edn., Chicago: University of Chicago Press, 2003).

Stovall, D., 'Urban Poetics: Poetry, Social Justice and Critical Pedagogy in Education', *The Urban Review*, 38(1) (2006), 63–80.

Swidler, A., 'Culture in Action: Symbols and Strategies', *American Sociological Review*, 51(2) (Apr 1986), 273–286.

Swift, R. 'Whose Streets? The Clampdown on Popular Rights', *New Internationalist*, Issue. 508 (Dec. 2017).

T

Tangherlini, T. R., '"Oral Tradition" in a Technologically Advanced World', *Oral Tradition*, 18(1) (2003), 136–38.

Taransaud, D., *I, Monster: Positive Ways of Working with Challenging*

Teens Through Understanding the Adolescent in Us (London: Routledge, 2016).

Tawada, Y., 'The Art of Being Nonsynchronous', in Perloff, M. & Dworkin, C. (eds.), *The Sound of Poetry: The Poetry of Sound* (Chicago: University of Chicago Press, 2009).

Taylor, S., *Left-Wing Nietzscheans: The Politics of German Expressionism 1910-1920* (1990, Reprint, Berlin: de Gruyter, 2012).

Tedlock, D., *The Spoken Word and the Work of Interpretation* (Philadelphia: University of Pennsylvania Press, 1983).

Teitler, N., *Freed Verse: Diversity in British Poetry 2015 – 2017* (London: The Complete Works, 2017).

Thomas, D., *Dylan Thomas Early Prose Writings*, Davies, W. (ed.), (London: Dent, 1971).

Thomas, L., 'Neon Griot: The Functional Role of Poetry Readings in the Black Arts Movement', in Bernstein, C. (ed.), *Close Listening: Poetry and the Performed Word* (New York: Oxford University Press, 1998).

Thompson, E. P., *The Making of the English Working Class* (1963, Reprint, Harmondsworth: Penguin, 1980).

Thomson, P. & Jaque, V. S., *Creativity and the Performing Artist: Behind the Mask*, (London: Academic Press, 2017).

Trévien, C. (ed.), *Verbs that Move Mountains: Essays and Interviews on Spoken Word Cultures Around the World* (Sabotage Reviews, 2018).

Tsur, R., 'Sound Affects of Poetry: Critical Impressionism, Reductionism and Cognitive Poetics', *Pragmatics in Cognition*, 5(2) (January 1997), 283–304.

Tsur, R., *What Makes Sound Patterns Expressive* (Durham, NC: Duke University Press, 1992).

U

Umiltà, M. A., 'The "Mirror Mechanism" and Motor Behaviour', in Falletti, C., Sofia, G. & Jacono, V. (eds.), *Theatre and Cognitive Neuroscience: Performance and Science: Interdisciplinary Dialogues* (London: Bloomsbury, 2016).

Utter! Spoken Word, 'Statements of Intent/The Obvious', *Utter! Manifesto,* (May 2018).

Uzendoski, M. A. & Calapucha-Tapuy, E. F., *The Ecology of the Spoken Word* (Urbana, IL: University of Illinois Press, 2012).

V

Vicinus, M., 'The Study of Nineteenth-Century British Working Class Poetry', *College English*, 32(5) (1971), 548–562.

W

Wade, S., *A Straightforward Guide to Writing Performance Poetry* (2nd edn., Brighton: Straightforward, 2011).

Wade, S., 'Interview with Adrian Mitchell', in Munden, P. & Wade, S. (eds.), *Reading the Applause: Reflections on Performance Poetry by Various Artists* (York: Talking Shop, 1999).

Wallis, M., 'Pageantry and the Popular Front: Ideological Production in the 'Thirties', *New Theatre Quarterly,* 10(38) (1994), 132–56.

Walton, J. K., *Chartism* (London; New York: Routledge, 2001).

Washington, R. E., *The Ideologies of African American Literature: From the Harlem Renaissance to the Black Nationalist Revolt* (Lanham, MD: Rowman & Littlefield, 2001).

Waterfield, R., *Hidden Depths* (New York: Brunner-Routledge, 2002).

Watts, R., 'The Cult of the Noble Amateur', *PN Review*, 44(3) (2018).

Weiss, J., Herndon, S. & Morris, T., *Brave New Voices: The Youth Speaks Guide to Teaching Spoken-Word Poetry* (Portsmouth, NH: Heinemann, 2001).

Welsh, A., 'Chant', in Preminger, A. & Brogan, T. V. F. (eds.), *The New Princeton Encyclopedia of Poetry and Poetics* (Princeton, NJ: Princeton University Press, 1993).

Welsh, A., 'Charm', Preminger, A. & Brogan, T. V. F. (eds.), *The New Princeton Encyclopedia of Poetry and Poetics* (Princeton, NJ: Princeton University Press, 1993).

Whalley, J. & Miller, L., *Between Us: Audiences, Affect and the In-Between* (London: Palgrave Macmillan, 2017).

Wheeler, L., *Voicing American Poetry* (Ithaca, NY: Cornell University Press, 2008).

Wilson, C., 'Edinburgh versus Austin: Poetry Slams and Ethics', in Trévien, C. (ed.), *Verbs that Move Mountains: Essays and Interviews on Spoken Word Cultures Around the World* (Sabotage Reviews, 2018).

Wojahn, D., '"A Kind of Vaudeville": Appraising the Age of the Poetry Reading', *New England Review and Bread Loaf Quarterly*, 8(2) (1985), 265–82.

Wordsworth, W., *Preface to the Lyrical Ballads* (1800, Reprint, CreateSpace Independent Publishing Platform, 2016).

Wyman-McGinty, W., 'The Body in Analysis: Authentic Movement and Witnessing in Analytic Practice', *Journal of Analytical Psychotherapy*, 43(2) (1998), 239–260.

Z

Zephaniah, B., 'Knowing Me', in *Too Black, Too Strong* (Tarset, Northumberland: Bloodaxe Books, 2001).

Zinn, H., *A People's History of the United States* (New York: Harper and Row, 1980).

Zumthor, P., *Oral Poetry: An Introduction* (Minneapolis: University of Minnesota Press, 1990).

Websites and Online Resources

Ailes, K., 'What Cult? A Critical Engagement with Watts' Essay', *Sabotage Reviews*, 6 March 2018, < http://sabotagereviews. com/2018/03/06/what-cult-a-critical-engagement-with-watts-essay/> [accessed 22 March 2019]

Ailes, K., 'Why "Slam Poetry" Is Not a Genre – Katie Ailes', 9 February 2016, <https://katieailes.com/2016/02/09/why-slam-poetry-is-not-a-genre/> [accessed 22 March 2019]

Al Jazeera, 'Dareen Tatour Sentenced to Five Months in Prison over Poem', 31 July 2018,<https://www.aljazeera. com/news/2018/07/dareen-tatour-sentenced-months-prison-poem-180731084215893.html> [accessed 29 March 2019]

Alleyne, R., 'Britain's "Me Culture" Making Us Depressed', *The Telegraph*, 6 November 2009, <https://www.telegraph.co.uk/news/science/science-news/6514956/Britains-me-culture-

making-us-depressed.html> [accessed 29 March 2019]

Anti-Slam Apocalypse, 'The Anti-Slam Apocalypse - #TeamTrending', *Process Productions*, YouTube, 6 February 2017, <https://www.youtube.com/watch?v=CZsdfk68I1I> [accessed 22 March 2019]

Anton, 'Corey Anton - YouTube' <https://www.youtube.com/user/Professoranton> [accessed 14 June 2019]

Apples and Snakes, 'Lemn Sissay: FULL INTERVIEW | Spoken Word Archive - YouTube', 20 December 2017, <https://www.youtube.com/watch?v=RqgWjwLDHE0&t=1374s> [accessed 16 April 2019]

Apples and Snakes, 'Producers Reflect on Some Recent Decisions - Apples and Snakes' <https://applesandsnakes.org/producers_blog/> [accessed 19 December 2018]

Apples and Snakes, 'The Apples and Snakes Story', *Spoken Word Archive*, <https://www.spokenwordarchive.org.uk/content/new-contributions/apples-snakes-story> [accessed 19 March 2019]

Apples and Snakes, 'Apples and Snakes - Wordsmiths & Co. Featuring Hannah Silva', *YouTube*, 11 July 2014, <https://www.youtube.com/watch?v=yCy9YS_UYeE&t=352s> [accessed 24 March 2019]

Assange, J., 'Julian Assange: "This Generation Is the Last Free Generation" - YouTube', *Daily Mail*, 24 September 2018, <https://www.youtube.com/watch?v=4vB05rZ6AMk&t=35s> [accessed 29 March 2019]

B

Bailey, Ben, 'Poets Vs MCs 2018 Review', *Brighton Source*, 24 January 2018, <https://brightonsource.co.uk/reviews/poets-vs-mcs-2018-review/> [accessed 21 March 2019]

Barron, J., 'Amiri Baraka, Newark Poet, Looks Back on a Bloody

Week in 1967', *The New York Times*, 10 October 2012, <https://
www.nytimes.com/2012/10/11/nyregion/amiri-baraka-newark-
poet-looks-back-on-a-bloody-week-in-1967.html> [accessed 22
March 2019]

Barton, L., 'The Beat Women - BBC Sounds', *BBC*, <https://
www.bbc.co.uk/sounds/play/b06084ks> [accessed 22 March
2019]

BBC Front Row, 'BBC Radio 4 - Front Row, Exit the King,
Man Booker Longlist, Tony Walsh, Nick Drnaso', *BBC*, 24 July
2018, < <https://www.bbc.co.uk/programmes/b0bbn6vs> >
[accessed 22 March 2019]

BBC News, 'BBC - Words First: Radio 1Xtra Launches BBC's
First-Ever Spoken-Word Season - Media Centre' <https://www.
bbc.co.uk/mediacentre/latestnews/2015/1xtra-words-first>
[accessed 24 March 2019]

BBC News, 'Egypt Protests: Army Rules out the Use of Force',
BBC News, 31 January 2011, <https://www.bbc.co.uk/news/
world-middle-east-12330169> [accessed 29 March 2019]

'BBC - Radio 4 Woman's Hour -Charlotte Smith', 28
December 2006, <http://www.bbc.co.uk/radio4/
womanshour/04/2006_52_thu.shtml> [accessed 26 April 2019]

Behrle, J., 'How to Write a Love Poem — Mindful Living', *Utne
Reader*, January–February 2012, <https://www.utne.com/arts/
how-to-write-a-love-poem> [accessed 22 March 2019]

Bernstein, C., 'Charles Bernstein - Interviewed by Payam
Fotouhipour' <http://www.bbk.ac.uk/readings-old/r1/
bernstein.html> [accessed 25 March 2019]

Bingham, J., 'Britain the Loneliness Capital of Europe', *The
Telegraph*, 18 June 2014, <https://www.telegraph.co.uk/lifestyle/
wellbeing/10909524/Britain-the-loneliness-capital-of-Europe.
html> [accessed 29 March 2019]

BP or Not BP, 'Problems with BP – BP or Not BP?' <https://bp-or-not-bp.org/problems-with-bp/> [accessed 29 March 2019]

Brady, A., Cleary, S., and Willey, S., 'British Poetry in Performance, 1960-2008 _ Beyond Text' <http://projects.beyondtext.ac.uk/poetryinperformance/index.php> [accessed 9 May 2019]

Brook, O., O'Brien, D. & Taylor, M., *Panic! Social Class, Taste and Inequalities in the Creative Industries*, 2018 <http://createlondon.org/wp-content/uploads/2018/04/Panic-Social-Class-Taste-and-Inequalities-in-the-Creative-Industries1.pdf> [accessed 25 March 2019]

Brown, M., 'Brexit Is Black Cloud for UK Arts, Says Former National Theatre Boss | Politics', *The Guardian*, 12 October 2018, <https://www.theguardian.com/culture/2018/oct/12/brexit-is-black-cloud-for-uk-arts-says-nicholas-hytner-national-theatre> [accessed 29 March 2019]

Butnotfamous, R., '1. Introduction to Poetry Busking', *YouTube*, 14 January 2019, <https://www.youtube.com/watch?v=DnFr7oB9jC0&index=1&list=PLeCXFZk-4Y8BYgHsHFXFFgtT6jizfQ60s> [accessed 24 March 2019]

Butnotfamous, R., 'Mission — Rich Butnotfamous - Performance Poet & Wordsmith' <https://www.richbutnotfamo.us/vision> [accessed 26 March 2019]

C

Carlo, S., and Krueckeberg, J., *THE STATE OF SURVEILLANCE IN 2018*, <https://bigbrotherwatch.org.uk/wp-content/uploads/2018/09/The-State-of-Surveillance-in-2018.pdf> [accessed 29 March 2019]

Chivers, Danny, 'Shop a Scrounger on Vimeo', 2011, <https://Vimeo.com/17295443> [accessed 21 May 2019]

Clinton, D., Annotation of Deleuze, G. & Guattari. F., 'Rhizome', in *A Thousand Plateaus*, (Theories of Media, 2003), http://csmt.uchicago.edu/annotations/deleuzerhizome.htm

Coates, D., 'Kate Tempest – Let Them Eat Chaos – Dave Poems', 8 February 2017, <https://davepoems.wordpress. com/2017/02/08/kate-tempest-let-them-eat-chaos/> [accessed 29 March 2019]

Cook, E., interview with Hollie McNish 'Poetry, Breastfeeding and Sex', *The Guardian*, 13 February 2016, <https://www. theguardian.com/lifeandstyle/2016/feb/13/poetry-breastfeeding-and-sex>

Crisp, J., 'Sexism in Genre Publishing: A Publisher's Perspective', *Panmacmillan.com*, 10 July 2017, <https://www.panmacmillan. com/blogs/science-fiction-and-fantasy/sexism-genre-publishing-publishers-perspective>

D

Democracy Now, 'Remembering Amiri Baraka Part 2 Featuring Sonia Sanchez, Felipe Luciano, Larry Hamm, Komozi Woodard', *Democracy Now*, 10 January 2014, <https://www. democracynow.org/2014/1/10/remembering_amiri_baraka_part_2_featuring> [accessed 22 March 2019]

Diggs, D., and Smith, D., 'Why Poetry Is The Best Medium For Kids Who Want To Change The World', *Huffington Post*, 19 July 2016, <https://www.huffingtonpost.co.uk/entry/why-poetry-is-the-best-medium-for-kids-who-want-to-change-the-world_us_578c0c57e4b03fc3ee5146d3?guccounter=1> [accessed 21 March 2019]

Dizraeli, 'My Brother Can't Help Himself', <https://www.facebook.com/Dizraeli/videos/10154853842292611/> [accessed 28 March 2019]

Donaldson, Jesse, 'This Is Why You Probably Hate Slam Poetry, According to a Linguistic Scholar', *VICE*, 6 February 2017, <https://www.vice.com/en_uk/article/aejne8/this-is-why-you-probably-hate-slam-poetry-according-to-a-linguistic-scholar> [accessed 21 March 2019]

Door-to-Door Poetry, 'What Is This? – Door-to-Door Poetry' <https://doortodoorpoetry.com/about/> [accessed 24 March 2019]

E

El Crisis, 'Nat Nye - El Crisis - Performance at MUTABARUKA Show UK - YouTube', *Gotkush TV*, 14 January 2017, <https://www.youtube.com/watch?v=WavHE1gpk20&t=1428s> [accessed 29 March 2019]

English, L., 'The Growing Popularity of Performance Poetry Is a Boost for Mental Wellbeing | Culture Professionals Network', *The Guardian*, 2 June 2016, <https://www.theguardian.com/culture-professionals-network/2016/jun/02/performance-poetry-boost-for-mental-wellbeing> [accessed 27 March 2019]

'Ethnicity in the UK' <https://www.ethnicity-facts-figures.service.gov.uk/ethnicity-in-the-uk> [accessed 22 March 2019]

Evans, D., 'Michael Curry's Royal Wedding Sermon Will Go down in History | Diana Evans | Opinion', *The Guardian*, 20 May 2018, <https://www.theguardian.com/commentisfree/2018/may/20/bishop-michael-curry-sermon-history-harry-meghan-wedding> [accessed 29 March 2019]

Evaristo, B., 'Amiri Baraka: My Fiery Inspiration | Bernardine Evaristo | Books | The Guardian', 10 January 2014, <https://www.theguardian.com/books/booksblog/2014/jan/10/amil-baraka-inspiration-bernardine-evaristo> [accessed 22 April 2019]

F

Farrago Poetry, 'About Farrago Poetry, London' <http://london.e-poets.net/about-Farrago.shtml> [accessed 21 March 2019]

Fenton, J., 'A Voice of His Own | Books', *The Guardian*, 3 February 2007, <https://www.theguardian.com/books/2007/feb/03/poetry.whauden> [accessed 29 March 2019]

François, K., 'Kat Francois Shares 'Does My Anger Scare You' against Deaths in Custody', *YouTube*, 31 October 2012, <https://www.youtube.com/watch?v=kCOWzMnA3EU> [accessed 29 March 2019]

Freeverse.org, Kean, D., Massey, K., Mason-John, V., Nagra, D., Solomon, A., Sesay, K. G. & others, *Publishing Opportunities for Black and Asian Poets* <www.freeverse.org.uk> [accessed 22 March 2019]

G

Gardiner, B., 'Why I'm a Striking Lecturer: I Want to Stop the Slow Death of Public Education | Becky Gardiner | Opinion', *The Guardian*, 12 March 2018, <https://www.theguardian.com/commentisfree/2018/mar/12/striking-lecturer-slow-death-public-education> [accessed 24 March 2019]

Gardosi, J., 'Jasmine Gardosi - Unidentified Crying Objects (Howl, October 11, 2017)', *YouTube*, 28 February 2018, <https://www.youtube.com/watch?time_continue=55&v=og4l4bG43zQ> [accessed 10 April 2019]

Gilpin, C., 'Slam Poetry Does Not Exist: How a Movement Has Been Misconstrued as a Genre', *Litlive.Ca*, 2015, <http://www.litlive.ca/story/602> [accessed 22 March 2019]

Ginsberg, A., 'Allen Ginsberg - Face to Face - YouTube', *Odeen Rocha*, 25 March 2015, <https://www.youtube.com/watch?v=TnDH40K9UPs> [accessed 22 March 2019]

Godden, S., 'Salena Godden: Passion and Hard Work Are the Keys to Writing', *London Evening Standard*, 20 January 2014, <https://www.standard.co.uk/comment/salena-godden-passion-and-hard-work-are-the-keys-to-writing-9071749.html> [accessed 24 March 2019]

Godden, S., 'Salena Godden - Voodoo - Live at Tongue Fu', *YouTube*, 25 June 2015, <https://www.youtube.com/watch?v=dl9oQ0rnGhU> [accessed 24 March 2019]

Godden, S., 'Salena Godden | March 4 Women | "Courage Is A Muscle" | "Pessimism Is For Lightweights"', *YouTube*, 16 March 2018, <https://www.youtube.com/watch?v=wjTVyBcJR7I> [accessed 29 March 2019]

Goody, J., 'Oral Literature', *Brittanica.com*, 27 August 2016, <https://www.britannica.com/art/oral-literature> [accessed 22 March 2019]

Gräbner, C., 'Performance Poetry and Academic Theory in the Trenches: Suggestions for a New Dialogue – Poetics of Resistance – Las Poéticas de La Resistencia' (first published 2008/2009, original reference unavailable) <https://poeticsofresistance.wordpress.com/2019/04/07/performance-poetry-and-academic-theory-in-the-trenches-suggestions-for-a-new-dialogue/> [accessed 8 May 2019]

Groff, D., 'The Perils of the Poetry Reading: The Page Versus the Performance', *Poets.org*, 26 January 2005, https://www.poets.org/poetsorg/text/peril-poetry-reading-page-versus-performance [accessed 22 March 2019]

H

Ha, Thu-Huong, 'History of Reading: The Beginning of Silent Reading Changed Humans' Interior Life', *Quartzy*, 19 November 2017, <https://qz.com/quartzy/1118580/the-beginning-of-silent-reading-was-also-the-beginning-of-an-interior-life/> [accessed 22 March 2019]

Harris, R., 'The Loneliness Epidemic: We're More Connected than Ever – but Are We Feeling More Alone?', *The Independent*, 30 March 2015, <https://www.independent.co.uk/life-style/health-and-families/features/the-loneliness-epidemic-more-connected-than-ever-but-feeling-more-alone-10143206.html> [accessed 29 March 2019]

Harrison, A., 'Is There More to Spoken Word Than All Those Terrible Adverts?', *VICE*, 1 February 2017, <https://www.vice.com/en_uk/article/jpd57x/is-there-more-to-spoken-word-than-all-those-terrible-adverts> [accessed 22 March 2019]

Hip Yak Poetry Shack, 'The HIP YAK Poetry Shack | Spoken Word Poetry of the Shack, Stage, School & Slam', 2019, <http://www.hipyakpoetryshack.co.uk/> [accessed 26 March 2019]

Historical Association, 'The Chartists / Podcast Series: Politics, Reform and War. / Historical Association', *Historical Association*, <https://www.history.org.uk/student/categories/495/module/4701/podcast-series-politics-reform-and-war/4703/the-chartists> [accessed 22 March 2019]

Holloway, D., 'Flash-Slam – National Flash-Fiction Day', 28 December 2011, <https://nationalflashfictionday.co.uk/index.php/category/flash-slam/> [accessed 21 March 2019]

Howlett, R., 'How We Reclaimed the Bard from BP – BP or Not BP?', 11 January 2013, <https://bp-or-not-bp.org/2013/01/11/how-we-reclaimed-the-bard-from-bp/> [accessed 29 March 2019]

Hyde, L., 'Lewis Hyde: & "Common As Air: Revolution, Art, and Ownership"; - YouTube', *WGBH Forum*, 15 Aug 2012, <https://www.youtube.com/watch?v=2HQVBmKsVhI> [accessed 21 March 2019]

I

Inquest.org.uk, 'BAME Deaths in Police Custody', Updated 10 January 2019, <https://www.inquest.org.uk/bame-deaths-in-police-custody> [accessed 29 March 2019]

Institute of Biodynamic Medicine, 'Biodynamic Psychotherapy - Institute of Biodynamic Medicine', <https://biodynamic.org/what-is/biodynamic-psychotherapy/> [accessed 24 March 2019]

J

Jack, S., 'Joygernaut (Andy Craven-Griffiths, Attenborough Arts Centre, Leicester, 11 October 2018)', *Sabotage Reviews*, 14 October 2018, <https://sabotagereviews.com/2018/10/14/joygernaut-andy-craven-griffiths-attenborough-arts-centre-leicester-11-october-2018/> [accessed 24 March 2019]

Jacob, L., 'Groundless in the Museum: Anarchism and the Living Work of Art', *Anarchist Developments in Cultural Studies* (Trent University, 2010), <https://journals.uvic.ca/index.php/adcs/article/view/17813/7434> [accessed 25 March 2019]

'John Cooper Clarke - Evidently Chickentown - YouTube' <https://www.youtube.com/watch?v=3KgB-sI2H-c> [accessed 20 May 2019]

Johnson & Alcock, <http://www.johnsonandalcock.co.uk/> [accessed 20 June 2018]

'Joolz Denby Has NO FEAR | Spoken Word Archive - YouTube', 2. January 2018, <https://www.youtube.com/watch?v=vMZxI9Lbq_M&t=2s> [accessed 20 May 2019]

K

Kadir, N., 'I'm Glad I Eschewed a Career in Academia – There Are Plenty of Alternatives for PhDs | THE Opinion', *Times Higher Education*, 31 July 2017, <https://www.timeshighereducation.com/blog/im-glad-i-eschewed-career-academia-there-are-plenty-of-alternatives-for-phds#survey-answer> [accessed 25 March 2019]

Kirmayer, L., 'Cultural Psychiatry: Lecture #10 Healing, Ritual and Psychotherapy Pt 1 – YouTube', *Transcultural Psychiatry*, 19 April 2013, <https://www.youtube.com/watch?v=JnxcMhH_-n4&t=4379s> [accessed 29 March 2019]

Kisuule, V., 'Vanessa Kisuule, Sexy – The Wardrobe Theatre', <http://thewardrobetheatre.com/livetheatre/sexy/> [accessed 24 March 2019]

KRS-One, *KRS-One at Sonoma State University*', *YouTube*, 2008, <https://www.youtube.com/watch?v=gjJDhyW2BaY&t=31s> [accessed 25 March 2019]

L

Lakoff, G., 'George Lakoff on Embodied Cognition and Language', *Central European University*, YouTube, 22 October 2013, <https://www.youtube.com/watch?v=XWYaoAoijdQ&t=2254s> [accessed 27 March 2019]

'Langston Hughes | Poetry Foundation' <https://www.poetryfoundation.org/poets/langston-hughes> [accessed 18 April 2019]

Liberty, 'Free Speech and Protest | Liberty' <https://www.libertyhumanrights.org.uk/human-rights/free-speech-and-protest> [accessed 29 March 2019]

Liberty, 'Human Rights in the UK after Brexit | Liberty', <https://www.libertyhumanrights.org.uk/human-rights/human-rights-uk-after-brexit> [accessed 29 March 2019]

Liberty, 'Protest around Parliament | Liberty' <https://www.libertyhumanrights.org.uk/human-rights/free-speech-and-protest/protest/protest-around-parliament> [accessed 29 March 2019]

Livingstone, K., 'Waking Hypnosis' <http://www.hypnosis101.com/hypnosis-tips/waking-hypnosis/> [accessed 29 March 2019]

M

Macnicol, F., 'Biodynamic Massage - an Introduction' <http://www.yobeely.f2s.com/articles/massintro.html> [accessed 24 March 2019]

Madera, John, 'Magic and Music Steer This Vessel: On Jorge Luis Borges's This Craft of Verse | Fiction Writers Review', 29 October 2009, <https://fictionwritersreview.com/essay/magic-and-music-steer-this-vessel-jorge-luis-borges-this-craft-of-verse/>

Mali, T., 'I Could Be a Poet', <https://www.stpatricktheatre.org/uploads/4/9/2/7/4927337/taylor_mali_poetry.pdf> [accessed 26 March 2019]

Marsh, S., 'Combat Loneliness with "Social Prescribing", Says Theresa May | Society', *The Guardian*, 14 October 2018, <https://www.theguardian.com/society/2018/oct/14/loneliness-social-prescribing-theresa-may> [accessed 29 March 2019]

Massey, G., '"Gerald Massey: Chartist, Poet, Radical and Freethinker" - Chapter 9.' <http://gerald-massey.org.uk/massey/cbiog_part_09.htm> [accessed 22 March 2019]

McKenna, T., 'Terence McKenna - A Crisis of Consciousness (Lecture)', *YouTube*, 16 June 2016, <https://www.youtube.com/watch?v=djm9KDW1sXE> [accessed 1 April 2019]

Melia, J., 'Burning Eye Books', *Bristol247.com*, 25 October 2017, <https://www.bristol247.com/culture/books/burning-eye-books-bristol/> [accessed 22 March 2019]

Michel, Lincoln, 'Lit Mag Submissions 101: How, When, and Where to Send Your Work - Electric Literature', 1 December 2016, <https://electricliterature.com/lit-mag-submissions-101-how-when-and-where-to-send-your-work/>

Monbiot, G., 'George Monbiot: How Do We Get out of This Mess?', *The Guardian*, 9 September 2017, <https://www.theguardian.com/books/2017/sep/09/george-monbiot-how-de-we-get-out-of-this-mess>

Mongiovi, J., 'Hypnotic Suggestion' <http://johnmongiovi.com/pages/hypnotic-suggestion> [accessed 29 March 2019]

Monologue Slam, 'Monologue Slam | Part of TriForce Creative Network' <http://monologueslamuk.com/> [accessed 21 March 2019]

Morgan, D. L., 'IndieFeed: Performance Poetry : David Lee Morgan (Music by Michael Harding) - BEAST MARKET (Capital, by Karl Marx, Chapters 1-4, The Beast Speaks)', 6 January 2014, <http://indiefeedpp.libsyn.com/david-lee-morgan-music-by-michael-harding-east-market-capital-by-karl-marx-chapters-1-4-the-beast-speaks> [accessed 29 March 2019]

Morgan, D. L., 'THE GIFT OF PAIN - YouTube', 25 December 2015, <https://www.youtube.com/watch?v=liCARIpQk1o&feature=youtu.be> [accessed 28 May 2019]

Morrison, J., 'The International Poetry Incarnation: The Beat Goes On', *The Independent*, 22 September 2005, <https://www.independent.co.uk/arts-entertainment/books/features/the-international-poetry-incarnation-the-beat-goes-on-314324.html> [accessed 22 March 2019]

Morrison, T., 'No Place for Self-Pity, No Room for Fear', *The Nation*, 23 March 2015, <https://www.thenation.com/article/no-place-self-pity-no-room-fear/> [accessed 29 March 2019]

N

National Rural Touring Forum, 'About Us | National Rural Touring Forum' <http://www.ruraltouring.org/about> [accessed 24 March 2019]

Novara Media, 'Radical Happiness: Lynne Segal', *Novara Media*, 11 December 2017, <https://novaramedia.com/2017/12/11/radical-happiness-lynne-segal/> [accessed 29 March 2019]

Nunberg, G., 'The Rise of Mass Literacy in History of Information', UC Berkeley School of Information, PDF presentation, 2 March 2017, https://bcourses.berkeley.edu/courses/1457197/files/708127/dwnload?verifier=jwPo16PWNuIxNi8FVkWlx0BAUUeGjUytlzfm2oAK [accessed 22 March 2019]

Nunes, A., 'The Mindscape of Alan Moore', Alexandre Nunes, *YouTube*, 27 June 2013, <https://www.youtube.com/watch?v=moRkHk-q9Rg>

Nymphs & Thugs, 'Nymphs & Thugs – Spoken Word Record Label' <https://nymphsandthugs.net/> [accessed 26 March 2019]

NYU Center for the Humanities, 'Theorizing Sound Writing', *YouTube*, 16 May 2017, <https://www.youtube.com/watch?v=WH0IhN6zZeM&t=1728s> [accessed 28 March 2019]

O

O'Hagan, E. M., 'The Fortnum & Mason Protest Verdict: A Farcical Injustice | Ellie Mae O'Hagan | Opinion', *The Guardian*, 17 November 2011, <https://www.theguardian.com/commentisfree/2011/nov/17/fortnum-mason-verdict-uk-uncut-protesters> [accessed 29 March 2019]

O'Keeffe, A., 'Hollie McNish: The Politics and Poetry of Boyfriends, Babies and Breastfeeding', *The Guardian*, 16 June 2017, <https://www.theguardian.com/books/2017/jun/16/hollie-mcnish-politics-

of-poetry-ted-hughes-prize-winner> [accessed 22 March 2019]

Oliver, M., 'Mary Oliver "Listening to the World" On Being with Krista Tippett', *The On Being Project*, 17 January 2019, <https://onbeing.org/series/podcast/> [accessed 22 March 2019]

Olson, C., 'Projective Verse', originally published 1950, <http://writing.upenn.edu/~taransky/Projective_Verse.pdf> [accessed 25 March 2019]

O'Sullivan, N., 'Remembering the Death of the Performance Poet', 2014, <http://niallosullivan.co.uk/index/remembering-the-death-of-performance-poetry/> [accessed 22 March 2018]

Otten, C., 'The Last Poets: America in Poetry from Black Power to Black Lives Matter', *The Guardian*, 21 November 2016, <https://www.theguardian.com/books/2016/nov/21/the-last-poets-america-in-poetry-from-black-power-to-black-lives-matter> [accessed 22 March 2019]

P

Patel, B., 'A Verse to Go, Please: Street Poets and the Lives They Touch', *The Atlantic*, 1 November 2013, <https://www.theatlantic.com/national/archive/2013/11/a-verse-to-go-please-street-poets-and-the-lives-they-touch/281035/> [accessed 24 March 2019]

Penlington, N., 'Nathan Penlington - Don't Need English Lessons to Learn Our Lines', 1999, <http://nathanpenlington.com/post/157016614067/dont-need-english-lessons-to-learn-our-lines> [accessed 22 March 2019]

Popova, M., 'James Baldwin on the Creative Process and the Artist's Responsibility to Society', *Brain Pickings*, 20 August 2014, <https://www.brainpickings.org/2014/08/20/james-baldwin-the-creative-process/> [accessed 29 March 2019]

Potter, G. 'How Do You Respect Fuck All?', *IndieFeed: Performance Poetry*, 3 August 2012, < http://indiefeedpp.libsyn.com/gerry-potter-how-do-you-respect-fuck-all/> [accessed 22 March 2019]

R

Reclaim Shakespeare, *Do We Sleep?*, 2012, <https://notbpblog.files.wordpress.com/2012/04/reclaim-shakespeare-company-script2.pdf> [accessed 29 March 2019]

Riley, P., 'Peter Riley: Is There No Modern Poetry of the "Low and Poor"?', *The Fortnightly Review*, 20 December 2012, <http://fortnightlyreview.co.uk/2012/12/working-class-poetry/> [accessed 22 March 2019]

Rohter, L., 'Is Slam in Danger of Going Soft?', *New York Times*, 2 June 2009, <https://www.nytimes.com/2009/06/03/books/03slam.html> [accessed 22 March 2019]

Romer, C., 'Lottery Shortfall Forces ACE to Cut 2018-22 Budget by £156m | News', *ArtsProfessional*, 24 January 2018, <https://www.artsprofessional.co.uk/news/lottery-shortfall-forces-ace-cut-2018-22-budget-ps156m> [accessed 24 March 2019]

S

Sam-La Rose, Jacob, 'The Rise of Spoken Word Educators in UK Schools | Teacher Network', *The Guardian*, 3 October 2013, <https://www.theguardian.com/teacher-network/teacher-blog/2013/oct/03/spoken-word-educators-poetry-schools> [accessed 27 March 2019]

Sanders, M., 'Making Better Rhymes: Chartist Poetry and Working Class Struggle', *Culture Matters*, 22 January 2016, <https://culturematters.org.uk/index.php/culture/festivals/item/2209-making-better-rhymes-chartist-poetry-and-working-class-struggle> [accessed 22 March 2019]

Scottish Poetry Library, 'The State of Poetry and Poetry Criticism in the UK and Ireland. Report by Scottish Poetry Library', *National Library of Scotland & International Writing at Liverpool University*, 2012, <https://www.liverpool.ac.uk/media/livacuk/centrefornewandinternationalwriting/Longform,post,-,The,State,of,Poetry,and,Poetry,Criticism,in,the,UK,and,Ireland,FINAL.pdf> [accessed 24 March 2019]

Shamaan Freeman-Powell, 'The Rock Stars of Poetry Explain Why the Art Is in Demand - BBC News', 28 Jan. 2019 <https://www.bbc.com/news/entertainment-arts-47005108> [accessed 14 June 2019]

Shatayeva, L., 'Aitys: Gem of Kazakh Spoken Literary Tradition, Platform for Human Rights', *The Astana Times*, 6 January 2017, <https://astanatimes.com/2017/01/aitys-gem-of-kazakh-spoken-literary-tradition-platform-for-human-rights/> [accessed 21 March 2019]

Shmoop.com, 'Lolita Narrator Point of View', <https://www.shmoop.com/lolita/narrator-point-of-view.html> [accessed 27 March 2019]

Shorthouse, R., 'Loneliness Should Be Recognised as a Signal of Poverty in Today's Britain', *The Guardian*, 26 February 2014, <https://www.theguardian.com/commentisfree/2014/feb/26/loneliness-signal-poverty-britain-iain-duncan-smith> [accessed 29 March 2019]

Shouse, E., 'Feeling, Emotion, Affect', *Media and Culture*, 8 (2005) <http://journal.media-culture.org.au/0512/03-shouse.php> [accessed 27 March 2019]

Sissay, L., 'Lemn Sissay: FULL INTERVIEW | Spoken Word Archive - YouTube', *Apples and Snakes*, 20 December 2017, <https://www.youtube.com/watch?v=RqgWjwLDHE0> [accessed 21 March 2019]

Sissay, L., 'Lemn Sissay on Slam Poetry | Spoken Word Archive - YouTube', *Apples and Snakes*, 2017, <https://www.youtube.com/watch?v=Z36iCiLgzFQ> [accessed 22 March 2019]

Slater, R., 'Verse Goes Viral: How Young Feminist Writers Are Reclaiming Poetry for the Digital Age', *The Guardian*, 27 November 2016, <> [accessed 22 March 2019]

Smith, M., 'SlamCulture 2011 - Marc Smith Interview - Sept11 - Slam In Europe', *YouTube*, 5 April 2013, <https://www.youtube.com/watch?v=MmH_ePoYCOM> [accessed 26 March 2019]

Somers-Willett, S., 'Susan B.A. Somers-Willett - "Can Slam Poetry Matter?"', *Rattle* <https://www.rattle.com/rattle27/somerswillett.htm> [accessed 21 March 2019]

Spencer, K., 'Politicians Could "Learn a Lot" from the Power of Poetry', *Sky News*, 28 May 2017, <https://news.sky.com/story/politicians-could-learn-a-lot-from-the-power-of-poetry-10895834>

Sundiata, S., 'Sekou Sundiata on music, poetry, East Harlem and activism', *HoCoPoLitSo*, *YouTube*, 1 May 2012, < https://www.youtube.com/watch?v=M0FIzRj7prY >

T

Take Art, 'Word/Play | Take Art' <https://takeart.org/word-play> [accessed 29 March 2019]

Taylor, A., 'Gig Theatre at Edinburgh Festival & Edinburgh Fringe', *The Skinny*, 29 July 2016, <https://www.theskinny.co.uk/festivals/edinburgh-fringe/theatre/gig-theatre-not-theatre-not-a-gig-a-movement> [accessed 27 March 2019]

Tempest, K., 'Kate Tempest - End Times', *YouTube*, 7 December 2009, <https://www.youtube.com/watch?v=jYMtmQ_H570&t=152s> [accessed 29 March 2019]

Tempest, K., 'Kate Tempest - Live Glastonbury Festival – 2017', *Land Pirates, YouTube*, 28 June 2017, <https://www.youtube.com/watch?v=mLzJUalxZYM> [accessed 29 March 2019]

Tempest, K., 'Kate Tempest – 'People's Faces'; | LIVE AT GLASTONBURY 2017', *Left Voice, YouTube*, 25 June 2017, <https://www.youtube.com/watch?v=CmHgQT9zP_c> [accessed 29 March 2019]

That's How the Light Gets In, 'The Mersey Sound – That's How The Light Gets In', *That's How the Light Gets In*, 18 June 2009, <https://gerryco23.wordpress.com/2009/06/18/the-mersey-sound/> [accessed 22 March 2019]

Thomason, T. C., 'The Role of Altered States of Consciousness in Native American Healing - The Cuyamungue Institute', Northern Arizona University, <http://www.cuyamungueinstitute.com/articles-and-news/the-role-of-altered-states-of-consciousness-in-native-american-healing/> [accessed 28 March 2019]

Travis, A., 'UK Mass Digital Surveillance Regime Ruled Unlawful | UK News', *The Guardian*, 30 January 2018, <https://www.theguardian.com/uk-news/2018/jan/30/uk-mass-digital-surveillance-regime-ruled-unlawful-appeal-ruling-snoopers-charter> [accessed 29 March 2019]

Tremlett, S., 'Exploring Contemplative Effects in Text-Based Video Poems by Sarah Tremlett – Poetry Film Live' <http://poetryfilmlive.com/exploring-contemplative-effects-in-text-based-video-poems/> [accessed 28 March 2019]

Trévien, C., 'About – Sabotage', *Sabotage Reviews*, <https://sabotagereviews.com/about/> [accessed 24 March 2019]

Trévien, C., 'The Challenges of Reviewing Spoken Word', *Sabotage Reviews*, 22 November 2017, <https://sabotagereviews.com/2017/11/22/the-challenges-of-reviewing-spoken-word/>

[accessed 24 March 2019]

Trévien, Claire, '"We Want Spoken Word Theatre to Go Global, so We Have to Be the Force Making That Happen": In Conversation with Sophia Walker', *Sabotage Reviews*, 8 December 2017, <http://sabotagereviews.com/2017/12/08/we-want-spoken-word-theatre-to-go-global-so-we-have-to-be-the-force-making-that-happen-in-conversation-with-sophia-walker/> [accessed 24 March 2019]

TyTe & Defenitial, 'Part 1: The Pre-History of Beatboxing', *HumanBeatbox.com*, 28 February 2005, <https://www.humanbeatbox.com/articles/history-of-beatboxing-part-1/> [accessed 22 March 2019]

U

UNESCO, 'Aitysh/Aitys, Art of Improvisation - Intangible Heritage - Culture Sector', *UNESCO*, 2015, <https://ich.unesco.org/en/RL/aitysh-aitys-art-of-improvisation-00997> [accessed 21 March 2019]

University of Twente, BMS Lab, *GSR Everything You Need to Know about Galvanic Skin Response to Push Your Insights into Emotional Behavior*, 2017, <https://imotions.com/gsr-guide-ebook/> [accessed 28 March 2019]

V

Vallance, C., 'Saying It with Words: Why Ads Are Getting More Chatty', 26 March 2018, <https://www.campaignlive.co.uk/article/saying-words-why-ads-getting-chatty/1460385> [accessed 24 March 2019]

Varjack, P., 'Is Performing at the Fringe Worth the Costs?', *WhatsOnStage*, 15 August 2017, <https://www.whatsonstage.com/edinburgh-theatre/news/performing-fringe-costs-festival-paula-varjack_44381.html> [accessed 24 March 2019]

Vermeersch, P., 'Why I Hate "Spoken Word" Poetry | WORD UP 411', 23 January 2014, <https://wordup411ng.com/why-i-hate-spoken-word-poetry/> [accessed 24 March 2019]

W

Walsh, J., 'All the Awards for Young Writers Amount to Discrimination | Joanna Walsh | Books', *The Guardian*, 8 September 2017, <https://www.theguardian.com/books/booksblog/2017/sep/08/all-the-awards-for-young-writers-amount-to-discrimination> [accessed 24 March 2019]

War on Want, 'A Resource Pack for Educators Cultural Resistance Youth at the Frontlines', *YouTube*, 2015, <https://www.youtube.com/watch?v=ozsOLdgp_y0> [accessed 29 March 2019]

Ward, D., 'Lost Voices of Victorian Working Class Uncovered in Political Protest Poems', *The Guardian*, 15 March 2007, <https://www.theguardian.com/uk/2007/mar/15/books.booksnews1> [accessed 22 March 2019]

Wasmuth, J., and Lindstedt, E., *Unreliable Narration in Vladimir Nabokov's Lolita*, 2009, <http://lup.lub.lu.se/luur/wnload?func=downloadFile&recordOId=1415031&fileOId=1471697> [accessed 27 March 2019]

Wells, T., 'Oi the Poetry – Garry Bushell | Standupandspit', <https://standupandspit.wordpress.com/2014/07/08/oi-the-poetry-garry-bushell/> [accessed 22 March 2019]

Wells, T., 'Radical Poetry In The 80s | Standupandspit' <https://standupandspit.wordpress.com/2017/04/14/radical-poetry-in-the-80s/> [accessed 22 March 2019]

Williams, H., 'The Women Poets Taking Over the World', *BBC*, 14 July 2017, < http://www.bbc.com/culture/story/20170713-the-women-poets-taking-over-the-world >

'Why Brands Are Using Spoken Word', 24 May 2016, <https://www.canvas8.com/content/2016/05/24/rhymes.html> [accessed 15 May 2019]

Yakubovskaya, I., 'Emotions, Empathy and Drama | Emotion on the Brain', 10 October 2014 <https://sites.tufts.edu/emotiononthebrain/2014/10/10/82/> [accessed 21 May 2019]

Interviews

Full length filmed interviews with the following artists can be found at 'Stage Invasion: Poetry & The Spoken Word Renaissance, (Full Interviews)', Vimeo, https://Vimeo.com/album/5871870:

Auton, Rob
Beard, Francesca
Berkson, Sam
Birnie, Clive
Gardosi, Jasmine
Godden, Salena
Gwynne Jones, Mark
Harvey, Matt
Hegley, John
Jarrett, Keith
Lola, Theresa
Makoha, Nick
McCabe, Rowan
McKay, James
Monkey Poet (Matt Panesh)
Morgan, David Lee
Nelson, Lee
Pepper, Penny
Raby, Henry
Redmond, Chris
Reid, Rachel Rose
Rolls, Jem
Seagrave, Jonny Fluffypunk
Slater, Alex
Taylor, Joelle
Thick Richard
Thompson, Keisha

Other titles by Out-Spoken Press:

The Neighbourhood
Hannah Lowe

Nascent
Vol 1: A BAME Anthology

Ways of Coping
Ollie O'Neill

A Greek Verse for Ophelia & Other Poems
Giovanni Quessep

The Games
Harry Josephine Giles

Songs My Enemy Taught Me
Joelle Taylor

To Sweeten Bitter
Raymond Antrobus

Dogtooth
Fran Lock

How You Might Know Me
Sabrina Mahfouz

Heterogeneous, New & Selected Poems
Anthony Anaxagorou

Titanic
Bridget Minamore

A Silence You Can Carry
Hibaq Osman

Email:
press@outspokenldn.com